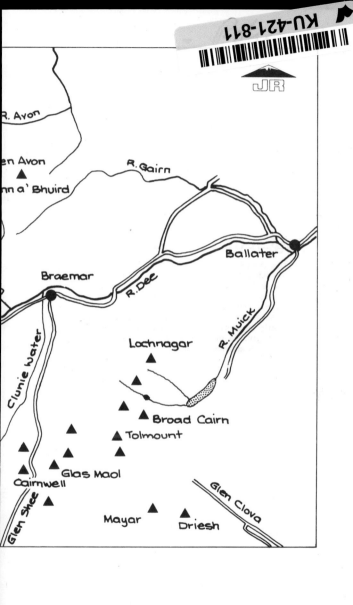

JR

R. Avon

en Avon

nn a' Bhuird

R. Gairn

Ballater

Braemar

R. Dee

R. Muick

Clunie Water

Lochnagar

Broad Cairn

Tolmount

Glas Maol

Cairnwell

Glen Shee

Mayar

Driesh

Glen Clova

ii

Published in Great Britain by the Scottish Mountaineering Trust,
1995
Copyright © The Scottish Mountaineering Club

First Edition   1961
Second Edition 1973
Third Edition   1985
Reprinted   1990
Fourth Edition   1995

British Library Cataloguing in Publication Data
A Catalogue record for this book is available from
the British Library

Maps drawn by Jim Renny
Diagrams by Kev Howett and T. Train
Production by Scottish Mountaineering Trust (Publications) Ltd
Typeset by Westec, North Connel
Colour Separations by Arneg, Glasgow
Printed by GNP Booth, Clydebank
          and St Edmundsbury Press, Bury St Edmunds
Bound by Hunter and Foulis, Edinburgh

Distributed by Cordee, 3a DeMontfort Street, Leicester, LE1 7HD

Contents

Introduction	1
Geology	2
History	4
Notes on the Use of this Guide	16

Lochnagar 23

North-East Corrie	24
Southern Sector	24
The Cathedral	26
Sinister Buttress	27
Northern Sector	28
Shadow Buttress Group	29
Tough-Brown Ridge and Face	41
Black Spout Pinnacle Group	52
West Buttress	66
Coire na Saobhaidhe	70
Coire Loch nan Eun	70
Cnapan Nathraichean	71

The Dubh Loch Cliffs 72

Eagles Rock	72
Green Slab	72
The Waterfall Climbs	73
The Mid-West Buttress	74
The Mid-East Buttress	75
A Likely Story Slab	76
Plateau Buttress	78
Creag an Dubh-loch	78
South-East Buttress	82
Broad Terrace Wall	83
The Hanging Garden	91
The Central Slabs	93
Central Gully Wall	103
False Gully Wall	123
North-West Buttress	128

North-West Gully Buttress   128
Girdle Traverses   129

Broad Cairn Bluffs   131
The Diamond Slab   131

Glen Clova   134

Bassies   134

Boustie Ley   134

Driesh   134

Mayar   139
Corrie Fee   139
South Wall   139
North Wall   144

Glen Doll   144
Craig Rennet   144
Craig Maud   144

The Upper South Esk Valley   145
The Strone   145
Juanjorge   145
Craig of Gowal   146
Hunt Hill   147

Southern Outlying Areas   148

Carn an Tuirc   148

Creag an Fhleisdeir   148

Glas Maol   149

Glas Tulaichean   150

Carn Binnein   150

Beinn a' Bhuird   151

Coire na Ciche   152
Slab Buttress   161

Coire an Dubh Lochain   163
Bloodhound Buttress   164
Glaucous Buttress   167

The Dividing Buttress 169
Gable Wall 170

Coire nan Clach 171

Garbh Choire 173
Squareface Buttress 174
Mitre Ridge 179

Stob an t-Sluichd 189

Graded List of Summer Climbs 190

List of First Ascents 194

List of Illustrations

Front Cover
  King Rat, Creag an Dubh-loch
    (Climber, Alastair Cain)   *Alan Shand*

Between pages 54 and 55
  High on Eagle Ridge, Lochnagar
    (Climber Sammy Dring)   *Kathy Murphy*
  Black Spout Wall, Lochnagar
    (Climbers, Dougie Dinwoodie and Bob Smith) *Greg Strange*

Between pages 86 and 87
  Polyphemus Gully, Lochnagar
    (Climber, Jane Naismith)   *Rab Anderson*
  The Shetlander, Creag an Dubh-loch
    (Climber, Wilson Moir)   *Niall Ritchie*

Between pages 118 and 119
  Voyage of the Beagle, Creag an Dubh-loch
    (Climber, Murray Hamilton)   *Rab Anderson*
  Cannibal, Creag an Dubh-loch
    (Climber, Murray Hamilton)   *Rab Anderson*

Between pages 150 and 151
  B Gully Chimney, Corrie Fee, Glen Clova
    (Climber, Doug Lang)   *John Hunter*
  Cumming-Crofton Route, Mitre Ridge, Beinn a' Bhuird
    (Climber, Geoff Cohen)   *Rab Anderson*

Back Cover
  Yeti, Creag an Dubh-loch
    (Climber, Chris Forrest)   *Andy Nisbet*

List of Diagrams and Maps

Lochnagar and Creag an Dubh-loch (Map)   25
Lochnagar, The Northern Sector   31
Lochnagar, The Tough-Brown Face   43
Lochnagar, Black Spout Pinnacle   53
Creag an Dubh-loch   81
Creag an Dubh-loch, Broad Terrace Wall   85
Creag an Dubh-loch, Central Slabs   95
Creag an Dubh-loch, Central Gully Wall   112-113
Glen Clova (Map)   135
Glen Clova, Winter Corrie   137
Glen Clova, Corrie Fee, South Face   141
Beinn a' Bhuird (Map)   153
Beinn a' Bhuird, Coire na Ciche   157
Beinn a' Bhuird, Coire an Dubh Lochain   165
Beinn a' Bhuird, Garbh Choire   175
Beinn a' Bhuird, Mitre Ridge, West Wall   183

The Climber and the Mountain Environment

With increasing numbers of walkers and climbers going to the Scottish hills, it is important that all of us who do so should recognise our responsibilities to the mountain environment in which we find our pleasure and recreation, to our fellow climbers, and to those who live and work on the land.

The Scottish Mountaineering Club and Trust, who jointly produce this and other guidebooks, wish to point out to all who avail themselves of the information in these books that it is in everyone's interest that good relations are maintained between visitors and landowners, particularly when there might be conflicts of interest, for example during the stalking season. The description of a climbing, walking or skiing route in any of these books does not imply that a right of way exists, and it is the responsibility of all climbers to ascertain the position before setting out. In cases of doubt it is best to enquire locally.

During stalking and shooting seasons in particular, much harm can be done in deer forests and on grouse moors by people walking through them. Normally the deer stalking season is from 1st July to 20th October, when stag shooting ends. Hinds may continue to be culled until 15th February. The grouse shooting season is from 12th August until 10th December. These activities are important for the economy of many Highland estates. During these seasons, therefore, consideration should be given to consulting the local landowner, factor or keeper before taking to the hills.

Climbers and hill walkers are recommended to consult the book HEADING FOR THE SCOTTISH HILLS, published by the Scottish Mountaineering Trust on behalf of the Mountaineering Council of Scotland and the Scottish Landowners Federation, which gives the names and addresses of factors and keepers who may be contacted for information regarding access to the hills.

It is important to avoid disturbance to sheep, particularly during the lambing season between March and May. Dogs should not be taken onto the hills at this time, and at all times should be kept under close control.

Always try to follow a path or track through cultivated land and forests, and avoid causing damage to fences, dykes and gates by climbing over them carelessly. Do not leave litter anywhere, but take it down from the hill in your rucksack.

The number of walkers and climbers on the hills is leading to increased, and in some cases very unsightly erosion of footpaths and hillsides. Some of the revenue from the sale of this and other SMC guidebooks is used by the Trust to assist financially the work being carried out to repair and maintain hill paths in Scotland. However, it is important for all of us to recognise our responsibility to minimise the erosive effect of our passage over the hills so that the enjoyment of future climbers shall not be spoiled by landscape damage caused by ourselves.

As a general rule, where a path exists walkers should follow it and even where it is wet and muddy should avoid walking along its edges, the effect of which is to extend erosion sideways. Do not take short-cuts at the corners of zigzag paths. Remember that the worst effects of erosion are likely to be caused during or soon after prolonged wet weather when the ground is soft and waterlogged. A route on a stony or rocky hillside is likely to cause less erosion than on a grassy one at such times.

Although the use of bicycles can often be very helpful for reaching remote crags and hills, the erosion damage that can be caused by them when used 'off road' on soft footpaths and open hillsides is such that their use on such terrain must cause concern. It is the editorial policy of the Scottish Mountaineering Club that the use of bicycles in hill country may be recommended on hard tracks such as forest roads or private roads following rights of way, but it is not recommended on footpaths or open hillsides where the environmental damage that they cause may be considerable. Readers are asked to bear these points in mind, particularly in conditions when the ground is wet and soft after rain.

The proliferation of cairns on hills detracts from the feeling of wildness, and may be confusing rather than helpful as regards route-finding. The indiscriminate building of cairns on the hills is therefore to be discouraged.

Climbers are reminded that they should not drive along private estate roads without permission, and when parking their cars should avoid blocking access to private roads and land, and should avoid causing any hazard to other road users.

Finally, the Scottish Mountaineering Club and the Scottish Mountaineering Trust can accept no liability for damage to property nor for personal injury resulting from the use of any route described in their publications.

Acknowledgements

A great many people have contributed to this guidebook over a number of years. First we must thank the authors of previous SMC guides; Mac Smith, Bill March, Dougie Dinwoodie and Greg Strange, whose work provided the backbone for this edition. Thanks also to Donald Bennet and Roger Everett, Publications Manager and Editor of Climbing Guidebooks respectively. Kev Howett produced the outstanding diagrams and Jim Renny the maps.

Many thanks to those who submitted slides for consideration, it is unfortunate that we could only include a small selection of the excellent contributions. A large number of people contributed with suggestions, corrections and information, while others read texts, checked proofs, graded routes and generally provided encouragement, not least by climbing with the authors. Their names are listed alphabetically. We apologise for any inadvertently missed out.

Rab Anderson, Rob Archbold, John Ashbridge, Steve Blagbrough, Jim Blyth, Colin Bruce, Martin Burrows-Smith, Rick Campbell, Andy Cunningham, Brian Davison, Ian Dillon, Sam Dring, Dougie Dinwoodie, Graeme Ettle, Brian Findlay, Chris Forrest, Andrew Fraser, Bruce Goodlad, Donald Green, Jas Hepburn, Alec Keith, Alan Kerr, Doug Lang, Gary Latter, John Lyall, James Maclaurin, Richard Mansfield, Alastair Matthewson, Wilson Moir, Neil Morrison, Kathy Murphy, Grahame Nicoll, Iain Peter, Jonathon Preston, Tom Prentice, George Reid, Niall Ritchie, Ged Reilly, Doug Rennie, Simon Richardson, Alastair Robertson, Alf Robertson, Alastair Ross, Mark Ryle, Malcolm Slater, Colin Stewart, Peter Stewart, Greg Strange, Walter Taylor, Andy Tibbs, Roger Wild and Blyth Wright.

Introduction

This, the latest of the SMC Rock and Ice guides to the Cairngorms, sees the area divided into northern and southern sections. One volume for the whole region would now be too large. Any division of the Cairngorms is not totally satisfactory as they are best considered as a single climbing area. However, the present arrangement produces two guides which are of manageable size and fairly logical in that most of the area described in this volume is best approached from Deeside, and most of the area of Volume 1 is reached from Strathspey.

This guide now contains all routes, although some may only be noted. Routes which have been climbed in summer and winter are given descriptions for both seasons. Modern summer grades have been used, with individual pitch grades for routes of VS and above if available. Modern winter grades are also given, using the 'dual system' for routes of grade IV and above.

Cairngorm rock is, to quote Mac Smith the writer of the first climbing guide to the area, 'honest granite'. It is generally sound and much of it is of an overlapping slab structure. This often gives superb climbing, particularly in the upper grades, where guile, footwork and friction may be the keys to success. Protection is average overall, certainly not as poor as once was thought, and with a rack of modern gear most of the climbs can be made safe enough. Vegetation, particularly lichen, can be a problem on some of the less popular climbs, but this is not unique to the Cairngorms.

In winter the climbing can be as much on rock and frozen turf as on snow and ice, particularly away from the gullies. Good neve is less common here than in the west as the area receives fewer freeze-thaw cycles. However, this may give more consistent conditions for longer periods. The approaches to the corries range from very short to long and arduous, and fitness, mountaineering ability and experience all play a part in success and safety.

It will be obvious that we have relied on the work of previous guidebook authors such as Bill March, and the information on new routes published annually in the SMC Journal. The foundation, however, remains Mac Smith's two-volume masterpiece of 1961 which turned the Cairngorms into a major climbing ground and established many of its traditions and legends.

Geology

The area covered in this guide and its companion Volume 1 consists of two roughly circular granite masses, that of Lochnagar and Creag an Dubh Loch in the south and the main Cairngorm massif in the north. These large granite plutons were formed about 500 million years ago during the Caledonian orogeny, when they formed the roots of a vast mountain chain. These were, with wind, weather and time, worn down to below sea-level and covered with sediment. About 50 million years ago they rose again to form a great flat plain which was eroded to reveal the old mountain roots which, because of their resistant nature, were left higher than the surrounding area.

The present day appearance of the Cairngorms is one of a high plateau with gently rolling slopes. This shape was produced by a period of tropical and sub-tropical weathering during the Tertiary period. It was then modified by the action of ice during the Quaternary period. These ice sheets and glaciers were selective in their erosion and left us pre-glacial features such as the rounded hills and tors, but also gouged out great troughs such as the Lairig Ghru and Loch Avon, and the many corries that cut into these mountains. It is these features of glacial erosion which provide the climbing in the Cairngorms.

The rock itself is a remarkably homogenous granite, although that in the Lochnagar region differs somewhat from that in the central Cairngorm area. It is generally fairly coarse-grained and pinkish in colour when freshly exposed, but it weathers to grey. The three joint systems are regular and approximately at right angles to each other. Because of the uniform nature of the rock there has been little to encourage preferential weathering, giving many cliffs their massive appearance. The majority of gullies are the lines of small vertical faults or crush lines, and many of them are of poor and shattered rock. Typical of Cairngorm granite is its 'woolsack' appearance, due to its vertical joints and sheeting, a type of joint which roughly parallels the surface and becomes thicker with depth, probably due to pressure release as the deeply buried rock was revealed by erosion. These rounded blocks are seen in many cliffs but are most notable in No.4 Buttress of Coire an Lochain.

The rock may also be cut by pegmatite or aplite veins. The former consist of large crystals and the latter are veins of fine grained rock. Several routes use these veins, which sometimes weather to give a ladder of tiny square holds. Occasionally, cavities in these veins contain crystals of quartz, which may be tinted to give it a smoky yellow to dark brown colour, the semi-precious Cairngorm stones that lured the first explorers onto these cliffs. Gas pockets or druses, which may contain crystals, can also be found in places.

History

LOCHNAGAR AND
CREAG AN DUBH-LOCH

(modified from notes by D.Dinwoodie and G.Strange)

The earliest known visitors to the cliffs were the quartz diggers and botanists on Lochnagar. In the earliest explorations of the SMC, Lochnagar naturally attracted attention. The mountain was accessible and its bold cliffs were clearly visible to the traveller through the glens. The more secluded Dubh Loch cliffs were found disconcertingly smooth and left untouched.

The first way made up the cliffs, in 1893, was a snow climb, Black Spout by the left-hand branch. The earliest rock climb was Tough-Brown Traverse in 1895, the outcome of a bold assault on the massive buttress in the middle of the crags. Raeburn attempted a number of lines with scant success, the main reward being the great central gully now named after him. This was a popular climb in later years until the best pitch was obliterated by rockfall in 1940. The remaining major gully was of more evil character – the disintegrating Douglas-Gibson. The SMC's efforts in this oppressive gash did little to foster enthusiasm for Cairngorm granite. By 1902, five attempts had been made, three by Raeburn. An abseil inspection (the start of a modern trend?) was even made in 1902 and the upper gully reported as "not being impossible".

Scottish climbing virtually died out in the years around the Great War and for almost two decades Lochnagar was abandoned to enjoy the same peace as Creag an Dubh-loch. Exploration was resumed by two members of the Cairngorm Club, Symmers and Ewen, the first of the local campaigners. The climbs of this pair have gained a notoriety rather than popularity, an unfair reflection on their enterprise. Performing heroics on loose rock and vegetation, they climbed most of the remaining gullies and chimneys, and three major buttresses. Symmers also made the first recorded climb on Creag an Dubh-loch, South-East Gully (1928).

Symmers and Ewen had been aware of the better possibilities on Lochnagar, naming such features as Parallel and Eagle buttresses and examining the line of Eagle Ridge. The field was left open however, to Dr. J.H.B.Bell, whose outstanding climb was the afore-mentioned Eagle Ridge. Building on a previous skirmish (Eagle

Buttress) and the work of Scroggie and Ferguson of Dundee, he completed his Lochnagar masterpiece in 1941. It remains a milestone in Cairngorm history, the only earlier climb of comparable quality being the remote and unsung Cumming-Crofton Route on Mitre Ridge. Other examples of Bell's pioneering skills were Parallel Buttress and the hard Direct Route on Tough-Brown Ridge. Bell, like Symmers, paid the odd visit to Dubh Loch and made the first important climb there, the difficult Labyrinth Route (1941).

Soon to come were the first probes of a new generation (partly inspired by Bell's climbs and writings), namely, the various bands who were to make up the Aberdeen School of the fifties. At this time, entire untouched corries and crags abounded all over the vast Cairngorm region and the number of existing climbs would soon be doubled. In the early years of this era, the easier breaks between the bare faces were climbed at Dubh Loch, as were the remaining classic lines on Lochnagar. Sutherland and Brooker led off with Route One on Black Spout Pinnacle, the last of the great Lochnagar buttresses to fall. In 1952, an eight-man party stormed the last of the classic lines, Parallel Gully B. The leader was Tom Patey, the most energetic explorer of the day.

The time was now ripe for the breakthrough on the bolder 'impossible' faces. It was obvious that these would provide the best climbing. The first of the big climbs was the huge intimidating corner of Vertigo Wall, climbed by Patey, McLeod and Will. Forced in the same year as Sassenach on Nevis (1954), Vertigo does not compare technically but must have been a similar psychological undertaking. Climbed in nails and bad conditions, it was an inspired achievement. Astonishingly, attempts were later made to climb an even more frightening line on the gully wall, while the slabbier frontal face remained virgin. This was the very exposed line of slabby shelves leading high up into The Giant. On the boldest attempt, Dick Barclay and Sticker Thom free-climbed up into the corner only to find themselves trapped. Friends on the plateau threw down ropes and hauled them to safety. Their pegs were to baffle the Squirrels on their subsequent direct ascent.

Perhaps even more important than Vertigo Wall was Jerry Smith's Pinnacle Face on Lochnagar the following year. Using rope-soled shoes, he threaded the big slab-apron avoided by Route One. Pinnacle Face was the first of the 'overlapping slab' routes which provided much of the best modern climbing, especially south of the Dee. It proved that the smooth open faces ran to better holds than appearances suggested. The next year, Bill Brooker and Ken Grassick, wearing Vibrams, repeated Pinnacle Face and continued up the steep Black Spout face to make The Link. This success was an eye-opener for Brooker and a clear indication of the great possibilities open in the Cairngorms. In 1958, with Dick Barclay, he applied this knowledge to Central Gully Wall and made the first open face route there, Waterkelpie Wall. The big Waterkelpie climb was paralleled by Ronnie Sellar's impressive Citadel on Shelter Stone Crag the same year. As the fifties drew to an end, the energy of the Aberdeen movement seems to have fizzled out, just as great things were being achieved. Mac Smith's guide was written at this time, winding up the era and stamping the Cairngorms as one of Scotland's main climbing areas.

The end of this campaign coincided with the arrival of the first modern invaders, the Edinburgh climbers. Jimmy Marshall had already plundered Parallel Gully B in the winter of 1958. The next year, in the unlikely month of November, he turned up at Dubh Loch to climb Mousetrap, later to become the trade route at Dubh Loch, a line unaccountably missed by the locals who had failed to find an entry into the recess. As far as exploration is concerned, a lull fell over the whole region in the early sixties. In 1964, a new generation of Aberdeen and Edinburgh men started tentative probings at Dubh Loch, soon to be joined by Dundee climbers. Jim McArtney provided Waterkelpie Wall with a long direct start. Later he was to open up Eagles Rock and do early work on King Rat and Goliath. Jim Stenhouse and Brian Lawrie finally answered the stark challenge of the Central Slabs with Dinosaur. Better pegs and PAs had taken some of the sting out of the naked slabs. The following year, Dave Bathgate and the Squirrels climbed the long-sought Giant, an epic ascent requiring many pegs. Lochnagar was forgotten in the Dubh Loch boom, apart from efforts on the forbidding Tough-Brown Face, which was opened up by two young Aberdonians, Mike Forbes and Mike Rennie, with Mort and Crypt (1967). At Dubh Loch, Brian Robertson led the technical Blue Max, a direct ascent of the Central Slabs. The most important event of the year, however, was an English intrusion; the Barley brothers forced a most impressive line up the middle of the impregnable-looking Broad Terrace Wall. Shrouded in mystery for a number of years, Culloden remains an impressive route for its time.

In 1968, Rennie's partly artificial Cougar was also impressive, a bold and committing climb up the most intimidating part of Central Gully Wall. Meanwhile, the great plum of King Rat fell to Allen Fyffe and John Bower at a surprisingly reasonable standard. Activity reached its height in June 1969 when the three classics of Black Mamba, Falseface and Goliath were climbed on the same day by rival teams. Fyffe and John Grieve stayed on for another four routes that week, including Pink Elephant. Subsequently, Predator, Sword of Damocles, Dubh Loch Monster and Gulliver fell in another short spell in 1970 and with these rapid developments a new guide was written by Fyffe, the most active pioneer of these years. Ian Nicolson's bold on sight lead of the Red Wall of Gulliver had produced the hardest pitch in the new guide.

In the seventies, Creag an Dubh-loch became the most popular summer crag in the Cairngorms. While the climbing was at last being appreciated, the place had sadly lost much of its mystique. Exploration shifted towards the dripping Broad Terrace Wall, while aid was being whittled away on the established lines. The most active pioneers were Dougie Dinwoodie and Bob Smith. This pair and others of the Etchachan Club also dispelled the myth that Lochnagar had little to offer in summer, with a series of fine routes on the Tough-Brown Face and Black Spout Pinnacle, culminating in the magnificent Black Spout Wall (1976). Dougie Dinwoodie and Greg Strange's guide appeared in 1978.

A new era focusing on the monolithic walls of Creag an Dubh-loch started in 1977 when Dave Cuthbertson and Murray Hamilton made free ascents of Cougar and The Giant. (It was not known at the time that The Giant had been freed previously by Nick Estcourt in 1974, but many found it difficult to accept this late claim which would have probably made The Giant the hardest route in Scotland at that time.) Four consecutive wet summers delayed the onset of yet harder climbs, but Murray Hamilton's Sans Fer (E4, 1979) was the start. The fine summer of 1982 saw Pete Whillance, Murray Hamilton and others produce six excellent routes of E3 and above, starting with Slartibartfast on the False Gully Wall. The remaining five routes were on Central Gully Wall, with pride of place going to Whillance's The Naked Ape (E5) and Hamilton's Ascent of Man (E5), both on the long-admired 'impossible' wall between The Giant and Cougar. These routes proved that the seemingly blank steeper walls did run to holds which the modern armoury could exploit. Gardening on abseil was a crucial factor which combined with the jump in technical ability.

Hamilton, with partners Anderson, Spence and Whillance, continued exploration in 1983. Most notable was the breach of the overhanging wall left of Culloden with Flodden (E5). Voyage of the Beagle (E4) started the criss-crossing of routes on Central Gully Wall. Also significant was Perilous Journey, Dinwoodie's first E5 after his reluctant adoption of the modern style of climbing. 1984 saw

Dinwoodie take over the leading role, but not before Hamilton and Anderson climbed the first E6, provocatively named Cannibal, after Dinwoodie's previous cleaning and attempts. Dinwoodie's answer was three routes on False Gully Wall, although the crux of The Improbability Drive (E6) was led by Graeme Livingston and became the hardest route in the 1985 guide.

After publication of the guide, the Dubh Loch became increasingly more popular, and all the modern rock routes were repeated. Climbers such as Wilson Moir and Rick Campbell were to the forefront, and the repeats usually resulted in rave reports of the climbs' quality. Naked Ape claims first prize with more than 10 ascents, and Cougar has certainly become the most popular E3. Dinwoodie continued to find even harder lines, and in 1987 peaked with Fer de Lance and The Web of Weird, which now gets the rating as the hardest route on the cliff. Dinwoodie considered the line of The Web of Weird as incomplete, but made his claim after the route was climbed by Rick Campbell and Paul Thorburn (with a direct start). Exploration has died down, largely because the best lines have been climbed, but rising standards of regular climbers are bringing increasing numbers able to climb these excellent routes. A few new routes have been found, notably due to Wilson Moir's enthusiasm for the slabs on the left end of Broad Terrace Wall; The Bedouin and The Eye of Allah have been produced and the quality of Alice Springs confirmed.

But Lochnagar has continued to be neglected, partly because of the high quality and wide selection of routes at the neighbouring Dubh Loch, but also because the existing routes were not cleaned on abseil; the existing lichen created a vicious circle. Alastair Ross was not discouraged, and in 1989 he climbed Lochnagar's first E4, An Saobh-chreideach, unrepeated and unpronounceable to the majority, so it has been nicknamed Shabby Creature. However, Black Spout Wall (E3) has had several enthusiastic ascents, but the classic Eagle Ridge continues to dominate. For those of a more exploratory nature, Lochnagar has some very fine if under-rated rock routes, particularly in the E grades.

The summer of 1995 saw the addition of The Existentialist by Moir, the hardest route by far on Lochnagar at E6, but offset by the loss of Nymph (one of the best HVSs) destroyed by a rockfall.

Winter

It is appropriate that the first recorded ascent of Creagan Lochnagar was made under winter conditions. This was in March 1893, when

Douglas and Gibson climbed the left-branch of The Black Spout. The previous day they had made an audacious attempt at the gully now named after them, but they were turned back below the 60m headwall. Another 57 years were to elapse before the gully was eventually climbed under winter conditions.

Apart from the classic Raeburn's Gully by Symmers and Ewen in 1932, few notable climbs were recorded before the Second World War. This is quite surprising considering the level of achievement attained elsewhere. Things were to change after the War. In the space of a single decade, from 1948 to 1958, snow and ice climbing on the mountain progressed from the ascents of easy gullies to the climbing of some of the most difficult face and buttress routes in the country. During these golden years, the North-East Corrie of Lochnagar was the crucible of modern winter climbing in Scotland. Each new season seemed to produce climbs of greater difficulty. Giant's Head Chimney, Douglas-Gibson Gully, The Stack, Polyphemus Gully and Eagle Ridge all represented significantly more serious and psychologically harder undertakings. Although there were a number of local climbers involved with these developments, Brooker, Patey and Taylor were probably the most active. Their 4½ hour ascent of Eagle Ridge proved how well they had mastered the art of climbing snow-covered rock. It was during the mid fifties that Patey and Smith started work on the climbers' guide to Lochnagar and the Cairngorms (edited by Smith), and at the same time devised the basic Scottish grading system of categorising winter climbs, only recently adapted to meet modern needs.

By 1958, ideas were changing and a new force emerged from Edinburgh in the shape of the crampon-shod Jimmy Marshall. His ascent of Parallel Gully B in icy conditions not only grieved the local climbers but represented a breakthrough in pure ice climbing, by clearly demonstrating the advantages of crampons over nailed boots for climbing ice. Local climbers took advantage of a good winter in 1959 to climb the first big winter routes on Creag an Dubh-loch. Sellars, Annand and Jerry Smith climbed Labyrinth Route and Brooker climbed Labyrinth Edge; the obvious potential of the Dubh Loch had at last been realised.

Lochnagar went into the sixties with all its major gullies and buttresses climbed. In later years several important climbs were made; notably Grassick, Light and Nicol's ascent of Pinnacle Face — the swan-song of the tricouni tricksters — but ironically a route of modern concept and difficulty, repeated only twice until the eighties. Apart from

Pinnacle Face, technical standards rose very little beyond those of the golden years. Crampons with front-points became the accepted footwear, but it was not until the early seventies that the technique of front-pointing steep ice began to supersede the tradition of step cutting. Once mastered, the new technique enabled ice climbs and climbs involving frozen turf to be ascended in faster times, and more and more parties began to tackle harder routes. In 1970, Bower and Simpson climbed the difficult Bower Buttress in the Hanging Garden and recorded the first winter route on Eagles Rock. Two years later, James Bolton made his bold ascent of Labyrinth Direct, thus creating the most difficult gully climb of its type in the country. The new technique had at last been successfully applied to a long-standing problem. The mid-seventies saw further climbs in the Hanging Garden and a rapid development of the watercourses on Eagles Rock as a worthwhile ice climbing alternative to the main Dubh Loch faces.

The mid-seventies saw a great increase in the number of winter climbers, with Lochnagar particularly popular. Confidence in the new techniques was growing slowly and the hard routes began to see regular ascents, with Eagle Ridge the major testpiece. For those with exploratory ideas, there was much to be climbed on pure ice; further climbs were made in the Hanging Garden and a rapid development of the water courses on Eagles Rock provided a less serious ice-climbing alternative. Norman Keir was more forward-thinking and determined efforts on the ice-glazed slabs of Pink Elephant with Dave Wright cost an involuntary bivouac but showed the way ahead. Influenced by Keir's audacity, Andrew Nisbet and Alfie Robertson adopted a more clinical approach in a two-day ascent of the formidably steep Vertigo Wall in 1977. Although not a technical advance, a psychological barrier had been broken and all the big VS routes were now winter targets. The technical advance came soon with John Anderson's ascent of The Link (1979).

January 1980 saw excellent conditions on the Dubh Loch, and an influx of Edinburgh climbers. Pink Elephant was the first of three great routes to fall in a week; the Aberdonian's answer was Goliath. The long sought Mousetrap was the third, and Murray Hamilton, Alan Taylor and Kenny Spence had achieved the first route on the front face of the Central Gully Wall. By March, the exceptional conditions had shifted to Black Spout Pinnacle and there were repeats of Pinnacle Face and The Link, as well as first ascents of the prominent line of Pinnacle Grooves and the desperate Epitome by visiting Polish climber Jan Fijalkowski, along with Aberdonian Bob Smith.

Three mediocre winters, a switch in emphasis to rock climbing and the deaths of three of the keenest pioneers (John Anderson, Bob Smith and Brian Sprunt) limited activity until 1984, when Lochnagar returned to its role as "the crucible of modern winter climbing". The start was Arthur Paul's ascent of Psyche. His partner Dinwoodie teamed up with Colin MacLean to try Trail of Tears, the first E grade route to be attempted in winter, while MacLean later roped in Nisbet for the big layback cracks of Nymph. Pantheist (Dinwoodie and Nisbet), completed the year of the initiation of axe torquing.

Several hard routes, including Solstice and Tough-Guy, fell in 1984/85, but 1986 was a great year on Lochnagar. Two big routes fell and a third in 1987, each after a long campaign. Trail of Tears (Nisbet's project) was first after 5 attempts; followed soon after by Dinwoodie's Diedre of the Sorrows, perhaps the hardest of the three, involving 13 hours over 3 attempts on the crux; finally Livingston's serious Torquing Corpse was ascended; the name reflects his expectations on the crux pitch. Also in 1986, but on Creag an Dubh-loch, Nisbet and Sandy Allan spent 19 hours climbing The Rattrap.

Although the rise in popularity of Cairngorm mixed climbing has provided many with the skill to repeat or even exceed these routes, the co-operation and competition of several committed winter climbers on the dole has not yet been matched. A heroic attempt by MacLean on Mort in 1985 reached within 10m of easy ground (2 rest points). A more recent attempt by Brian Davison freed past the rest points before gravity reclaimed all the gain. Mort remains the definition for the next generation.

While Lochnagar has remained popular, with Eagle Ridge, Parallel Buttress and Parallel Gully B becoming trade routes, and repeat ascents of Psyche, Tough-Guy and (nearly) Nymph, Creag an Dubh-loch saw a lull during the poorer winters of 1988-92. Conditions were excellent during January 1993 and Doug Hawthorn claimed three big ice lines, the hardest being The Sting, but word did not spread fast enough for general advantage. Despite the occasional excellence of its ice, futuristic mixed climbing possibilities exist here too.

CREAGAN A' CHOIRE ETCHACHAN, COIRE SPUTAN DEARG AND BEINN A' BHUIRD

These cliffs are in the remote plateau most accessible from Braemar, and although the former two are described in Volume 1 of this guidebook, their histories are closely intertwined. They have never achieved the popularity of the big cliffs of Shelter Stone, Lochnagar or Creag an Dubh-loch, nor do they have the accessibility of the Northern Corries or Loch Avon. Consequently development has been fairly recent and almost exclusively by Aberdonians.

Before 1948, activity was confined to easy snow climbs on Beinn a' Bhuird and to Mitre Ridge, the focus of pre-war attention and at 200m high, the only feature to rival the bigger cliffs. Determined efforts resulted in ascents of the ridge and Cumming-Crofton Route on the same day in July 1933. Only Eagle Ridge could rival these for difficulty in the pre-war period. Two further routes on Mitre Ridge were climbed by the Armed Forces during the War.

Early guides had described the rock of Creagan a' Choire Etchachan as "rather fragmentary" and Sputan "not suited for climbing, the rocks being rounded and devoid of holds". Once the post-war move was made out from the gullies onto the buttresses, these descriptions were quickly proved wrong. Sputan Dearg, with its clean juggy rock and fine, low grade buttresses, was the first to attract attention. After Pinnacle Buttress and the excellent Crystal Ridge were climbed in the summer of 1948, a further eight routes, including most of the main buttresses, followed in 1949. The main activists were Bill Brooker, J. Tewnion and Mac Smith. In the fifties, Brooker, Smith, Tom Patey and others, including the 'Kincorth Club' (Freddy Malcolm, Alec Thom, and Dick Barclay) moved away from Sputan Dearg and began to develop the Beinn a' Bhuird corries. Standards were rising and by 1956 most of the obvious lines up to Mild VS had been climbed. Important climbs were Hourglass Buttress (1953), Squareface (1953) and The Carpet (1955). In September 1955, Patey and John Hay made a move on to the Crimson Slabs, the first attempt on one of the smooth Cairngorm faces. The result was The Dagger, the hardest route in the Cairngorms at that time. Hay returned to the slabs the following year to put up the companion route, Djibangi. These routes opened up great possibilities and became the major test pieces in the area for almost a decade. Also from 1956 were Talisman and another test piece, Amethyst Wall.

A temporary lull fell over this area and in 1961 Mac Smith's climbers' guide to the Cairngorms was published.

Such had been the level of activity in the early fifties that further development required a rise in standards. This was to come in the mid-sixties, with the arrival of a new generation. They called themselves 'The Spiders' and included John Bower, Mike Forbes, Brian Lawrie and Mike Rennie. VS routes became commonplace and PAs replaced boots, although Ronnie Kerr's very early first ascent of The Sheath (1961), perhaps the earliest HVS in the Cairngorms, was achieved in boots. Although Beinn a' Bhuird was largely neglected, several fine routes were established on Sputan Dearg, such as Grey Slab and Terminal Wall (1963) and Jim McArney's free finish to Amethyst Wall (1964). Meanwhile, at Creagan a' Choire Etchachan in 1966, Mike Forbes and Mike Rennie made an impressive ascent of the oft-tried Stiletto, the fore-runner of a new rise in technical standards. A few months later they climbed the popular Scabbard.

In the period from 1970 to 1972 there was a new burst of activity before the publication of Greg Strange's guide to the area in 1973. Strange, along with Dougie Dinwoodie, Brian Lawrie and others of the Etchachan Club, tidied up many of the good VS lines. Since 1973, the rock climbing standard has risen relentlessly and the attention of those leading HVS and above, an increasing number, has switched to the bigger, steeper cliffs such as Creag an Dubh-loch or the Shelter Stone Crag. The competitiveness of modern rock climbing has caused accessibility of rock to often overshadow the traditional mountain day. Even so, the classic routes of VS and below have remained popular, while exploration has been sporadic, at least partly because these remote cliffs have limited area of steep or smooth rock for E-grade routes. Some recent finds of smaller and more obscure buttresses, such as Black Crag, have yielded routes in the modern idiom to those who are prepared to make the effort.

Although it remains a rock climbing backwater, Beinn a' Bhuird saw a burst of activity when the HVS grade was explored in the late 1970s by members of the Etchachan Club (including Greg Strange, Rob Archbold, Norman Keir, Gordon Stephen and Andy Nisbet). The west face of Mitre Ridge became established as a fine modern face with several routes, including Slochd Wall (free, 1979) and The Empty Quarter (1983). Since then, remoteness and limited high quality rock has caused it to revert to a quiet venue. In a similar way, Sputan Dearg has restricted modern style rock and although the middle grade routes are of high quality, they are short and have received little encouraging publicity. Aberdeen-based climbers, particularly Simon Richardson and Greg Strange, have recently climbed a number of new routes.

Creagan a' Choire Etchachan is now by far the most popular of the three, both for classic and new routes (although not since 1986), but it is limited somewhat by the stubborn seeps typical of south-facing Cairngorm slabs. Scalpel (Dinwoodie and Strange, 1977) and Sgian Dubh (Nisbet and Mary Bridges, 1978) were two obvious HVS lines but a number of harder routes were established in the mid 1980s. Henchman (Hamilton and Anderson, 1983) and Talking Drums (MacLean and Nisbet, 1986) are two fine routes on the wall right of the classic Talisman, but most of the activity was concentrated on the Crimson Slabs by the granite slab-loving Aberdeen climbers who squeezed in nine more routes. Although *Classic Rock* has condemned Talisman to permanent popularity, the fine VS routes of Dagger, Djibangi and Scabbard continue to see many ascents.

Winter

In the fifties, the standards of winter climbing were advancing rapidly, as well as the growing attitude that all rock climbs were potentially winter routes. Many of the buttresses as well as the gully climbs received ascents by the Aberdeen climbers, although the remoteness kept progress at a lower pace than in summer. The south-facing Sputan Dearg was rarely visited and many of the best routes on the icy Creagan a' Choire Etchachan were left for the crampon-shod later generations, apart from The Corridor (Freddy Malcolm and Alec Thom, 1954). Garbh Choire of Beinn a' Bhuird gave the best routes such as Mitre Ridge, by Brooker and Patey in 1953 and South-East Gully, by Ronnie Sellars and George Annand in 1959.

Development was slow for a period, but it was revived in the late sixties by the Spiders, now in crampons but still step-cutting. John Bower and Jim McArtney were particularly to the forefront, with McArtney on ice (Djibangi, 1965) and Bower on technical winter rock; The Carpet and Hourglass Buttress (1970) were several years ahead of their time. With the advent of front-pointing, ice-climbing was suddenly in vogue and the icy Creagan a' Choire Etchachan became popular. New ice routes included Carmine Groove (1974) and The Dagger (1977). Equally popular was the remote and serious Garbh Choire, with Flume Direct (1974), East Wall Direct (1974) and Crucible Route (1978). Only in the late seventies did technical winter rock re-emerge, one of the first and hardest being Cumming-Crofton Route by Dick Renshaw and Greg Strange in 1977. This was the year when powder lay deep and unchanged for 3 months and their round trip to the Mitre Ridge and back took over 24 hours. Mitre Ridge itself was repeated in 1974, and twice more in 1977, to become established as a classic winter route.

Winter development of these cliffs has been steady but slow throughout the 1980s into the 1990s. Many of the existing routes up to grade V, and some of the new ones, have been repeated occasionally, with Sputan Dearg the neglected exception. During the poor winters of the early 1980s, the snowy rock theme continued with the development of Grey Man's Crag at Sputan Dearg and the east face of Mitre Ridge. These routes, often accomplished by Nisbet and partners, did not gain universal approval as valid winter climbs, although they were quite snowy by present standards. Creagan a' Choire Etchachan saw repeats of many of the harder ice routes, although Avalanche Gully and the free ascent of the icicle of Square-Cut Gully both waited until 1985. Mixed climbing must always be an option here, as the crag is susceptible to morning sun, and recent routes, many by Richardson and partners in early season, have not usually been icy. However, Andy and Gill Nisbet took advantage of exceptional conditions in December 1992 to climb three icy routes. This icy climbing and the proximity of the Hutchison Hut have maintained the popularity of Creagan a' Choire Etchachan, with Djibangi, once thought to be rarely in condition, seeing many ascents and the more reliable Red Chimney as a common option.

Notes on the Use of the Guide

Classification of Routes

Summer

For summer rock climbs the following grades have been used: Easy, Moderate, Difficult, Very Difficult, Severe, Hard Severe, Very Severe (VS), Hard Very Severe (HVS), Extremely Severe. The Extremely Severe grade has been subdivided into E1, E2, E3, E4, E5, E6 and E7 in keeping with the rest of Britain.

Technical grades are given for routes of VS and above where known. Much effort has been made to elicit information from active climbers about routes, some of which will have all the relevant pitches graded while others will have only the crux pitch so described. The normal range for technical grades expected on routes of the given overall grade are as follows; VS – 4b, 4c, 5a; HVS – 4c, 5a, 5b; E1 – 5a, 5b, 5c; E2 – 5b, 5c, 6a; E3 – 5c, 6a; E4 – 5c, 6a, 6b; E5 – 6a, 6b. Routes with technical grade at the lower end of the range will be sustained or poorly protected, while those with grades at the upper end of the expected range will most likely have a shorter and generally well protected crux.

Although the British system is thought second to none by those familiar with it, it is known to confuse visitors from abroad. For their benefit, it can be assumed that 5a, 5b, 5c and 6a correspond to the American grades of 5.9, 5.10a/b, 5.10c/d and 5.11a/b respectively. Eurocraggers should note that there is little or no fixed protection on these routes and if they are used to cruising bolted French 6c, they may suffer some distress while attempting the corresponding 6a pitches here, with their sometimes spaced and fiddly protection. Grading information is in some cases scanty or even lacking, particularly in some of the older or more obscure routes; climbers should therefore be even more circumspect in their approach to such routes. Further information about any routes is always welcome.

Winter

Winter climbs have been graded using the two-tier system in which the Roman numeral indicates the overall difficulty of the climb and the accompanying Arabic numeral represents the technical difficulty of the hardest sections of climbing. This is built on the old Grades of I to V, which was previously used, but it is only for climbs of Grade IV and above (occasionally grade III) that the two-tier system has been applied. Both parts of the grading system are open-ended.

Grade I — Uncomplicated, average-angled snow climbs normally having no pitches. They may, however, have cornice difficulties or dangerous run-outs.

Grade II — Gullies which contain either individual or minor pitches, or high-angled snow with difficult cornice exits. The easiest buttresses under winter conditions.

Grade III — Gullies which contain ice in quantity. There will normally be at least one substantial pitch and possibly several lesser ones. Sustained buttress climbs, but only technical in short sections.

Grade IV — Steeper and more technical with vertical sections found on ice climbs. Buttress routes will require a good repertoire of techniques.

Grade V — Climbs which are difficult, sustained and serious. If on ice, long sustained ice pitches are to be expected; buttress routes will require a degree of rock climbing ability and the use of axe torquing and hooking and similar winter techniques.

Grade VI — Thin and tenuous ice routes or those with long vertical sections. Buttress routes will include all that has gone before but more of it.

Grade VII — Usually rock routes which are very sustained or technically extreme. Also sustained routes on thin or vertical ice.

Grade VIII — The very hardest buttress routes.

The technical grades which are shown by the Arabic numbers, are based on the technical difficulty of classic winter routes of Grade III, IV and V. This is used as a basis for assessing the technical difficulty of the route, while the Roman numeral gives an indication of the overall seriousness of the climb, in a very similar way to which the E grades and the numerical grades are used in summer. In this way a V,4 is normally a serious ice route, V,5 would be a classic ice route with adequate protection, V,6 would be a classic buttress route and V,7 would indicate a technically difficult but well protected buttress route. Each route is of the same overall difficulty (V) but with differing degrees of seriousness and technical difficulty.

Equipment and Style
It is assumed that a good range of modern nuts and camming devices will be carried for the harder climbs, both in summer and winter. The summer climbs described in this guide are graded assuming the

presence and stability of any of the *in situ* pegs that are mentioned. If pegs are essential on new routes, it is hoped that they will be kept to a minimum and left in place; please keep to the Scottish tradition of bold climbs with leader-placed protection. Please make every attempt to find a safe alternative to pegs before resorting to them. Unfortunately pegs are still necessary on some winter routes to make them acceptably safe. This tends to be more often the case on the harder gully climbs than on the better rock of the buttress routes.

Many of the hardest rock climbs that are described in this book will have been cleaned or otherwise inspected prior to the first ascent, but most routes of E2 and many of E3 were climbed on-sight. Although every attempt is made to grade them for an on sight lead, this should be borne in mind. Many of the difficult winter routes were also initially climbed with prior knowledge; sometimes unintentionally gained by a summer ascent of the route, some through previous failure and sometimes by deliberate inspection prior to a winter ascent. Again, every attempt has been made to grade for an on-sight ascent.

Left and Right
The terms left and right refer to a climber facing the direction being described, i.e. facing the cliff for route descriptions, facing downhill in descent.

Pitch Lengths
Pitch lengths are in metres, rounded to the nearest 5m. The lengths are usually estimates, rather than measurements. 45m ropes are sufficiently long for the Cairngorms, although 50m is also popular, especially for the harder winter climbs. Where lengths greater than 50m are given this does not indicate moving together, merely belay where required or desired.

Recommended Routes
No list of recommended routes has been given, instead a star grading system for quality has been used. Stars have been given as a selection guide for occasional visitors and consequently have been allocated somewhat sparingly and spread throughout the grades, although vegetation and poor rock limits the number of stars below VS. Many of the routes without stars are still very good. Higher grade routes tend to be more sustained and on better rock but somewhat higher standards have therefore been applied. Grade VII and VIII winter routes have not been starred unless they have had sufficient repeat ascents, but

most aspirants are unlikely to be influenced by a starring system. Equally, starred routes on different cliffs may vary slightly according to the quality of the cliff, but it is necessary to apply stars as a route selection aid. Winter stars are a problem because quality will vary with conditions, so stars, like the grade, are applied for average conditions which may not exist at the time. Stars have been reduced for rarely-formed ice routes, but one should never be committed to any particular route before inspecting conditions anyway.

*** An outstanding route of the highest quality, combining superb climbing with line, character, situation and other features which make a route great. Could compare with any route in the country.

** As above, but lacking one of the features while having similar quality of climbing.

* Good climbing, but the route may lack line, situation or balance.

First Ascensionists

The year of the first ascent is given in the text. The full date and first ascensionists are listed cliff by cliff in chronological order at the back of the guide. The original aid is also listed, usually with the first free ascent. Details of variations are given under the parent route. Whether the route was ascended in summer or winter conditions is indicated by an S or W at the left end of each line. Winter ascents are listed separately from their corresponding summer route, with different forks of gullies also listed separately. Aid eliminations in winter are noted when known, although these were rarely recorded before the 1970s.

Litter and Vandalism

Litter is a continuing problem at popular camping sites and bothies, despite a slow improvement in recent years. All litter, including spare and unwanted food, should be taken out of the mountains. The justifications for leaving food that is bio-degradable is spurious in these areas, as the breakdown of material in such a cold environment takes years. Likewise, leaving food for birds and animals is misguided as this only attracts scavengers into the area where they prey on the residents. Birds such as the ptarmigan have their eggs taken while hoodie crows become increasingly obvious. If you take it in, take it out again; this includes finger tape and chalk wrappers, litter that climbers cannot blame anyone else for. Another problem is rings of stones used round tents; if you must use them, return the boulders where they came from. In the end, justified complaints by landowners can lead to access problems. Please co-operate by not leaving any traces behind you.

Mountain Rescue

In case of an accident requiring rescue or medical attention, telephone 999 (police). This will usually mean a return to habitation, with the exceptions of the public telephones at Derry Lodge (Map Ref 041 934), the Coire Cas car park (Map Ref 991 059) and at Spittal of Glenmuick (Map Ref 308 850). Give concise information about the location and injuries of the victim and any assistance available at the accident site. Try to leave someone with the casualty. In a party of two with no one nearby, there will be a difficult decision to make. If you decide to go for help, make the casualty warm and comfortable and leave them in a sheltered, well marked place. However, it is often better to stay with the victim.

There is a first-aid box in the corrie of Lochnagar at the usual gearing-up point (Map Ref 251 857) on a small flattening about midway between the Loch and the right side of Central Buttress (cairn). Its contents vary, but there is often a casualty bag and avalanche probes.

Avalanches

Every year avalanches occur in the Cairngorms, sometimes with tragic results. Climbers venturing onto the hills in winter should aquaint themselves with the principles of snow structure and avalanche prediction. There are a number of suitable books on the subject. A knowledge of what to do if involved in an avalanche, either as a victim or an observer, may help to save lives. A knowledge of first aid and artificial resuscitation is an obvious necessity.

Avalanches most often occur following heavy snow fall or during periods of strong thawing conditions, when slopes between 22 and 60 degrees are suspect, with the main danger area being between 30 and 45 degrees. Any danger will last longer in colder conditions when the snow pack takes longer to stabilise. The main danger in the Cairngorms is windslab avalanche, which occurs when snow is redeposited by the wind. This snow bonds poorly with underlying layers and in these conditions lee slopes are the main danger areas, but pockets of windslab can be found in any sheltered location. Knowledge of the preceding weather, especially wind direction, is of great importance in predicting which slopes and climbs are avalanche prone and this must always be borne in mind.

Climbers and walkers, however, should be able to make their own predictions by studying the pattern of snow deposition from the past and present weather conditions. Being able to dig a snow pit, study the snow profile and assess the relative strengths of the various snow layers and draw sensible conclusions from a profile is an important skill for those venturing on the hills in winter. The shear test and the Rutchblock test can be very useful tools in assessing avalanche risk, although their application requires some knowledge and experience. A simple indication of severe avalanche risk is when the snow splits easily into slabs with defined boundaries when walked on; these small slabs indicate that much bigger ones may be waiting to peel off. Along with the means to make a realistic risk assessment it is also necessary to understand the principles of movement in avalanche terrain to minimise any risk.

If avalanched, try either to jump free or anchor yourself for as long are possible. If swept down, protect your access to oxygen by 'swimming' to stay on the surface, by keeping your mouth closed and by preserving an air space in front of your face if buried. Wet snow avalanches harden rapidly on settling, so try and break free if possible at this point. If trapped, try to stay calm to reduce oxygen demand.

If a witness to an avalanche, it is VITAL to start a search immediately, given that it is safe to do so. Victims will often be alive at first but their chances lessen quickly if buried. Unless severely injured, some 80% may live if found immediately but this drops rapidly to about 30% after 1 hour and 10% after 3 hours. Mark the burial site if known, the site when last seen and the position of anything else found and search until help arrives. Again, a working knowledge of first aid may save a life, as many victims may have stopped breathing. Remember that IMMEDIATE SEARCHING CAN SAVE LIFES.

Whilst the ability to make your own assessment of risk is vital to anyone venturing into this area, avalanche predictions produced by the Scottish Avalanche Information Service are readily available during the winter. These can be found at police stations, sports shops, tourist information centres and many hotels throughout the area. There is also a display board at the head of Coire Cas car park. This information is also available on local radio and in the local and national press and from the Police SAIS Avalanche Information Service on 01463 713191. For the computer literate to get a report on e-mail, simply mail-avalanches dcs.gla.ac.uk.

On World Wide Web, access the information by typing in URL. The URL for the avalanche service is:

http://www.dcs.gla.ac.uk/other/avalanche/

Maps and other sources of information

The maps recommended for use are the following Ordnance Survey 1:50,000 maps: Sheets 44 (Ballater) and 36 (Grantown and Cairngorm) cover the area, which is also partly covered by Sheet 33 (Braemar). The 1:25,000 Outdoor Leisure Map entitled the *High Tops of the Cairngorms* is also suitable for the northern section of this guide. The map references of the larger crags and corries in this guide indicate the approximate centre of these features.

The meaning and pronunciation of local place names can be found in *Scottish Hill and Mountain Names* by Peter Drummond, published by the SMT (1991). Much useful information about the hills and the area as a whole can be found in the SMC District Guide *The Cairngorms* by Adam Watson and published by the SMT (1992).

Lochnagar

Lochnagar is understandably one of Scotland's most famous mountains. Its distinctive outline rises gracefully above a complicated mass of lower hills and wooded slopes and provides a noble mountain landscape for all residents and approaching climbers on Royal Deeside. The name really refers to the loch above which "the dark frowning glories" loom, while the mountain should be called Beinn na Ciochan. The 1155m summit, Cac Carn Beag, is at Map Ref 244 861.

Most of the climbing on the mountain is situated in the magnificent north-east corrie whose cliff-front extends for 1½km, reaching a height of 250m and encircling the loch. It is split by great gullies into many important buttresses giving long natural routes. Lochnagar's infamy attributed to its vegetation and loose rock is not altogether unfounded. Considerable areas of cliff are grassy and with few exceptions the gullies are loose. The rock climbing Aberdonian, however, would rightly defend his "citadel of vegetatious granite", for on the steep clean faces and ridges of the buttresses are to be found climbs of the highest calibre.

In winter the buttresses and gullies excel. Conditions are particularly reliable; its deep enclosure protects the snow from the effects of a thaw and shelters the climber from strong south or west winds. Another consequence is the collection of windslab, for which the corrie is notorious on days of spindrift, although some of the buttresses should offer safe options. A criticism is that powder may lie unconsolidated for long periods in January and February. But the classic buttress climbs are only a little harder, and perhaps more intricate under powder, progress being dependent on the abundant frozen turf instead of snow and ice.

Access

Lochnagar, lying wholly in the Royal Estate of Balmoral, has restrictions placed on the use of approaches to the corrie from Deeside, but the route from Glen Muick gives unhindered access at all times, even during the stalking season. There is a ranger and naturalist service at Spittal of Glenmuick, where full access information is available. Camping is prohibited near the picnic site at Spittal Wood.

The car park is reached from Ballater by 15km of motor road (sometimes blocked by snow in winter). From the car park, walk through the wood past the visitor centre, turn immediately right (signpost) and follow a private unsurfaced road across the Muick to a T-junction beside an out-building of Allt-na-giubhsaich Lodge. A path follows a fence westwards from this out-building. Take this path which leads through pine trees to join a landrover track. This is followed all too obviously out of the pines and up the open hillside to the Muick-Gelder col. Here the path branches off the track to the left and is well marked to the summit plateau. Leave this main path beyond the spring known as Foxes' Well and go over the col between Meikle Pap and Cuidhe Crom to descend into the corrie. The total distance is 7km.

Descents

In summer, the quickest descent to the corrie floor is by the main (right) branch of The Black Spout. If this is snow-filled, follow the corrie edge and descend beyond West Buttress. In winter, either branch of The Black Spout can be descended with care, but the main branch is recommended as the cornice is almost always easily passed on the left (looking down). The normal return to the valley is to follow the cliff edge back to the Meikle Pap col (beware of cornices). In stormy weather, a foolproof but longer descent can be made *via* Glas Allt and Loch Muick. From any point near the cliff top, head south (if at the top of West Buttress, beware of The Black Spout which cuts into the plateau). Gentle slopes soon lead into the upper basin of Glas Allt, which is followed to Loch Muick.

THE NORTH-EAST CORRIE

The corrie has two sectors of differing aspect. The northern, with its great amphitheatre of buttresses and gullies, forms the main climbing arena and its domination has limited visitors to the Southern Sector.

SOUTHERN SECTOR

This forms a wide bay with a frieze of rock under the plateau. The line of demarcation is Central Gully, an open chute sending its screes to the lochside on the left of Central Buttress, the first major buttress on the Glen Muick approach.

At the back of the Southern Sector is a short prominent chute of distinctly red scree, **The Red Spout**. This is (almost) at the lowest point

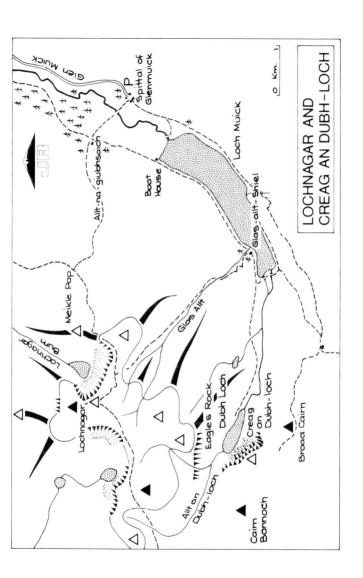

LOCHNAGAR AND
CREAG AN DUBH-LOCH

0 Km. 1

Glen Muick

P
Spital of
Glenmuick

Loch Muick

Allt-na giubhsaich

Boat
House

Glas-allt-Shiel

Meikle Pap

Glas Allt

Lochnagar
Burn

Lochnagar

Eagles Rock

Dubh Loch

Creag
an
Dubh-loch

Allt an
Dubh-loch

Cairn
Bannoch

Broad Cairn

of the plateau rim and rarely cornices. To the left of the spout are some ribs, then a well defined buttress with a steep lower section. This is **Sunset Buttress** (Very Difficult with combined tactics; III,5 in winter). The obvious gully in the right flank of the buttress is **Sunset Gully** (III, left fork taken). Towards the left side of the front face is a vegetated groove which leads to a prominent wide crack on the left edge. This is **Quick Dash Crack** (IV, 5). The chokestoned gully between Sunset Buttress and a slabby buttress on the left is **Iffy** (an early season IV,4). The only other recorded climb between this and the Meikle Pap col is **Jacob's Slabs** (Difficult; III,4 in winter), which takes the right side of the isolated piece of rock high under the plateau rim near the top of the 'ladder' section of the tourist path.

To the right of The Red Spout, the rocks gain in stature as they approach Central Gully, presenting a trio of buttresses. The leftmost is indeterminate. The central is The Cathedral, separated from the right buttress by Forsaken Gully. The right buttress is Sinister Buttress, the largest of the trio and descending lower into the corrie than The Cathedral.

THE CATHEDRAL

Towards the left end of The Cathedral is an impressive mummy-shaped tower (the cathedral spire). To its right are four slender ribs divided by chimneys and grooves (the cathedral body) which provide most of the routes. Above these ribs is a left-rising terrace ending at a deep chimney taken by three routes. Cathedral Chimney, then another buttress with a higher base, are the next features to the right before Forsaken Gully.

Transept Groove 90m IV,4 (1983)
Climb the broken groove line immediately left of the mummy-shaped tower and finish by the left and deepest of two chimneys at the top of the terrace.

Transept Route 100m V,6 * (1994)
Climb the groove right of the mummy-shaped tower to the terrace, finishing by the chimney. The crux is a technical overhang on the first pitch, but the climbing is sustained throughout. The summer route (Severe) trends right across the grooves to the chimney finish.

Sepulchre 80m V,6 *   (1987)
A good short climb, taking the central groove of the crag. Start from
the left side of a slight bay and climb a narrow groove twisting up right.
From ledges above, climb twin grooves, then trend left to finish by the
chimney of Transept Route.

Judas Priest 100m V,5   (1986)
This follows the larger right-hand groove rising from the bay. Climb a
corner on the right before moving left to enter the main groove, then
follow it to easy ground. Work right through a slot to finish at the top of
Cathedral Chimney.

Trinity 110m V,7   (1995)
This route follows the rightmost corner system. Start as for Judas
Priest, then continue up the slabby corner above and its continuation
above a ledge to easy ground. Climb up and right to a steepening
groove (Judas Priest moves right through the obvious slot). Climb
straight up to belay below an alcove, then take the right-hand corner
past a small chokestone.

Cathedral Chimney 60m III   (1977)
Climb the obvious deep narrow chimney left of the rightmost buttress.

No Worries Groove 90m IV,6   (1993)
The rightmost buttress on the edge of Forsaken Gully gives a poor rock
climb but a better winter route, following a prominent left-facing corner
in the centre of the face above the start of Forsaken Gully. A short wall
high up is the crux.

Forsaken Gully 90m II   (1950)
A narrow gully, generally without pitches, but quite steep and often
heavily corniced.

SINISTER BUTTRESS

This triangular buttress is steep in its lower half and named with
reference to its lichenous and vegetated rock.

Forsaken Rib 90m III   (1970)
The rib on the right of Forsaken Gully.

Gremlin 90m V,6   (1982)
The steep wall left of Direct Route. From the toe of the buttress, easy
ledges lead up left to a steep wall. Go up right *via* an ice bulge, then
back left to a little corner. This leads to a left-trending ramp and easy
ground.

Direct Route 90m Severe   (1955)
A prominent chimney cleaves the lower buttress slightly right of centre.
Climb its left side, then go across and up its right side to belay below
an overhung corner. Climb this and the true crest *via* a little tower to
the top.
Winter: **Terrorist** 90m IV,5 (aid)   (1975)
Start right of the prominent chimney, join the direct route for its
overhanging corner, and go right then left to finish up a pronounced
runnel beyond the little tower. Some aid was used.

Gully Route 60m II   (1995)
This starts someway up Central Gully and leads to the tower of Direct
Route. Moderate in summer.

Central Gully 200m I
Defining the right limit of Sinister Buttress is the open funnel of Central
Gully. Quite straightforward.

NORTHERN SECTOR

The great semicircle of cliff beyond Central Gully is entirely continuous,
but for ready identification a division of the buttresses into five natural
groups is made. These groups are determined by the four largest
gullies cutting through the cliff. The gullies, whose positions may be
pinpointed in thick weather by their great scree or snow fans, are from
left to right:
    Douglas-Gibson Gully presents a straight-cut gash between high
walls. It is bounded on the left by a trio of buttresses forming the
distinctive Shadow Buttress group, to the right of Central Gully. Snow
lies longer here than elsewhere in the corrie and a tongue usually lasts
into July. It is bounded on the right by Eagle Ridge.
    Parallel Gully B is a very distinctive as a narrow chimney in smooth
rock which leads to a wider gully in its top half. Parallel Buttress is to
its left and the steep, smooth Tough-Brown Face is on the right.

Raeburn's Gully lies right of Tough-Brown Ridge, and its lower Tough-Brown Face, in a recess where the corrie angles round from north to east-facing. It is inconspicuous from most viewpoints because of its left-slanting course. Its screes, however, can be seen joining those of The Black Spout.

The Black Spout is unmistakable; a wide corridor slanting right and scree-filled to the plateau. To its left is the Black Spout Pinnacle Group and on the right is West Buttress.

The standard place for gearing up is the first aid box, situated on a platform below the screes of the northern sector. The magnetic bearings from the box to some of the major routes are as follows, but it should be noted that all the direct approaches cross regular avalanche paths.

Central Buttress (initial gully): 190 degrees
Shadow Buttress A, Original Route: 214 degrees
Parallel Gully A: 258 degrees
Raeburn's Gully: 278 degrees
The Black Spout: 286 degrees

SHADOW BUTTRESS GROUP

This group is composed of three buttresses angling down left from Douglas-Gibson Gully. Central Buttress is the obvious and lowest descending crest on the left. Shallow Gully, ill-defined, separates Central Buttress from Shadow Buttress A, which is easily recognised by its prominent curving band of grass or snow (The Spiral Terrace) starting low down below the large overhangs. Rightmost is Shadow Buttress B, narrow and well defined by steep walls dropping into Douglas-Gibson Gully on the right and Polyphemus Gully on the left. Its base lies at a higher level than that of Shadow Buttress A, and in the angle formed between them is Shadow Couloir, a bay into which falls Shadow Chimney and Giant's Head Chimney.

1 Central Buttress 300m Moderate   (1928)
The easiest of the major buttresses and the first on the left. The left flank is composed of easy-angled grassy ledges, but the steep slabby face dropping into Shallow Gully has continuous rock in its lower reaches. The best route starts up an introductory gully leading left from the foot of Shallow Gully. At its top, traverse right as soon as practicable and climb the crest to two gendarmes set on a level arete. From there

about 120m of scrambling leads to the plateau. The climb on the whole is spoiled by the ever-present easy ground on the left.

Winter: II *   (1948)

The technical, turfy climbing offers a good introduction to Lochnagar buttresses, but the slopes above the arete can avalanche and will funnel down Shallow Gully. There are numerous easy possibilities on the left flank, but follow the summer line to get the best from the route.

2 Mantichore 60m E1   (1976)

A short but good and sustained climb. Just above the start of the introductory gully of Central Buttress there is a steep rippled slab bounded on its right by a groove. The line ascends this slab then follows the right-hand twin groove.

1. 25m 5b An easy ramp leads *via* a little groove to the rippled slab. Climb the slab to its apex, then step down to a mossy ledge and belay.

2. 35m 5b Move up to a higher ledge, then step right and climb a tapering slab-flake into a V-groove. Continue up this to near its top, move left, then go up to a grassy ledge below a square-cut roof. Go up left to easy ground.

3 Central Buttress Direct 90m IV,6   (1975)

Above and right of the steep Mantichore wall is a straight line of grooves parallel to the initial gully of Central Buttress. The route is Hard Severe in summer.

4 Chevalier 110m V,7   (1995)

This route takes a parallel line of the shallow grooves just left of Centrist, finishing by the same easy groove. Start at the foot of Central Buttress Direct and trend right.

5 Centrist 140m V,5 *   (1974)

A direct winter ascent of the right face of Central Buttress. It gains the normal buttress route at the gendarmes from where one can follow the ordinary route or descend ledges on the left to return to the corrie floor. Start close to the groove line of Central Buttress Direct, just right of the lowest rocks. Climb a shallow groove slanting slightly right and go over a chokestone, then go up into a big groove with an overhang at its top. Avoid this on the left (crux) and continue curving left up ramps until an easier angled groove leads right to the crest just before the gendarmes.

LOCHNAGAR

THE NORTHERN SECTOR

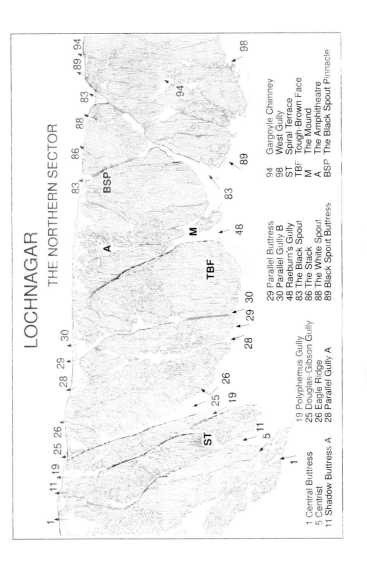

1 Central Buttress
5 Centrist
11 Shadow Buttress A

19 Polyphemus Gully
25 Douglas-Gibson Gully
26 Eagle Ridge
28 Parallel Gully A

29 Parallel Buttress
30 Parallel Gully B
48 Raeburn's Gully
83 The Black Spout
86 The Stack
88 The White Spout
89 Black Spout Buttress

94 Gargoyle Chimney
98 West Gully
ST Spiral Terrace
TBF Tough-Brown Face
M The Mound
A The Amphitheatre
BSP The Black Spout Pinnacle

6 Sciolist 150m IV,4   (1978)
A vague line of grooves left of Shallow Gully, including an obvious
V-groove and ending beside a prominent square tower.

7 Shallow Gully 300m IV,4   (1959)
The shallow depression between Central Buttress and Shadow Buttress A. Graded for some ice, but not being recessed, it fills up less
readily than the major gullies and is therefore variable in standard.
Difficulties are confined to the lowest 60m, which are poorly protected,
after which snow leads to the upper slopes of Central Buttress. The
route is Very Difficult in summer, but with bad rock and vegetation.

8 Shadow Rib 300m V,5   (1970)
This is the slabby rib immediately right of Shallow Gully and separated
from the Original Route on Shadow Buttress A (via the Spiral Terrace)
by large overhangs. Start at the foot of the slabby rib just right of
Shallow Gully. Climb twin left-facing grooves overlooking Shallow Gully
and continue up the crest to a steep wall. It is a grade easier to start
up on the right by a cave left of Original Route's introductory gully.
Traverse right below the steep wall to a short awkward flake crack
which leads to a ledge returning left. Where the ledge ends, make an
exposed step round a corner, then go up left and climb an easy gully
to a small col on the upper crest. Climb the crest, as for Original Route,
to the plateau. In summer, the climb is Difficult (or Severe direct) and
vegetatious.
Variation: **Slime Lords** V,6   (1984)
A direct line starting out left from the cave, then going straight up
passing near the awkward flake crack of the normal route. Continue to
Original Route.

9 Shadowlands 250m V,7   (1995)
An intimidating direct route through the steep lower buttress. A super-
direct combination with the Direct Route would be worthwhile. Start at
the cave up left from the introductory gully of Original Route.
1. 30m Climb up left to a good stance, as for the easier option of
Shadow Rib.
2. 25m Trend right over short steep walls until it is possible to make
an awkward step down and right to the base of an imposing left-trending fault (junction with Shadow Buttress A Direct Route).

3. 20m Gain the fault from the right, and climb it for 15m until it is possible to break out right into an overhanging niche. Pull over this to reach a good ledge.

4. 25m Make a difficult step left and follow the fault to its end.

5. etc. 150m Move up and right to the crest, soon joining Original Route.

10 Shadow Buttress A, Direct Route 250m VI,7   (1984)

A direct winter route taking a ramp which cuts through the steep lower buttress. Start at the cave up left from Original Route's introductory gully.

1. 30m Move out left for 10m until it is possible to break right up an awkward slab into the bottom left corner of a roofed recess. Leave the recess immediately by a steep corner to belay overlooking Shadow Rib.

2. 30m Curve up and right to a ledge system, then go up to enter the base of the ramp by a wild move up a short wall.

3. 40m Climb the ramp and a prominent V-groove to reach the apex of the lower buttress.

4. etc. 150m Continue up the easier crest, soon joined by the normal route, to the plateau.

Variation: **The Time-Out Finish**

This takes a lower ramp leading out right from the ledge system on pitch 2, at technical grade 5.

11 Shadow Buttress A, Original Route 300m III,4 ***   (1949)

A first class mountaineering route and a good choice for strong parties in poor conditions (it is safe from avalanche once the route is reached). Start in the bay below the large overhangs. Climb up right towards the overhangs, then follow the Spiral Terrace round right underneath them to a balcony. From its end, climb a vague rib alongside Shadow Chimney, including a steep section which is a notorious short crux. It is possible to turn up from the Spiral Terrace too soon and encounter extra difficulties (see Vortex). Now trend left and regain the crest by a shallow gully. Follow the crest to a small tower, passed by a short descent on the right (or climbed direct, 5).

The route gives an interesting summer Moderate, but it is very vegetated and rarely climbed nowadays.

There are four variation starts, which can also be considered as independent routes. They are sometimes sheltered on a stormy day, when one can descend back into the corrie without braving the plateau.

12 Shadow Chimney IV,4 (1952)
The prominent chimney on the left side of the Shadow Couloir leads
back and knee past the right side of Original Route's crux. Very Difficult
in summer.

13 Bell's Route III (1953)
The rocks on Shadow Chimney's immediate left, joining Original Route
at the balcony. Moderate in summer.

14 Vortex IV,4 (1994)
Start 20m down from Bell's Route, just above the lower buttress's
steepest section. Move up left to grooves, then climb these to the
balcony. Continue directly to the left of Original Route's crux.

15 Katabatic Corner V,5 (1985)
From the base of the lower buttress, climb the turfy leftmost of three
corner lines before moving right into the top part of the central and
most obvious corner.

16 Moonshadow 225m V,5 (1992)
The well defined buttress between Shadow Chimney and Giant's Head
Chimney Direct. Start at the foot of Giant's Head Chimney.
1. 40m Climb diagonally up and left for 15m to enter a steep, right-facing corner. Climb this and exit left on turf. Continue up behind a large
boulder to belay in Shadow Chimney.
2. 25m Leave the chimney immediately by climbing an awkward wall
on the right, which leads to a hidden ramp cutting back right to the
crest of the buttress. Pull over the small roof above to reach a good
ledge.
3. 40m Continue easily for 15m to reach a steep slabby wall cut by
parallel cracks. Climb the right side of the wall *via* a left-facing corner,
and finish up easier ground to a ledge.
4. 40m The short steep corner behind the belay leads to a rightwards
trending line of weakness.
5. and 6. 80m Continue up mixed ground to reach Shadow Buttress
A below the final tower. Climb this to the top.

17 Giant's Head Chimney Direct 200m V,5 (1972)
Giant's Head Chimney is the right-hand of the Shadow Couloir chimneys and is hidden behind Shadow Buttress A when viewed from the
first aid box. Polyphemus Gully branches out from the chimney a short

distance up (the branch banks out in winter). Climb the narrow lower chimney with one ice pitch, usually short, to a large overhang. Move out right to belay. Traverse left across the overhang (exposed and technical) to a stance. Enter the shallow upper chimney and follow it to a snow bowl. From this, gain Giant's Head Arete on the right which leads to the crest of Shadow Buttress A and the top. Very Difficult in summer.

18 Giant's Head Chimney 220m IV,4 *   (1950)
A fine climb, graded for good ice. Climb the initial chimney to the overhang and move right to belay as for the Direct. Follow a terrace round the corner on the right into a trough. The initial 30m of the trough may contain much ice, and in these conditions it gives a superb exposed pitch. Higher up the trough becomes an easy snow scoop. Here, more difficult climbing may be found by moving right on to the 'Feathered Arete'. Very Difficult and unpleasant in summer.

19 Polyphemus Gully 200m V,5 ***   (1953)
An excellent gully with good rock belays below the two hard pitches, and a soft touch for the grade in good conditions. The gully cuts deeply into the left side of Shadow Buttress B and is reached by traversing on steepening snow from the base of Giant's Head Chimney. There are two big pitches separated by 60m of steep snow. The upper pitch can be climbed directly on ice above a cave. In thinner conditions, either take a little corner on the right, or more commonly, an obvious V-groove on the left. The cornice is often huge but can usually by outflanked by a traverse right on Shadow Buttress B. Severe in summer.
Variation: **Multiple Chimneys** V,5   (1949)
On the left wall above the lower pitch, a prominent tower cleft by a V-chimney can be seen high up on the left under the plateau. Leave the gully immediately above the initial pitch, then head for and climb the chimney. Difficult in summer.
The Tower Variation: V,5   (1974)
Leave the main line higher up and follow the first corner on the right of the tower.

The next five routes lie on Shadow Buttress B, which presents the classical buttress form. A steep lower section, built on broad austere lines, leads to easier-angled ground before tapering to a narrow crest at the top.

20 Raeburn's Groove 70m VI,7 *   (1986)
A recommended but harder start to Shadow Buttress B. Climb the
obvious groove on the left edge of the buttress to where it ends under
a steep wall. Traverse left beneath the wall and climb its left edge (crux).
Go left again and up a short groove to reach the crest and the junction
with other routes.

21 Bell's Route 200m Severe   (1934/1941)
A fine line but with bad rock and vegetation. Start just inside the foot
of Douglas-Gibson Gully where a grassy break leads left to the centre
of the buttress. Go up a crack on the right until two teeth are encountered below a vertical wall. From a perch on the left tooth "flit quickly
across a holdless wall to grasp a flake handrail". The flake is loose!
Beyond this, ascend a groove to belay on a large platform at the top
of the steep section. Scrambling now follows until the final rocks
steepen below the plateau. The best way is on the left.
Winter: V,6 **   (1955)
A rewarding climb, typical of the best of the winter buttresses. A
technical lower section is followed by enjoyable climbing up the crest
via snow aretes and short steps leading to a steep finish and
occasionally a difficult cornice.

22 Original Route 200m IV,4 **   (1972)
This provides a route of more consistent standard, also recommended.
Start inside Douglas-Gibson about 10m above Bell's Route and follow
shallow turfy grooves to the crest. Severe and dangerous in summer.

23 Eclipse 120m VI,5   (1988)
A fine route which climbs the Douglas-Gibson face. It is serious,
requires ice, and is not often in condition. Start well below the gully
narrows, about 10m up from a smooth corner and beyond a blunt rib.
Climb the shallow groove, then move left across the rib to gain and
follow snow and ice up and right through a prominent slot. Move up left
to a big snow ramp and climb this rightwards to a peg belay on the
right. The line of the ramp ends at overhangs below Penumbra. Climb
the next groove left of the ramp which leads directly to the summit
rocks.

24 Penumbra 110m V,5 *   (1972)
This interesting line follows the larger corner running from the narrows
of Douglas-Gibson Gully to the top of Shadow Buttress B. The more

ice the easier, but serious. From the point where Douglas-Gibson Gully suddenly narrows, climb the obvious discontinuous corner for three pitches to the cornice. Sometimes it is necessary to traverse left below this to exit on the true crest of Shadow Buttress B.

25 Douglas-Gibson Gully 200m V,4 ** (1950)
The great gully between Shadow Buttress B and Eagle Ridge provides a historically important climb. Although it has lost much of its original aura of impregnability, the gully still provides a fine and serious climb in impressive surroundings. Under normal conditions, straightforward snow with perhaps one short pitch leads up through the narrows to the foot of the top wall. Move left and climb a groove to a small rock fault, until it is possible to move left into an easier snow runnel leading to the cornice. This is sometimes huge and unavoidable. The route is also good early in the season when there is much ice and a smaller cornice. When free from winter's grip, it is a death-trap. The upper wall is totally rotten, wet and ungradeable.

Variations: **The Forks**
Three other forks diverge from the base of the top wall. All are about 60m long and may offer a smaller cornice than the normal (left) fork. The **Right Fork** (V,5 1973) runs up the Eagle Ridge side of the top wall. It is Severe and nearly as dangerous in summer.

The **Central Fork** (VI,5 1984) requires good conditions. An icicle forms at the base of the top wall. Climb the icicle, then an icy groove to a bulge. Pass this on the right (not by the obvious chimney). A hidden right-trending line leads to the finish.

The **Far Left Fork** (V,5 1980) traverses left and slightly up into a far left gully with a huge chokestone.

EAGLE RIDGE AND
THE PARALLEL BUTTRESS GROUP

These two famous features lie between Douglas-Gibson Gully and Parallel Gully B. First from the left is Eagle Buttress. The narrow, soaring crest on its left edge is Eagle Ridge, from which huge undercut walls plunge into Douglas-Gibson Gully. To the right of Eagle Buttress, cleaving the central cliff, are Parallel Gullies A and B. Parallel Gully B commences as a thin 80m chimney before funnelling outwards in its upper reaches. Sandwiched between them is flat-fronted Parallel Buttress which tapers to a slender ridge near the plateau.

26 Eagle Ridge 250m Severe *** (1941)

One of the finest climbs in the country, and very popular. The ridge dries quickly after rain, but it is possible in the wet, as the crampon cleaned rock is not too slippery (VS?). Start just inside the screes of Douglas-Gibson Gully.

Climb the first obvious 20m groove. Easier climbing follows up a shallow gully and an awkward short chimney leading towards the Eagle Buttress face. Head back left towards the crest by a choice of routes, all going *via* a 10m inset corner on the right. Here the ridge steepens in a rugged 15m tower. Swing up into a recess on the right, then continue up steep rock and go left to a splendid sentry box. The next pitch follows a smooth arete and finishes up a little corner to a ledge on the crest (do not go further right here). Follow the crest over the 'Whaleback' for 20m to a ledge at mid-height in a short slab corner, the top of which ends in an airy knife-edge forming the crest.

The vertical wall against which the knife-edge abuts is traditionally the crux. Climb it by a crack on the left to reach another level arete. Climb the crest to a projecting square-cut overhang. The winter route traverses right here. Instead, swing up onto the coping slab above and, from some cracked blocks, mantelshelf into a V-recess (the loss of turf has made this move harder, 4b. The winter route on the right is easier). Finish up the final slabs which dip into Douglas Gibson Gully.

Winter: VI,6 *** (1953)

The Queen of Lochnagar's winter climbs. Viewed from the corrie floor, the ridge sweeps up majestically in a series of alluring snow crests and intimidating walls. In calm weather and with good snow a technically reasonable climb may be enjoyed; in powdery conditions the ridge becomes a big undertaking. The Tower provides the winter crux. Some parties have avoided the summer crux section by climbing further right of the crest (Dundee Route). This should not be missed however, as it provides an exciting problem, one of the highlights of the climb. The summer crux is short but technically very hard, although it can build up with snow. For the final pitch, a corner on the right of the summer route is usually taken.

The big slabby corner on the Eagle Ridge wall of Douglas-Gibson Gully, springing up from the narrows (opposite Penumbra) gives a 60m V.5 (1989). A 15m right traverse joins Eagle Ridge below the summer crux; a more direct finish would be possible with good snow.

27 Eagle Buttress 250m IV,3 (1956)

The buttress holds snow well and is often in condition, but it is a serious route, with poor protection and the crux near the top (perhaps under-graded). Start midway between Eagle Ridge and Parallel Gully A. For about 120m, the climbing is straightforward up to the head of the central snow scoop. The line of least resistance then veers right to below the steep upper wall. Here a ledge leads right to three parallel V-grooves overlooking Parallel Gully A. Climb the central groove (crux). Turn left and follow the edge close to Parallel Gully A, joining it at the very top.

Variation: **Eagle Groove** IV,5 (1988)

A good alternative finish is to climb the obvious groove line trending left from the central snow scoop to finish up Eagle Ridge. Difficult in summer.

28 Parallel Gully A 270m III ** (1948)

A variable but always enjoyable climb which may have several long ice pitches or completely bank out into a snow chute. The direct first pitch may give as much as 30m of sustained ice, but it can be avoided by a traverse from the left. There is a shallow chimney in the gully bed above. It can be climbed, but it is better to go left on ice to a long stretch of snow leading past a minor gully on the right to a bifurcation. A rising traverse left gains entry to the left fork which is straightforward to the cornice, often by-passed on the left.

Right Fork Variation: IV,4 ** (1958)

From the bifurcation, take the steep and more direct right fork.

1930 Route Variation: V,5 (1978)

This is closer to the summer line (Severe). Follow the narrow minor gully on the right to a *cul de sac* on the side of Parallel Buttress. Move left onto the buttress, which leads steeply to the top.

29 Parallel Buttress 280m Severe (1939)

A route with character, history and of course a fair amount of vegeta-tion. Start up a wide groove just right of Parallel Gully A. Enter the groove from the right and finish at a grassy corner. Above are twin grooves (these form the variation start; start in the right groove and transfer to the left, VS). Instead move right along a ledge into a defined chimney. Straddle this and exit to a ledge on the right. Slant right up two recessed corners to a big flake, from where easy ground slants left to a grassy section where Tough-Brown Traverse crosses it. Work up easy ground until forced, by the great slabby face of the buttress. to move right to the edge of Parallel Gully B. Gain a shelf overlooking the gully and climb it to its end, almost in the gully (30m). Move left onto the face and ascend the right-hand of two faults for 30m to a ledge girdling the buttress, The Necklace. From the centre of the ledge, either climb a groove and recess to the crest above, or move right and climb the crest directly. Continue up the crest *via* a pointed block to a platform beneath the Tower. Gain a small ledge up on the left, then climb the shallow groove above for 3m to a large jammed spike (crux). There is a large ledge beyond the crest on the left, but continue up and right to the top of the Tower. Scrambling remains to the plateau.

Left Edge Variation: VS 4c   (1976)
Take the twin grooves start as described above, then follow the left edge of the buttress above, joining the normal route just below the Tower. In winter, this is VI.7 (1980).

Winter: VI,6 **   (1956)
An excellent climb with continuously interesting climbing all the way, but escapable. As with Eagle Ridge, consolidated snow will considerably ease the difficulties. The most likely points of difficulty are the defined chimney in the lower section, the ramp overlooking Parallel Gully B, the initial moves above The Necklace and the Tower. At the jammed spike on the Tower, move left to a sloping snow shelf and follow it until it is possible to return to the crest behind the Tower. A graceful snow arete leads to the plateau.

30 Parallel Gully B 280m VS   (1952)
A huge rock fall in June 1995 from the right edge of the lower chimney across the Tough-Brown Face may have altered this route. The chimney contains some debris, perhaps dangerous. Since at the time of going to press the details were unknown, the description has been left unchanged; decide for yourself whether the climb is justifiable.

  Uncharacteristic of a Cairngorm gully, both in appearance and in the quality of the rock which is clean and sound. It is only recommended when dry. The continuity of the gully is broken by two large grass bays, the lower of which is the scoop crossed by Tough-Brown Traverse. The first section is a narrow 80m chimney which starts from the screes as a steep crack, normally wet. When dry, it gives a good pitch, 4c. Otherwise start well to the left and enter the chimney after 15m. Follow the chimney to the scoop (4b). Above, the true line of the gully continues easily to a large rounded chokestone which bars further progress. This section of the climb, up to the second grass bay, is taken on the right of the gully bed to a ledge about 10m below a large overhang. Immediately above, on the left, is a 4m groove, The Contortion Groove. Climb it and exit left to a sloping ledge (4c). Work up left to gain the second bay. The big pitch above is loose and an easy ramp leading right is vegetated, so it is better to take a horizontal ledge leading out left from the back of the bay onto Parallel Buttress. Continue by this route, including the fine Tower pitch.

Winter: V.5 *** (1958)
An outstanding route. Climb the gully directly throughout. The left-hand start is usually easier and leads to the chimney; this is sustained but well protected. Entry to the top pitch is blocked by a bulge, sometimes easier on the left side. An alternative here is a groove on the right which leads to the top of Tough-Brown Ridge.

TOUGH-BROWN RIDGE AND FACE

The massive buttress left of Raeburn's Gully presents a forbidding facade of steep boiler-plate slabs, known as the Tough-Brown Face, which taper gradually upwards to form a defined ridge. The true crest of the buttress commences near the foot of Raeburn's Gully and follows the extreme right end of the frontal slabs before merging with the upper ridge.

31 Tough-Brown Traverse 300m Very Difficult (1895)
A devious ascent of the ridge outflanking the lower slabs by starting on Eagle Buttress and gaining the ridge in its ledged upper half. It has little interest as a summer route, consisting mostly of short walls and grassy ledges, but it serves as an exit route, either upwards or in descent, from the Tough-Brown Face. Start on Eagle Buttress some distance left of the initial pitch of Parallel Gully A and traverse into the gully above the pitch. Continue to traverse right and up over the easy section on Parallel Buttress to the grassy scoop above the chimney of Parallel Gully B. Use a short chimney to gain the Great Terrace, which runs across the buttress above the Tough-Brown Face. There is a network of possible lines above the Great Terrace. The original route leaves the Great Terrace about 10m before its upper end by climbing a wall to a ledge. Continue right up a slabby ramp which is soon left by a horizontal ledge to the left. A zigzag course then leads to the crest.

Winter: IV,3 *   (1952)
One of the classics of the mountain. With successful route-finding the
line of the pioneer summer ascent is technically straightforward, but it
is easy to trend too far right at the end of the Great Terrace and
encounter more difficult climbing near the crest of the buttress (but
good; IV,4). In good conditions, a direct line has been followed from
the left end of the Great Terrace (close to Parallel Gully B) to join the
obvious ramp ascending from the upper bay of Parallel Gully B. This
route should not be underestimated in poor weather or late in the day
as retreat is difficult.

The great wall of slabs of the Tough-Brown Face which dominates
the lower half of the buttress is one of the finest rock faces in the
Cairngorms. The face is more vegetated than Creag an Dubh-loch,
although this is largely confined to the ledges. Those used to the
pre-cleaned lines of elsewhere may consider the routes a little dirty.
Sustained technical climbing is a characteristic of all the routes on this
face.

The most prominent feature on the face is a pair of corners (slightly
offset and one above the other) situated left of centre and trending
slightly left towards the scoop of Parallel Gully B. This is the line of
Crypt. All the lines eventually lead to easy ground on the upper buttress
where the Tough-Brown Traverse can be ascended or descended.

From Mort and routes to its right, the quickest descent is to abseil
into Raeburn's Gully. From the top of these routes, traverse right until
overlooking the initial groove of Backdoor Route. Descend easily right
on vegetation (away from Backdoor Route). After about 15m there is
a sling on a block and a peg from which a 45m abseil down a steep
wall reaches the scree fan of Raeburn's Gully.

The following three routes end at the scoop on Parallel Gully B, from
where a descent of Tough-Brown Traverse is the easiest option. Route
lengths are to the Great Terrace only.

A huge rockfall occurred in June 1995 during the final stages of
preparation of this guide. A one-metre thick and 25m high slab of rock,
extending from Parallel Gully B across to the corner of Psyche, slid off
to leave an enormous scar. The whole of the main pitch of Nymph has
gone, and this route has been omitted. Most of the second pitch of
Psyche was removed and the route appears dangerous. Sylph may
not have been altered so much, but it too appears dangerous. Crypt
and the routes to its right appear unaltered.

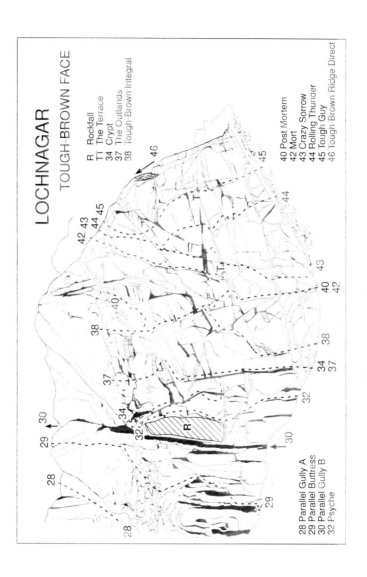

LOCHNAGAR
TOUGH-BROWN FACE

R Rockfall
TT The Terrace
34 Crypt
37 The Outlands
38 Tough-Brown Integral

40 Post Mortem
42 Mort
43 Crazy Sorrow
44 Rolling Thunder
45 Tough Guy
46 Tough Brown Ridge Direct

28 Parallel Gully A
29 Parallel Buttress
30 Parallel Gully B
32 Psyche

32 Psyche 90m   (1972/84)
This route follows the right edge of the rockfall scar. Originally this was
a corner, but it is now a flake crack. The finish used to traverse off left,
roughly along the top of the rockfall, and a different line will probably
be necessary. While this route is very dangerous at present, it may
ultimately provide a climb of good quality. The question of a winter route
is more doubtful.

33 Sylph 90m E1   (1978)
This route has also probably been affected by the rockfall, but despite
the possibility of dangerous debris the line may still exist. The description has been left unaltered. The climb takes thin cracks and grooves
between Psyche and Crypt; the finger cracks are excellent. Start up a
left-trending groove system just right of the similar starting grooves of
Psyche.
1. 40m 4c Climb the groove to below the big Psyche crack.
2. 40m 5b Climb the twin finger cracks just right of the big crack. Avoid
a blank section above by traversing right under a small roof to the rib
of Crypt. Step back left into the groove and climb it to an awkward pull
over a roof by a flake crack (the continuation of the big Psyche crack).
Continue up the rib above past the left side of a big roof to belay as for
Crypt.
3. 10m Finish up Crypt.

34 Crypt 80m HVS   (1967)
Follows the two main corners left of the centre of the face. The long
second pitch is good.
1. 30m 4b Climb the grassy right-hand corner to exit left to a ledge.
2. 40m 5b Traverse the ledge to the left-hand corner which is usually
wet and mossy. Step left and follow a layback crack to move back into
the corner. Climb the corner until below an overhung grass ledge, move
out left onto the rib and climb this to regain the corner above an
overhang. Belay on a grass ledge below a second overhang.
3. 10m Move left from below the overhang and climb clean rock to the
top.
Winter: VI,7 **   (1979)
In good conditions, ice forms down the main corner and its steep
mossy section which is avoided in summer (climbable with thin ice).
Occasionally it will continue down the slabs left of the summer start. If
not, start by the summer line (as for Trail of Tears).

35 Trail of Tears 130m VII 8   (1986)
A superb route, taking the easiest line up a futuristic piece of cliff. The
route climbs the first two pitches of The Outlands, then takes the big
ramp (as for Dirge) to join and finish up Post Mortem. The finish was
climbed free with ice present, but under powder it would probably be
necessary to use a peg for aid (as for Diedre of the Sorrows).

36 Dirge 140m E1   (1975)
An intricate line, now superseded by more direct routes but utilised by
some hard winter climbs. Start just right of the first Crypt corner.
1. 35m 5a Climb a shallow corner and go over a bulge at 10m, then
move right and go up to a tiny ledge. Follow the obvious horizontal
traverse right and climb up to below an obvious 10m corner.
2. 10m 5a Climb the corner and go up to a good ledge.
3. 30m 5b Climb the slanting cleft above (a distinctive landmark) and
step down left into a recess. Climb down left, then traverse left under
an overhang and go up a crevasse behind two great detached flakes.
Belay at the far end of the flakes (on Outlands).
4. 35m 4c Climb the shallow groove above to a grass ledge, then go
right up a big ramp to belay in a grassy niche as for Post Mortem.
5. 30m 5b Go up the steep groove above, then finish by vegetated
ground. (Post Mortem is a cleaner option).

37 The Outlands 100m E3   (1981)
A direct route straight up the cliff in the line of the first Crypt corner.
The crux is technical but the protection is always good. Start as for
Crypt.
1. 30m 4b Climb the first pitch of Crypt.
2. 30m 5b Continue straight up the corner over a bulge and to the top
of the great Dirge flakes. Continue up the groove to the grassy ledge,
then move right (as for Dirge) and go up to a grassy ramp and a good
stance.
3. 20m 6a Dirge goes right up the ramp. Instead, climb directly up the
short wall above to a good flake crack. Step down left and across to a
small slabby ramp running up to the overhangs. Move left round the
bulge, then go up into a diagonal crack (crux) in the upper slab. Climb
this, then move up left and back right by a finger flake and so to grassy
ledges.
4. 20m 4c Continue straight up the slab to the final groove, which
slants up right to the Tough-Brown Traverse.

38 Tough-Brown Integral 140m E2 ** (1983)

A constructed line based on the start of Dirge and joining Post Mortem. The fine crux section of Post Mortem is missed but this is often wet. The Integral gives a sustained and direct line on the cleanest available rock.

1. and 2. 45m 5a Climb the first two pitches of Dirge.

3. 30m 5b Traverse right along a narrow rising foot ledge to join Post Mortem in the crack line leading to the perched block.

4. 25m 5b Post Mortem, pitch 3.

5. 30m 5b Finish by either Dirge pitch 5, or Post Mortem pitch 4 (40m 5a; cleaner but less direct).

39 Diedre of the Sorrows 150m VIII,8 (1986)

A direct and very sustained route, climbed without ice, which takes a line of corners between Dirge and Post Mortem, passing the slanting cleft of Dirge. Start at the bottom of Post Mortem at the foot of twin snow ramps. The summer ascent of this route is E2 5c.

1. 30m Climb the left-hand ramp, then make a short traverse to the top of the right-hand ramp. Overcome an awkward bulge and go up a groove to belay below the cleft.

2. 15m Gain a grassy niche up on the left, either directly, or by a traverse from the top of the cleft. Climb the bulge above to gain the big groove and follow this to a semi-hanging stance on a good block.

3. 15m Climb up left over the hard bulge above, then follow the crack line to a shelf just left of Post Mortem. Climb the wall to the grassy niche of Post Mortem. This is the crux pitch; the peg runners were left in situ.

4. etc. 90m Finish by Trail of Tears (Post Mortem) as direct and free as ice allows (one peg for aid and a descent right of the final block were used).

40 Post Mortem 150m E2 * (1970)

This direct line up shallow cracks in the centre of the face gives a superb sustained route, unfortunately slow to dry. Start at a large pointed block 10m below the centre of the face.

1. 35m 4c Go up the obvious groove just on the left, then move right on a grass ledge to The Terrace, a long upper grass ledge. A better alternative start is the first pitch of Nevermore (5a).

2. 30m 5b From the left end of The Terrace, climb a short ramp leading left. Step left into a groove and follow it for 5m (crux) until it is possible

to traverse left to a resting place. Climb a short slab under a roof and traverse back right to regain the crack line above the groove. Follow the crack line, now a corner, passing a roof to a perched block.

3. 25m 5b Climb the corner above the block, step right underneath a roof into a second corner, then climb this and step back left to an awkward rest under a bulge. Climb the crack above to jammed flakes and work out left to reach a large ramp (Dirge joins here). Belay in a grassy niche.

4. 40m 5a Follow the ramp to a break, descend right to a lower ramp, make an awkward move round a corner, then climb up to the continuation of the main ramp. Follow cracks in the ramp to its tip, then make a big step up round a block.

5. 20m The way to the upper terrace of the Tough-Brown Traverse is now obvious as a line of flakes leading left. From there it is probably more satisfying and quicker to go to the plateau.

41 Nevermore 115m E2 (1981)

This route takes a line up into the prominent triangular niche high up in the centre of the face between Post Mortem and Crypt. Start 5 metres right of a large pointed block, close to Post Mortem.

1. 35m 5a Make a mantelshelf move onto a shelf. Continue up more shelves, then detour out right into a crack line (the lower continuation of the crack line of Crazy Sorrow, usually wet). Return left, finishing up a shelf to The Terrace.

2. 20m 5c Follow Mort for 10m to the down-pointing tooth, then move left round this to a recess. Move up and pull over the bulge and go straight up the crack to exit onto the next grass ledge left of the twin cracks of Mort. Now move left down the ledge to a recess under a groove system running down from the big niche.

3. 20m 5b Gain the groove above from the right rib and climb it to a grassy patch below a mossy leaning corner. Climb the corner into a niche which has good cracks but a sloping floor.

4. 20m 5c Take the continuation crack line above the left side of the niche. Climb a shallow groove above, step out left at the top, move up, then exit out left by a flake onto the ramp of Post Mortem.

5. 20m Finish up Post Mortem.

42 Mort 110m E1 * (1967)

This is the impressive crack line slanting right from near the centre of the face. At about 45m it breaks through a prominent roof beside a large down-pointing tooth of rock. A classic companion route to Post Mortem, only a little easier but with shorter difficulties.

1. 35m 4c Climb Post Mortem, pitch 1.

2. 35m 5b Climb steeply up for 10m to the right side of a down-pointing tooth in the roof. The roof is cut by twin cracks. Climb over the bulge and go up the right-hand crack to a poorly protected mantelshelf. To the left is a well defined rib; go up its right side and pull up left onto the top. Climb the left-hand crack above to a grassy ramp and go up this for 5m to a belay.

3. 40m 5a Traverse immediately left under a small roof to enter a continuation groove. A higher traverse into the groove is cleaner but 5b. Continue to a grass trough and a big perched block.

43 Crazy Sorrow 105m E3   (1982)
The next crack line right of Mort has a short and well protected crux section.

1. 40m 5a Start by the first pitch of Nevermore to reach The Terrace and belay at the right side of a block, just left of a huge standing block with a gap behind it.

2. 35m 6a From the top of the smaller block, move left and up to the crux roof (it is seldom completely dry under the roof). Surmount the roof to reach a crack line and follow it to a grass ramp. Follow this to its top (just right of the grass ramp of Mort and a junction with Rolling Thunder).

3. 30m 5a Finish by Rolling Thunder, pitch 4.

The following two routes roughly follow parallel left-slanting crack lines between Crazy Sorrow and the right edge of the buttress (Tough-Brown Direct). The crack lines pass either side of a large white scar, which is just below a long ledge which slants down from the crux of Tough-Brown Direct. The line of the left-hand crack meets the line of Crazy Sorrow (which slants slightly right) high up. This section of cliff is more vegetated than further left and dry conditions are required to appreciate the good rock that is present.

44 Rolling Thunder 95m E1   (1982)
This route approximates to the left-hand crack line, climbing up to the scar, passing it on the right, then going diagonally left. Start 15 metres from the right end of the lowest terrace (approached from the right) below a narrow jutting roof.

1. 25m 5b Climb the crack on the left of the roof, then work up left by cracks to a small terrace. Go right under a small roof to a horizontal crack and gain a crack which leads to the next terrace right of a huge block.

2. 20m 4c Move back right, go up a short corner and the continuation crack to the scar. Move right a few metres and trend back left to the long ledge.

3. 20m 5b Climb the fine diagonal crack going left and, when it ends, continue left then up to below a right-slanting roof (junction with Crazy Sorrow). Traverse right under the roof to a grassy trough.

4. 30m 5a Escape right is now possible, but go left round an edge, gain a higher slab, cross the overlap above, then continue *via* cracks and corners to easy ground.

45 Tough Guy 105m VS   (1980)

This vegetated route is based on the right-hand intermittent crack line, at the right edge of the face before it curves round towards Tough-Brown Direct. Start at the right end of the lowest terrace, adjacent to the scree fan of Raeburn's Gully.

1. and 2. 60m 4b Follow a series of cracks punctuated by grassy ledges to finish on the long ledge a few metres right of the scar.

3. 30m 5a Climb the wall above (well right of the diagonal crack of Rolling Thunder and to the left of two thin vertical cracks) using flakes and small ledges leading up left (crux). Cross a rake to the left (this rake is the escape below the final pitch of the last two routes) and continue diagonally left *via* large cracked blocks to a stance some 10m below another white scar.

4. 15m Trend up left into a grassy trough.

Winter: VII,7   (1984)

A fine sustained climb loosely based on the summer route. The thin crack right of the summer crux was the winter crux. An alternative start is *via* Mort and behind the huge block near Crazy Sorrow.

46 Tough-Brown Ridge Direct 250m VS   (1941)

This takes the easiest line on the extreme right-hand side of the face, then follows the ridge above. Most of the climbing is vegetated but the one VS pitch is good. Start just inside the scree shoot of Raeburn's Gully.

1. 45m A short wall, then a slabby ledge passing right, leads to a long grassy groove sloping up left. At its top, make a sharp right traverse to

a pile of huge blocks. Go left by a flake crack, then a short slab traverse ends at a wall.

2. 20m 4c Steep slabs rise in three ill-defined steps and bar access to easy ground. Climb the slabs to the second step, then move round the edge to a short vertical wall and pull up to a rounded ledge. Continue up slabs to ledges above.

3. etc. 185m Much easier climbing leads up the ridge to the plateau.

Winter: V,6   (1969)

The steep initial 60m is hard. Follow the summer route to the terrace below stepped slabs (45m). Instead of climbing the slabs, move round right and pass below a short vertical wall to a miniature arete poised above Raeburn's Gully. Climb the groove above the arete, or step down to the right beyond the arete, and climb a wall which leads to easier ground. A version of the summer line has also been climbed. Finish up grooves left of the prominent groove of Backdoor Route, or traverse right into Backdoor Route.

47 Backdoor Route 220m IV,4 *   (1954)

A good line with fine situations, which is relatively easy after the first pitch. Just right of the crest of Tough-Brown Ridge a prominent groove system descends in a direct line to a point immediately below the bend in Raeburn's Gully. Start up a big corner but traverse left after 10m, then go up across slabs and slant up right to gain the corner's top (it can be climbed direct: harder). Follow the groove system above to reach the crest about 50m below the plateau.

Variation: V,6

Climb a groove on the right of the big corner after 10m, then ascend a second groove and a wall to reach the crest.

48 Raeburn's Gully 200m II ***   (1932)

A classic climb which fills quickly in the course of a normal winter to leave one ice pitch. Early in the season it is excellent, with much ice and Grade III. There is often a very large cornice which may necessitate a steep traverse to the top of Tough-Brown Ridge.

Variation: **Lemmings Exit** III   (1977)

This is an obvious fault on the left wall well right of and parallel to Backdoor Route, starting just above the bend and below the main ice pitch. It requires good and probably unusual conditions.

Variation: **The Gutter** III   (1954)

A steep off-shoot of Raeburn's Gully, breaching the right wall above the easy intermediate section and about 80m from the top. Very Difficult in summer.

There have been many accidents in Raeburn's Gully caused either by climbers starting an avalanche or being hit by one. The gully has a large catchment area, including the corniced rim of The Amphitheatre, and for this reason it is probably more prone to avalanches than any other gully in the corrie.

49 Raeburn's Gully *via* **The Clam**   200m Hard Severe   (1954)
The Clam is the thin impressive slit on the Scarface (right) wall of Raeburn's Gully, a unique rock formation providing a strenuous route of character. There is loose rock but little vegetation. It is graded and 'recommended' for wet weather as the waterwashed rock does not become too slippery. From the scree tongue, Raeburn's Gully provides wet slabs and scree as far as two massive chokestones. These are not very difficult and beyond them is a sandy recess. The crux of the gully (and the whole route) follows: climb the left wall on small holds, then return to the gully bed. A little higher is a cave in the right wall; the huge boulders jammed in the gully immediately above form the winter crux, but are straightforward in summer. Leave the main gully 30m above the boulders to gain the start of the Clam. Surmount huge blocks to a square recess on the right, then pass over a short wall into the slit. "The scenery is remarkable, with chokestones jammed far out between the walls. From the innermost cranny, traverse out and upwards, back and toe, for 25 feet to a tiny bracket providing a welcome resting place on the very edge of the slit. There is a flake belay 6 feet up a slab on the outside. From the flake return directly into the narrow upper chimney. Exhausting work threading the chokestone on the inside, with an exit akin to that of a cork from a bottle." From there it is easy to the plateau.
Winter: V,6   (1977)
Short and fierce. The upper chimney above the flake belay was climbed on the outside in good conditions, but it may be easier inside if the chimney is not blocked.

50 The Straight-Jacket   85m VII,7   (1980)
This line is visible in summer as the prominent chimney-crack high on the Scarface wall of Raeburn's Gully. An inch by inch struggle, perhaps requiring icy conditions. In summer the route was reported to be VS but usually wet, and 4 pegs for aid were used on pitch 3.
1. 20m From immediately above the crux of Raeburn's Gully, cut back right and go up to a ledge below the chimney.

2. 10m In summer it is possible to get inside the chimney; in winter it is an off-width.

3. 10m Immediately above the chimney is a steep iced corner. Climb it and exit right to a slab.

4. 45m Traverse left and climb a spiral shelf which leads to the upper rib of Scarface. Continue easily to the plateau.

BLACK SPOUT PINNACLE GROUP

This region lies between Raeburn's Gully and The Black Spout. Scarface, the first buttress in the group, frowns down on Raeburn's Gully, its face marked by a great rockfall. Between the upper rib of Scarface and The Pinnacle is The Amphitheatre, a large grassy bowl with small ribs under the plateau. The Pinnacle itself, a massive wedge-shaped structure, culminates in a true peak which is separated from the plateau by a narrow col. The Pinnacle is demarcated by Pinnacle Gullies 1 and 2, which run up to the col from either side. Pinnacle Gully 1 starts from The Mound, a rock island at the foot of Raeburn's Gully; round its back is Pinnacle Gully 2, an offshoot of the Left Branch of The Black Spout. From the col to the plateau is 30m of easy rock.

From a rock climbing point of view, The Pinnacle's only rival is the Tough-Brown Face. The Pinnacle has two distinct areas of interest, namely the lower slabs and Black Spout Wall. The lower slabs form an apron of continuous rock which starts beside The Mound and stretches upwards for about 100m until the angle eases and the rock becomes broken and vegetated toward the summit of The Pinnacle. Moving up right into The Black Spout, the slabs become progressively steeper and merge with the very steep Black Spout Wall. This 150m wall is roughly triangular-shaped with Black Spout at its base and the two sides formed by the limits of the steep rock.

Climbs started on the lower slabs do not lead naturally to the upper part of Black Spout Wall, but tend to veer left to easy ground. The solution is The Springboard, a large platform of vegetated ledges about 35m above Black Spout and a thoroughfare between the lower slabs and Black Spout Wall. From The Springboard three lines of weakness fan upwards. From left to right these are the lines of Route1, Hood Route and The Link. Any of these climbs may be used to reach the summit after completing a route on the lower slabs. Alternatively, abseil from The Springboard into Black Spout, or reverse the first pitch of Route 1 (Severe).

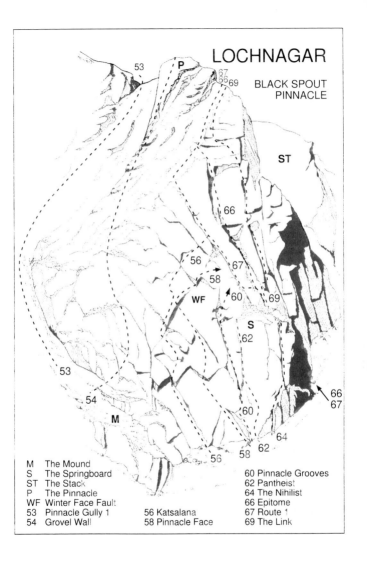

LOCHNAGAR

BLACK SPOUT PINNACLE

ST

P

WF

S

M

M	The Mound	
S	The Springboard	
ST	The Stack	
P	The Pinnacle	
WF	Winter Face Fault	
53	Pinnacle Gully 1	
54	Grovel Wall	56 Katsalana
		58 Pinnacle Face

60 Pinnacle Grooves
62 Pantheist
64 The Nihilist
66 Epitome
67 Route 1
69 The Link

51 Hiawatha 170m VI,8 (1995)

This direct ascent of the Scarface buttress is a late season route which requires ice on the first two pitches and a good build-up in Raeburn's Gully to bank out the initial overhangs. Start at the toe of the buttress, about 5 metres left of the icefall of Scarface.

1. 40m Climb a steep icy slab trending right, then step back left to enter the left-hand of twin open grooves. Follow this over several short walls and make an awkward exit onto a small stance below an overhanging V-groove.

2. 20m Climb the V-groove (crux) and exit right onto a steep ramp which leads to the left edge of the amphitheatre.

3. to 5. 110m Finish up the upper rib of Scarface, on the left.

52 Scarface 170m V.4 * (1972)

Start on the right wall of Raeburn's Gully, marginally above the bend, and climb a shallow depression as directly as possible into The Amphitheatre. At times, particularly towards the end of the season, or after a long thaw, the depression becomes very icy and thus provides a very fine climb. The summer line (Severe) follows ribs on the left, but the best winter line is to continue easily up the left edge of The Amphitheatre. Above, climb an ice groove (the leftmost of three faults above The Amphitheatre) and exit left to the final few metres of the rib.

53 Pinnacle Gully 1 200m III (1951)

This is the gully from The Mound to the col behind the Pinnacle; a safe choice in powder snow. Only the final section up to the col shows true gully formation; lower down the climb follows a diagonal fault which leads towards The Amphitheatre (when followed into The Amphitheatre and continued by the right-hand fault above, it gives Amphitheatre Route, III). Gain the top of The Mound from the lowest rocks. Go left and climb a chimney left-slanting to broken ground. At a point about 40m from the base of the chimney, traverse back right across a slab above a cave, climb a short chimney and exit right to easier ground. Two pitches, mostly snow, lead to the col, a fine knife-edge of snow. From the col to the plateau is easier, apart from a little rock step. Moderate and very vegetated in summer.

High on Eagle Ridge, Lochnagar (Climber, Sammy Dring)

A route has also been made between Amphitheatre Route and Pinnacle Gully 1 (**PG Corner**, 1981), leaving the diagonal fault above the traverse of Pinnacle Gully 1 and finishing by a big corner left of the upper gully of Pinnacle Gully 1 (III and good in lean conditions).

54 Grovel Wall   200m V,6   (1977)
A fairly direct line from the Mound to The Pinnacle summit. From the left edge of the Mound, climb diagonally right for 20m, then cut back left and go straight up to a short overhanging wall. Avoid this on the right, and climb a line of grooves and shallow chimneys parallel to Pinnacle Gully 1 to the top. Severe and very vegetated in summer.

The French Connection (1979) is a desperate direct start to Grovel Wall in winter. The first 15m are common with Winter Face, then take a groove line left to join Grovel Wall low down.

55 Winter Face   250m VI,6 *   (1974)
A diagonal line of weakness on the lower slabs which crosses Pinnacle Face before joining Route 1. It requires good conditions, when it holds ice. Start just right of and above the lowest rocks in the little chute between the Mound and the face, and opposite a conspicuous perched block. Slant up rightwards to below a prominent overhang (20m). Gain an inset slab on the right, pull back left and continue up the groove (20m, crux, ice required). Follow the obvious diagonal line up and right over a big flake, then climb a corner to belay in the niche of Pinnacle Face. Make a short descending traverse right round a corner, then go up a ramp to a shallow chimney which leads up left to join Route 1. Finish up this.

The frontal slabs of the Pinnacle are complex and the lines of the summer routes are difficult to pick out from below. The start of Pinnacle Face is the best landmark.

56 Katsalana   130m HVS   (1982)
Start 10m down from and left of Pinnacle Face.
1. 30m 5b Climb a prominent left-trending corner, passing left of a pale scar, to reach a recess marked by twin water streaks.
2. 30m 4b Continue up a corner, then go right and traverse left to reach

Black Spout Wall, Lochnagar (Climbers, Dougie Dinwoodie and Bob Smith)

a fault line taken by Winter Face. Follow the fault *via* a big flake to the large grass stance at the end of pitch 2 of Pinnacle Face.
3. 40m 5a Climb the left-hand crack of Pinnacle Face, traverse left below a bulge, then go right on good holds. Make a delicate traverse right, then continue up and right to a ledge beside a spike.
4. 30m Climb up right round a rib and continue with one awkward move to easy ground on Route 1.
Winter: VI,7   (1984)
Follow the summer route to Winter Face, then go diagonally left by a corner to join Grovel Wall.

57 White Mischief 125m HVS   (1978)
A line close to Pinnacle Face at times; on pitch 3 it merges with Winter Face. Start at the same point as Katsalana.
1. 25m 5b Gain and pull right into a shallow right-facing corner. Climb the corner and just before reaching Pinnacle Face swing out left into the start of a left-slanting corner line.
2. 20m 5a Pull out above the corner and climb cracks in the rib next to Pinnacle Face, then move back into the corner above a step and follow it past a bigger step to belay (on Katsalana).
3. 45m 4b Climb up right for 3m towards a peg and sling on Pinnacle Face. Hand traverse a thin crack to join Winter Face. Follow Winter Face over its big flake and corner to belay in the niche of Pinnacle Face.
4. 35m Follow Winter Face towards the Springboard and many options.
Winter: VI,8   (1992)
Follow the first 2 pitches of the summer line. If pitch 3 is well iced, climb directly past the peg and sling of Pinnacle Face to join Winter Face. With poor ice, follow the summer route (the horizontal crack is hard to find under snow).

58 Pinnacle Face 95m VS *   (1955)
A classic route with some fine climbing, following a not too obvious line covering a fair area of the impressive lower slabs. Start at the corner of Black Spout about 10m above the lowest rocks.
1. 35m 4a Two grooves slant left onto the face; either may be used to start. The shallow left-hand one starts as an awkward wall, then go up

the groove to a short chimney at 20m. The prominent V-shaped right-hand groove, again awkward at the start, leads in 10m to a delicate left traverse into the other line. Continue *via* the chimney, then by cracks trending left.

2. 25m 4b Climb a short distance to a corner and pull onto the right-hand slab. Work left up a slabby fault to a large grass stance (close to the obvious fault of Winter Face).

3. 25m 4b Continue left a short distance, crossing Winter Face, to twin cracks. Climb either crack, finishing at the top of the right-hand crack. Continue up the right-hand crack, then traverse right on flakes to a niche.

4. 10m 4b Climb the steep corner above to a ledge. From there, an easy traverse right on grass ledges leads to Route 1 about 30m above The Springboard.

Winter: VI,7 **   (1966)
A demanding climb of great quality, which is usually a mixed route with short technical sections, but pitch 2 requires a little ice. It is extremely hard without, but there is a peg and sling *in situ*. When very icy, it is one technical grade easier. Follow the summer line for two pitches, then join Winter Face and climb this *via* a turfy corner on the right of the summer line. The original ascent followed the summer route throughout, but this is rarely done nowadays. If conditions allow, climb as directly as possible from the junction with Winter Face to the summit of The Pinnacle (near pitch 3 of Katsalana).

59 Fool's Rib 80m HVS   (1976)
This is a direct version of Pinnacle Face, following the rib just left of Pinnacle Grooves.

1. 35m 5a Climb the right-hand starting groove of Pinnacle Face and step right at the top. There is a groove directly above which hugs the left side of the rib. Climb into the groove and go up to a short corner under an alarmingly detached flake. Climb the corner and the flake and go up steeply to small ledges.

2. 35m 5a Continue up left under the bulge of the rib for 5m. Pull out right onto the rib and climb it directly to a grass ledge below and right of the steep final corner of Pinnacle Face.

3. 10m Move out right to a flake edge and traverse diagonally up to the grass ledge at the end of Pinnacle Face (or traverse right to easy ground).

60 Pinnacle Grooves 70m VS * (1975)

Excellent, well protected climbing, following a direct line of grooves starting from the foot of Pinnacle Face and ending at easy ground on Route 1 just above and left of The Springboard.

1. 30m 5a Climb the right-hand starting groove of Pinnacle Face. At its top, move right then go left and up to a large down-pointing flake. Layback up its left side to step into a smooth groove on the left. Climb the groove to a grass stance.

2. 15m 5a Continue up the groove to a grass ledge on the right.

3. 25m Step left, then go up for about 10m until a series of grass ledges leads right to easy ground above The Springboard.

Winter: VII,7 * (1980)

An excellent short route. With more ice in the corner the climbing is easier, but the protection poorer. The grade is for difficult conditions of thin ice the step left from the pinnacle has yet to be done under powder.

61 Pantheist 55m E1 (1978)

A worthwhile climb, particularly for the second pitch where it follows the obvious groove right of Pinnacle Grooves. Start 5 metres right of the initial groove of Pinnacle Face.

1. 25m 5a Climb the obvious cracks *via* a square slot to a ledge. Move right up a little slab over a bulge, then break left and back up right to a grassy niche. Poorly protected.

2. 30m 5a Traverse left to climb the big groove to The Springboard.

Winter: VII,8 (1984)

Two hard pitches, with slabs and bulges followed by the steep corner-groove. Protection is adequate, but strenuous to place, and two axe rests were taken on the first ascent. From a ledge above the square slot, the winter line goes higher and further left before making a descending traverse under a bulge to rejoin the summer route.

62 Infidel 60m E3 (1989)

Starts as for Pantheist, but diverges right.

1. 30m 5b Climb the slot to the ledge and surmount a steep flake. Go straight up the slabs above and over a bulge to reach a short crack which leads to a sloping ledge 4m below a large left-facing corner.

2. 30m 5c Step up and left to stand on a booming flake. Go up the blind crack and climb a shallow left-facing corner (left of the large one) to reach sloping ledges. Climb a cracked wall to a small ledge and finish near The Springboard up a right-facing corner.

63 An Saobh-chreideach 50m E4 *   (1989)
Start just down left of Nihilist Direct.
1. 20m 5b Climb left up a short ramp, then go up a groove to ledges.
Follow The Nihilist past the mantelshelf to another ledge. Move up left
and go up to a jug at the base of twin blind cracks. Step across left to
the belay ledge of Infidel.
2. 30m 6b Move right and climb the blind cracks to the base of the big
left-facing corner. Go up this and the left-trending cracks above to a
good side-pull. Follow the horizontal break rightwards past a Friend
half placement to the base of another corner (crux). Finish up this to
gain grassy ledges above The Springboard.

64 The Nihilist 45m E1 *   (1976)
This excellent route packs a lot of climbing into its short length. Near
the foot of Black Spout a large smooth wall lies directly below The
Springboard. The climb follows a diagonal line up right close to the left
edge of the smooth wall, then ascends the prominent twin grooves
above to The Springboard. Start 10 metres right of the V-groove of
Pinnacle Face, immediately left of the smooth wall.
1. 25m 5b Climb to obvious holds and make a difficult move left before
swinging up to a large ledge. From a higher ledge, gain a steep narrow
slab with a bulging wall above, then traverse right to an apparently
desirable mantelshelf ledge. Continue right eventually to gain the main
groove and descend a little to a belay.
2. 20m 5a Make a long stretch to steep cracks above an obvious
hooded overhang. Relatively easy climbing now leads up right to a
hard exit by a wide crack to The Springboard.
Variation Start: 10m 5b
This is harder than the normal way. About 5 metres right of the normal
start is an obvious V-groove with a flat bottom. Climb into the groove
and continue straight up to join the normal route at the large ledge.

65 The Existentialist 40m E6 6b *   (1995)
This hard route climbs the large smooth wall to give a superb pitch.
Start 10 metres right of Nihilist Direct Start at a small corner line. Climb
boldly up into the little corner. Climb it and the crack line above to a
ledge. Continue up a superb flake crack until it is possible to exit by the
left-hand crack. Finish up The Nihilist to reach The Springboard.

66 Epitome 150m HVS   (1977)
This climb takes the prominent groove beneath The Springboard to
the left of the first pitch of Route 1, then follows the central fault and
hanging crack left of the roof skirted by Hood Route.
1. 30m 4c Traverse left to the foot of the prominent groove, then follow
it to The Springboard.
2. and 3. 60m 4b Climb the grassy central fault (as for Hood Route)
to the good ledge below the steep section.
4. 20m 5a Move left and climb the big hanging crack just right of the
corner (crux). Near the top, move left to a ledge on the arete, then climb
a delightful slab mantelshelf to gain easier ground on Route 1.
5. 40m Continue to the summit *via* Route 1.
Variation: VS 4c
An easier but inferior variation avoids the hanging crack by swinging
round the arete on the left from the top of a large down-pointing block
and climbing the rib to rejoin Epitome just below the mantelshelf. An
escape route traverses left round the arete from the belay, then
continues left to Route 1.
Winter: VII,8   (1980)
A desperate technical problem, which was climbed in exceptional
conditions with a lot of ice which formed to the right of the hanging
crack.

67 Route 1 200m V,6 *   (1956)
A classic winter climb, low in the grade, but with route-finding important
it provides continuously interesting climbing through particularly fine
situations. Start in Black Spout beyond a vertical groove in a steep
smooth wall below The Springboard (Epitome). Climb a prominent
slabby ramp passing an overlap (hard when no ice is present, as
graded). Traverse left soon above the overlap and gain The Springboard *via* a short wall, also hard. Go up the ledges above (the central
fault), then traverse left into the left-hand fault and follow it to the front
face. Here one can continue left, but a much better line goes up right
starting by a big flake to gain the crest at a point overlooking the fork
in Black Spout. A wall and an arete lead to the summit of The Pinnacle.
Severe in summer.

68 Hood Route 90m HVS   (1976)
The central fault above the Springboard passes the very large roof on
the right. A strenuous and unusual crux pitch, but the approach is very
vegetated. Start from The Springboard.

1. 35m Climb the fault easily up big grass ledges.
2. 25m 4b Continue more steeply up the fault to belay below the prominent hanging crack of Epitome.
3. 20m 5a Climb steeply towards the left side of the roof. From the top of a flake, make a long step right to a ledge and go along this for 5m to huge flakes stacked under the roof. Pull strenuously up right to a slab leading to a stance at the end of the Route 2 traverse.
4. 10m The groove of Route 2 leads to easier ground and the top of The Pinnacle.

69 Hoodwinked 70m E2   (1995)
A direct line right of Hood Route and a harder continuation from The Springboard.
1. 30m Climb turfy ground close on the right of Hood Route, then diverge right behind a big block on Hood Route's right arete.
2. 30m 5c Climb the arete to another flake, make a move up and traverse left for 3m to ledges. Return slightly right to follow a leftwards slanting line which ends with the pull-up to a slab on Hood Route and the belay at the end of the Route 2 traverse.
3. 10m The groove of Route 2 leads to easier ground.

70 The Link 100m VS *   (1956)
This traditional continuation to Pinnacle Face is a little mucky in places. As the name suggests, the climb connects Routes 1 and 2. Initially it follows the right-hand fault above The Springboard, then takes a slightly contrived line up across the Route 2 traverse to finish left of the summit crest. Start at the top of The Springboard in the rightmost of the three faults.
1. 15m Enter a V-groove by a short awkward right traverse. Climb the vegetated groove to a stance on the rib on the right.
2. 25m 4c Make a few moves up the rib, then step back into the groove and climb it to below a prominent triangular overhang. Move up and right round a huge block to a small recess under an overhang. Climb the overhang, then follow a good crack slightly right to behind another huge block.
3. 30m 4c Now a big vegetated groove slants left (taken in winter) and a prominent crack continues right. Follow the crack, and near its top move out left. Go awkwardly left (crossing Route 2) to a steep groove and climb this to a large overhang. Pass this on the right using a sometimes rotating block.

4. 30m 5a One can escape by swinging up and traversing left between two overhangs, but it is better to climb the overhang above by good cracks.

Direct Start: VS 4c *
This takes a line right of Route 1 (avoiding the grass ledges of The Springboard) and provides an independent start. Just right of Route 1 there is a recess with a steep vegetated groove above. Scramble to the foot of the groove and climb obvious parallel cracks in a short chimney on the left. Continue up left over vegetation, then steep slabs lead to the stance on the rib 20m above The Springboard.

Winter: **Link Face** VII,7   (1979/1984)
This superb and exposed climb is a composite selected as the most independent natural winter line. It usually has thin ice, but is easier with more. Start up the undercut vegetated groove immediately right of the direct start to The Link. Tension left to join the direct start above its steep section. Continue by the summer route until beyond the overhang, then take the big groove slanting left to join Route 2.

71 Black Spout Wall 170m E3 ***   (1976)

A superb route which climbs the formidable wall above and right of the start of Route 1 and finishes by cracks in the steep gable wall above the traverse of Route 2. There is a great overhung recess in the middle of the wall and the route follows the obvious crack line in the pillar to its left.

1. 40m 5c Traverse along a small ledge to a deep crack and climb this to a block at 15m. Climb the bulge above and continue up a smooth dwindling groove to cracks (protection and a big *in situ* peg). Descend to the lip of the overhang and swing left into the scoop at the base of a ramp. Climb the ramp and the overhang at its top to reach better holds. Go down diagonally right to a ledge and peg belay directly above the initial cracks; a great pitch.

2. 30m 5c Go up the corner above, then climb a bulge into the groove above and climb this to exit out left to ledges close to The Link.

3. 40m Climb out and up right by slabby shelves to gain the arete above the great overhangs. Climb this to the little ridge at the top of the chimney crack of Route 2.

4. 25m 5c To the left is the 'inhospitable crack', which goes left, and directly above is a forking crack system. Climb the long right fork to the apex of the wall.

5. 35m Climb the crest to the top of The Pinnacle.

The following routes take obvious lines up the steep wall right of Black Spout Wall and below the initial chimney of Route 2. Both climbs are slow to dry.

72 The Vault 35m E2 5b   (1982)
The left-hand chimney line. Climb a stepped wall to the base of the wide chimney, which has poor rock in the back. Move up the chimney and exit left to a flake formation and finish up a crack and groove line.

73 Drainpipe Crack 35m E2 5c   (1982)
The right-hand line provides a fine jamming crack, harder than The Vault. Climb the steep and strenuous crack into a recess under the final overhang (possible belay). Surmount the overhang (crux) to gain the right-hand crack, which leads to the top.

Above the fork in Black Spout, a broad sloping grass ledge cuts into the right side of Black Spout Wall. Four routes start from this ledge, which all lead to the summit of The Pinnacle. Route 2 goes out left up the prominent chimney-crack from the bottom left end of the ledge. From the top of the ledge, a huge corner runs up left to the crest of The Pinnacle (Ice Ox). Left of this is a parallel corner ending in a short steep wall (Solstice). Twin Chimneys Route takes the narrow deep chimney cutting into the well defined buttress of Settler's Rib on the right. Although short, these routes lie high on the mountain and come into condition early in the season. Further up the Left Branch of Black Spout is the obvious Pinnacle Gully 2.

74 Route 2 120m Severe *   (1953)
This is one of the few good routes below VS on Lochnagar, and it is very exposed. Start from the bottom left end of the large grass patch.
1. 35m Climb the prominent chimney-crack slanting left and ending at a little ridge projecting from the steep gable wall.
2. 25m Descend vegetated ledges left for 5m, then make a long traverse left into the middle of a big groove (taken throughout by The Link in winter). Climb the groove to large ledges.
3. and 4. 60m Easy climbing leads to Route 1 and the summit.
Winter: VI,6   (1962)
A serious climb with magnificent situations. The chimney-crack often contains ice and may be quite straightforward, but the traverse will always be hard and sustained.

75 Solstice 100m VI,7   (1984)
Start by a vegetated corner slanting up left from the start of The Ice
Ox, and reach a line up the left wall of its big corner. Overcome the
steep wall and continue by a steep crack line. Short but well worth
doing.

76 The Ice Ox 100m IV,4 *   (1984)
The big obvious corner.

77 Twin Chimneys Route 100m IV,5   (1961)
Start as for The Ice Ox, but continue straight up *via* the obvious
chimney to a rib. Follow this more easily to the top of The Pinnacle. It
is also possible to start from the bottom of the rib. An impressively
steep line, Very Difficult in summer.

78 Settler's Rib 90m IV,5   (1993)
Start just above the chokestone of Black Spout, Left Branch (after
mid-season this is only a steepening low down). Follow an easy turfy
crack leading left to a stance just below where the rib steepens (20m).
Traverse horizontally right for 5m until overlooking Slab Gully, then
climb straight up through a bulging crack just right of the buttress crest.
Continue right up awkward rounded cracks, then trend left to a good
ledge and finish up the crest.

79 Slab Gully 80m III   (1967)
Climb the central depression in the smooth face below Pinnacle Gully
2. Difficult in summer.

80 Reiver's Buttress 80m III,5   (1994)
Turfy grooves in the right side of the face lead to a fine technical finish
up the rounded arete overlooking the col at the top of Pinnacle Gully 2.

81 Pinnacle Gully 2 90m II   (1932)
The short prominent gully running up behind The Pinnacle from Black
Spout, Left Branch. In lean conditions, the chokestone can be difficult.
The gully is Moderate in summer and loose, but a good way to the top
of The Pinnacle. Continue to the plateau by the easiest line up the
crest.

82 Slice of Ice 60m IV,3 (1985)
Right of and parallel to Pinnacle Gully 2 is an inset slab which can accumulate ice. Start at the base of the gully and climb a thicker icefall up right to the slab.

83 The Black Spout 250m Easy *
This is the great scree corridor separating the main face from West Buttress. The Right Branch has no pitches. The Left Branch, hidden from the corrie floor, has one entertaining pitch, a huge chokestone with a small time-honoured through route.
Winter: I *** (1893)
The chokestone soon becomes buried and in these conditions both branches are straightforward snow, the Left Branch being slightly steeper and with occasional cornice difficulties. The scenery is attractive.

84 Crumbling Cranny 60m Easy (1926)
A wide chimney cutting into the right wall of the Left Branch, almost opposite Pinnacle Gully 2, provides a steep but dirty scramble finishing under a rock bridge under the plateau.
Winter: II (1913)
A short and surprisingly popular snow chute. The huge cornice often requires tunnelling, although it can be avoided by a harder variation to the right.

85 Sour Grapes 50m V,7 (1994)
On the right wall of Crumbling Cranny is a right-slanting chimney. Climb this, then step left into a hanging corner.

86 The Stack 150m Hard Severe (1952)
The buttress between the two branches of the Black Spout, following a line of chimneys high on the face overlooking the Left Branch, gives an enjoyable but dirty route with an intriguing variety of pitches. The crux is nearly VS; the rest is sustained but no more than Very Difficult. Start just below the pitch in Left Branch. Zigzag cracks in a slab lead to a steep wall 20m up on the right. Climb the wall by a strenuous corner (crux), then above this step off a block and keep passing right to reach a grass platform. Scramble left over vegetation to the base of an obvious chimney blocked by jammed boulders. From a few metres up the chimney, move left and follow a narrow ledge provided with a continuous handrail downwards for 10m. Return to the right by two

short cracks to an alcove above the jammed boulders. Follow the chimney directly ahead for a further 10m to a large bollard. Step boldly off this onto a sloping shelf on the right, then climb a short wall to a grass platform. Move left and climb slabs and walls leftwards to the plateau.

Winter: V,6 *   (1952)
Short, sustained and intimidating, this climb is usually very icy and often comes into condition before other routes. The first platform may be gained by the summer route or by a shorter line up an icefall which forms to the left. Above, follow the summer route. In good conditions the whole fault can be climbed direct to avoid the descent and the bollard move.

87 Torquing Corpse 130m VII,6   (1987)
A serious route with difficult route-finding which takes an intricate line through very steep rock on the nose of The Stack. Start on the left wall of the main branch of Black Spout, 10m up from the toe of the buttress beneath a steep corner groove.
1. 50m Climb the corner and belay at the extreme right end of the large terrace.
2. 20m Traverse right to reach some steep grooves.
3. 15m Ignore a groove with an old peg and an overhanging top. Climb the very last one on the right (this is the top half of a big inset slab which comes up from The White Spout) to a cave belay.
4. 20m Move out left, then pull up to reach a left-slanting fault. Climb the fault to a headwall 10m below the plateau.
5. 25m Traverse left with a step down to reach and climb an easy finishing groove.
   In icy conditions, it may be easier to continue left from the cave and climb straight up to the finish.

88 The White Spout 70m IV,4   (1974)
In good conditions, an icefall forms in a depression on the left wall of the main branch of Black Spout, right of the ramps of Torquing Corpse. Climb it trending right, with a short steep section near the top.

WEST BUTTRESS

This is the final section of the main corrie, right of Black Spout. At each end of its defined part, two buttresses extend unbroken to the screes; on the left is Black Spout Buttress, on the edge of the gully; on the right is West Rib, whose left flank plunges into the deep West Gully. Between these buttresses the lower face is indeterminate, with mixed rock and grass up to the Midway Terrace. However, above the terrace the climbs follow well defined features, four ribs separated by three gullies of which the central gully is the obvious narrow slit of Gargoyle Chimney leading to a high amphitheatre. The shallower gullies either side are West End on the left and Gargoyle Direct on the right. These enclose Causeway Rib on the left and Bell's Pillar on the right of Gargoyle Chimney. The leftmost rib is less well defined and split at its base by the square chimney of Isis; between it and Black Spout Buttress is the shallow fault of Western Slant. The rightmost rib, next to West Gully, is climbed by Dod's Diversion/Quasimodo. High on the right under the plateau is a prominent square, smooth wall at whose top right corner is the Gargoyle, a small but prominent feature jutting from the plateau rim.

Winter conditions on West Buttress are variable, as it catches the sun and in the second half of the season the buttress routes are often stripped of snow. West End to Gargoyle Direct are described from the Midway Terrace at the base of the middle tier, easily reached from the left or the right.

89 Black Spout Buttress 250m Difficult *   (1908)
The best of the easy routes in the corrie. The line on the lower buttress is heavily vegetated and may be avoided by traversing from Black Spout opposite its fork. The complete route starts at a chimney-fault at the top of a grass slope about 10 metres right of Black Spout. Climb the chimney, then scramble for about 60m to a level arete marking the end of the lower section. Above the arete, a ridge of piled blocks leads to a deceptively difficult short chimney. Easy climbing leads to a short wall which is started in the centre and finished by an awkward corner on the right. A steep 10m wall now bars the way. Taken direct, it is a fine pitch on good holds. Above, follow a ledge on the left and regain the crest which leads without difficulty to the top.
Winter: III,5 **   (1949)
A good winter route with several technical but very short sections. It comes into condition with the first snow and is a good choice under powder. The lower buttress is much improved in winter. The steep 10m wall is normally outflanked by a peculiar traverse right to a recess at the head of a flanking gully (Western Slant). Return left to the crest as soon as practicable, usually just below the plateau.

To the right of Black Spout Buttress, three little chimneys or gullies go up the indefinite face to the upper rocks. The leftmost (Difficult) contains a narrow cave and leads to the step on Black Spout Buttress. Use either of the others to reach Midway Terrace just below and right of Gargoyle Chimney. The central one is a scramble; the rightmost is Difficult.

90 Western Slant 250m II/III   (1954)
The fault tucked into the right side of Black Spout Buttress above its step. Use the left-hand chimney-gully on the broken face right of Black Spout Buttress to gain the Midway Terrace below a short square-cut gully. Move left, then go up and left to a long slanting groove. Climb this to a bottleneck, then gain the gully running alongside Black Spout Buttress to finish as for that route.

91 Isis 210m V,6   (1994)
The leftmost of the middle tier ribs. Start between Black Spout Buttress and Western Slant by climbing the obvious central corner, then trend up right to join Western Slant and reach an obvious square-cut gully in the rib. Ascend the gully to its close, then move right and climb a corner and its continuation to a *cul de sac*. Return left to the face of the rib and finish up this.

92 West End 130m IV,5   (1977)
Between Isis and Causeway Rib there is a vegetated depression which occasionally forms a prominent icefall. Climb the crest of Causeway Rib for 20m and move left into the depression, which should be chosen when well iced.

93 Causeway Rib 120m IV,5   (1975)
The rib bounding Gargoyle Chimney on its left. The best winter start is *via* the first 10m of Gargoyle Chimney, then move out left into a 6m grassy gully ending against a wall. Climb the right corner into a V-cleft and reach the crest. Traverse back right, then follow the rib past a little pinnacle and blocks overlooking Gargoyle Chimney to the level Causeway. Finish up a final tower. A pleasant climb in summer, Very Difficult.

94 Gargoyle Chimney 120m IV,4 *   (1952)
The prominent thin chimney in the centre of the face gives an excellent pitch, sometimes 30m of ice. Above this, go up and left on snow to a steep finish and sometimes a difficult cornice. Difficult in summer.

95 Bell's Pillar 120m V,5   (1992)
The rib right of Gargoyle Chimney. Start just right of Gargoyle Chimney
and climb a shallow left-facing corner until it is possible to swing right
to the crest. Follow this until under the smooth square wall, then skirt
left and finish up the fault just right of Gargoyle Chimney's final pitch.

96 Gargoyle Direct 140m V,6   (1954)
The rightmost gully, with diversions on the rib next to West Gully
(depending on the amount of ice). Start up the rib and move into the
gully above an overhang. A chokestone will force a section on the right
rib unless conditions are very good, then return to the gully. A difficult
finish slants right below the Gargoyle to go round the corner into a
small gully.

  This route is Very Difficult in summer, and it largely follows the rib
but is forced into the gully for a pitch after 30m (very unpleasant). A
genuinely direct version of Gargoyle Direct is **Dod's Diversion**, HVS,
which takes a direct crack line on the rib for pitch 2 (5a) and gains the
plateau by the obvious steep crack finishing a few feet left of the
Gargoyle block (5a).

97 Quasimodo 290m VII,8   (1995)
This is a winter ascent of the rib of Dod's Diversion with a direct start
and finish. Start 20 metres left of West Gully and climb an open gully
and mixed ground to the midway terrace. Climb the start of Gargoyle
Direct, then move right to the twin cracks of Dod's Diversion. Climb
these (crux), then continue up the rib to join Gargoyle Direct (summer)
at the final wall. Climb a stepped crack line and its continuation to exit
just right of the Gargoyle (the Direct Finish to Gargoyle Direct in
summer).

98 West Gully 250m IV,4 *   (1948/1966)
The lower section soon ices up and provides an ideal introduction to
steep ice climbing. The upper gully, although impressive, is relatively
straightforward. The final chimney to the plateau may be difficult if
taken direct and the blocks are uncovered. The left branch is easier.
Difficult in summer.

  Below the final chimney of West Gully, three prominent chimneys
cleave the right wall. Only the central one (**Shylock's Chimney**, a back
and knee VS) is worth the excursion from the plateau *via* the easy left

branch of West Gully. The left chimney is Difficult, the right is a tight Severe. The buttress to the right of West Gully is **West Rib**, Very Difficult in summer and an improved IV,4 in winter. The shallow gully to its right is **Gelder Gully**, II.

A girdle traverse has been made from Black Spout (starting up Route 2) to Central Buttress. Much of the climbing is very vegetated (Severe). Though equally pointless in winter, it gives good climbing and was done in two consecutive days, starting up Pinnacle Gully 2 (VI,5).

COIRE NA SAOBHAIDHE (Map Ref 247 865)

This is the shallow corrie which lies directly below the summit of Lochnagar. It is separated from the main North-East Corrie by the West Ridge (the ridge on the west side of the main corrie). The back wall of the corrie consists of an area of waterwashed slabs. A slanting 50m fault (Moderate) forms the junction between easy-angled slabs on the right and steeper foliated slabs on the left. An obvious watercourse runs down the centre of the steeper section. This gives a climb of about Severe in summer and it is a good short ice climb in winter (110m, Grade III).

COIRE AN LOCH NAN EUN (Map Ref 230 854)

This large western corrie of Lochnagar has very little continuous rock, but the prominent **Stuic Buttress**, a scramble in summer, gives a worthwhile climb under snow, Grade I.

CNAPAN NATHRAICHEAN (Map Ref 224 888)

This northern outlier of Lochnagar (about 3km south-west of Gelder Shiel), reveals two exposures of slabs on its north-east flank. The lower western slabs (just above the Ballochbuie Forest) are heavily vegetated, but near the centre there is a column of water-washed rock which gives an interesting ice climb, **The Plaid**, II/III. Another icefall of similar grade has been climbed near the left side.

Close under the summit there is a more attractive area of fairly clean slab known as Sleac Ghorm. Some slab routes of about 100m have been climbed. The prominent straight corner on the left side of the slabs is **Green Mamba**, Severe. **Venom**, E1, takes a line starting just right of Green Mamba, to finish up the wet slab passing the enormous moss overhang on the right. The crack line just left of Green Mamba is **Bushmaster**, VS. The obvious curving corner to the right of Green Mamba is **Boomslang**, VS. The overlapping slabs to the right of Boomslang (just right of a clump of young trees) give **The Padder**, Severe, while **The Grass Snake**, Severe, follows overlapping slabs well to the right, left of an easy grassy corner.

In winter, this slabby face largely banks out under a heavy build-up, but early in the season it may provide an accessible alternative to the unconsolidated higher areas. Four routes have been climbed, II or III, following obvious groove lines on early season ice. The broken ribs left of the main section have also been climbed (Grade II).

The Dubh Loch Cliffs

This chapter describes the climbing around the Dubh Loch, which lies between the Lochnagar and Broad Cairn massifs. Here some of the finest climbing in Britain may be found.

EAGLES ROCK
(Map Ref 235 835)

These slabby rocks are a long discontinuous band of cliff set high on the White Mounth escarpment, opposite Creag an Dubh-loch. The main feature of the rocks is the big waterfall away to the left. Also prominent is the open and easy-angled Diagonal Gully near the right end.

The rocks are too high above the loch to become the playground they might have been, but they are nevertheless a useful alternative to the main cliff. The climbs are short and light-hearted, following natural lines on sound granite. Those climbs which are not water-courses usually dry much more quickly than the bigger Creag an Dubh-loch routes. In addition, the south-facing aspect ensures that the routes catch a good deal of sun, a point worth bearing in mind in cold weather or in the afternoon when the sun has left the main cliff.

In winter, the drainage lines generally ice up readily, no snow being required. Early in the season after a hard frost, a number of fine icefalls form. Though shorter, they offer comparable quality to Hell's Lum Crag in early season, but their relative inaccessibility has limited popularity. Later in the season, some of the routes partially bank out with snow and the crag's sunny aspect can wreak havoc with the ice.

GREEN SLAB

This obvious slab is not far left of The Waterfall, and can be identified by the pink central fault of **Bumble**, Very Difficult. The quickest summer descent lies immediately down the west side, but this is tricky at the bottom. Alternatively, go further west to easy slopes. The slabs left of Bumble give **Jade Pavement**, Very Difficult. In the course of a normal winter, the slabs soon disappear under snow. When not banked out, they may be sheathed in snow and ice and have been climbed by two separate lines based on Bumble, Grade II.

Green Slab 90m Hard Severe *   (1968)
This route goes up the clean slab right of Bumble, with a good pitch
through and above the halfway wall. The protection is poor. Go up the
slab and the obvious corner just right of Bumble to ledges below the
steep halfway wall. Move up left to a ledge, then go diagonally right
across the wall using flakes (crux). Move on right and climb an overlap
to finish up cracked slabs.

THE WATERFALL CLIMBS

The waterfall cascades down a large slabby buttress which tapers up
to the right. After a dry spell, the longer the better, the left side of the
stream can be climbed, Severe. The best descent lies down broken
ground immediately alongside the fall on its west side.

In winter, enormous amounts of ice form here. In unusually cold
conditions the waterfall can freeze completely and the whole buttress
disappears under ice. The winter descent back to the start of the routes
is either awkward or long. One can make an easy descent away to the
west (beyond the Green Slab), or the east; climb up and over the
plateau edge and descend Diagonal Gully. The short but harder
descent is Green Gully, which lies between the corner of Lethargy on
the right and, on the left, an ice curtain draping the left wall of a vertical
outcrop. Although Green Gully is Grade I with a large build up, the best
line of descent is difficult to find and should be considered Grade II.

The Waterfall 150m II *   (1974)
Climb the continuous low-angled ice to the left of the flow of water.
Escapes are possible to the left. When frozen, the direct line would
give a steeper variation.

Spectrum 110m Very Difficult   (1971)
The obvious line of corners and grooves right of the Waterfall and
immediately right of black overhanging walls. On the rare occasions
that it is dry, it is the best route of its standard here. Start at the first
obvious break well up right from the foot of the fall.
1. 45m Climb into a corner leading to a recess below a dark slanting
crack.
2. 30m Climb the short steep wall right of the recess and follow slabs
up right to the base of a big V-groove.

3. 35m Climb the groove to the top, turning the final part on the left. (To continue straight up is VS; a better finish is the crack in the rib on the right, Hard Severe.)
Winter: III *   (1971)
A sustained climb on continuous water ice, which is distinguished by the big V-groove near the top which gives a fine finish. Just to its right, another groove system gives a shorter but not too separate line.

Just left of the grassy fault of Green Gully is a patch of clean slab which gives **Stratus** (VS 4c). In winter, this banks out with snow and low-angled ice.

THE MID-WEST BUTTRESS

This is the left-hand of two large zones of rock set roughly in the centre of the cliff. It is the highest and most continuous section and is recognised by the pink watercourse corner of Lethargy to the left and several obvious groove lines to the right. Descent is by Green Gully or by Diagonal Gully away to the east (see The Waterfall section).
    The rib between the grassy bank of Green Gully and the corner of Lethargy gives **Nimrod**, VS 4c.

Lethargy 120m Hard Severe   (1967)
The obvious corner on the left of the buttress is usually a watercourse, but pleasant when not. Follow the corner as directly as possible (starting 5 metres to its right) to a point where escape left is apparent. The Green Gully descent lies below; finish up the short steep left-hand corner above.
Winter: II *   (1970)
The corner forms a continuous ribbon of ice early in the season, but tends to bank out later. Above the corner, take the escape left, climb the summer finish, or follow the prominent steep icefall above the corner (IV,5).

Indolence 140m VS   (1967)
The first of the crack and groove lines right of Lethargy, although a drainage course, can be followed up the dry right side all the way. Good climbing. Start at a grassy fault forming the left margin of a big slab, 10 metres right of Lethargy's corner. Climb the fault or pad up the big slab (4c) for about 60m to a big overlap. Break through this by a short corner and an overhang just right of the watercourse. Continue up

cracks right of the upper gully, then follow a narrow rib and crack on the right to the top.
Winter: III   (1976)
The watercourse forms a fine icefall, the best part of which does not bank out. Very early in the season, a good combination is the first pitch of Lethargy, an easy right traverse and the upper icefall of Indolence.

Nomad's Crack 150m VS   (1967)
The next and best defined groove line right of Indolence. Climb slabs to a prominent V-chimney, go up this and more slabs to a wide V-groove system and finish up this (usually wet).
Winter: V,5   (1976)
A good sustained climb up the summer line on a narrow ice ribbon. The initial slabs soon bank out, but the climb is slow to come into good condition.

To the right of Nomad's Crack are two obvious corners; the left is **Taboo**, VS; the right is **Abstention** (VS 4c). A prominent icefall forms high on the summer line of Abstention (IV,5).

THE MID-EAST BUTTRESS

This roughly triangular face lies up and left of some broken slabs lining the left bank of Diagonal Gully. The most prominent feature is the big inverted L-shaped corner of Gibber set on the central pink slabs. Diagonal Gully is the obvious descent, in both summer and winter.

Sliver 150m III *   (1974)
The obvious winter line running up the right side of the broken ground between the Mid-West and Mid-East buttresses. A fairly continuous line of water ice will be reliably found.

Flamingo (HVS 5a) goes up the rocks to the left of the big corner of Gibber. A similar line has been climbed in winter, but it banks out readily (Grade III).

Gibber 120m VS *   (1969)
The big inverted L-shaped corner gives the best pitch on Eagles Rock when dry. Start at the lowest continuous rocks. Work up and across left to near the edge (45m). Go up the slabby ramp on the right, then continue up a short corner in a steep wall to a ledge. Climb up left into

the corner and follow it up and right round the roof to a glacis (5a). Easier rocks lead to the top.

Winter: 130m IV,3   (1977)

In winter, a sliver of ice forms which approximates to the summer route. The big corner may be seriously unprotected if the crack is inaccessible. The difficulty is very variable, depending on the amount of ice.

Right of Gibber are three corners. **Whisper** (VS 4c and IV,3) takes the middle groove while **Verbal Diarrhoea** (VS 4c) takes the corner right of Whisper.

Shiver 150m III   (1976)

This is the icefall which forms on the rocks right of the slabs of Whispers and the big corner of Gibber. There are no obvious escapes, but variations are possible.

A LIKELY STORY SLAB

This is the greenish disc of overlapping slab to the right of the lower part of Diagonal Gully. It is the most accessible of the climbing areas, dries very quickly and receives much sun. It provides fine climbing reminiscent of the Etive Slabs, including the poor protection. The easiest descent is to traverse into Diagonal Gully, but in dry weather a devious way can be made on the east.

There is a short route on the extreme left edge of the slabs (HVS but very artificial). A right to left girdle traverse (Severe) goes between the two main overlaps.

The Stretcher 80m E1   (1975)

In the centre of the lower slab is the obvious corner of A Likely Story; this route climbs the poorly protected slabs to its left. Start at a curious white trickle mark near the lowest left corner of the slab.

1. 20m 5a Climb to the first overlap, move left along the lip and go up a tiny corner just left of a scoop (Fraud Squad). Belay on the left.

2. 40m 5a Move about 5 metres right over slabs and go up to a short crack running back left to the main overlap. Climb the crack and the double overlap direct, then trend slightly right and back left to a ledge under a sharp nose in the upper overlap. An easier but indirect alternative is to traverse left after the double overlap, then to climb up to the ledge.

3. 20m Climb through the overlap just right of the nose and go up right to a grassy crack leading to heather.

Fraud Squad 70m E2 *   (1984)
A direct line just right of The Stretcher gives better climbing but is escapable, though not obviously, to that route. Start just right of the white trickle mark.
1. 30m 5b Climb direct to the first overlap (reaching it at the same place as for A Likely Story). Traverse left for 3m through the overlap and climb a scoop with horizontal quartz bands. Exit left from the top of the scoop (bold), return right above it for 2m and climb to a crack which penetrates the main overlap just right of a V-notch.
2. 30m 5b Climb the crack through the double overlap and go slightly right to follow a pocketed blind crack (or the slab on its immediate right) to the base of a thin curving flake. Above this, traverse left to belay near The Stretcher.
3. 10m 4c Go through the upper overlap just left of a good thread (right of The Stretcher) and finish up mossy cracks.

A Likely Story 80m HVS **   (1968)
This little gem, the best and most popular route on Eagles Rock, dries very quickly. Start in the middle of the lower slabs.
1. 30m 4c Go up slightly left to an overlap, move right 2m and cross the overlap to climb to an obvious corner leading to a ledge.
2. 20m 4c Go up by a flake to gain the corner above and follow this up to make a delicate right traverse under the overlap into a notch. Pull through the overlap and go up into a triangular depression.
3. 30m 4b Traverse left along a slab below a steep wall, then climb an obvious crack in the slab.
Variation Start:
1. 30m 5a Go through the overlap as for Fraud Squad, then traverse back right and go up to climb the left rib of the corner of A Likely Story.

Prohibition 90m Hard Severe
This takes the obvious line of cracks and grooves just right of the centre of the slab. Start near its lowest right corner. Climb straight up the slab and go up by a blunt flake. Move up and right into the crack system (this point can also be reached from the right), then continue up the crack system to the upper overlap. Climb over this into a long shallow corner which leads to the top.

Nameless 60m Severe   (1968)
A line on the right side of the slab, starting at an obvious left-leaning
corner with a bulge above (20m). Go straight up the slab above *via* an
open scoop, cross an overlap, and finish up slabs or traverse left to the
shallow corner of Prohibition.

PLATEAU BUTTRESS

Up right from A Likely Story Slab is a curious lattice of slab. Higher still
under the plateau is a little brown buttress housing a small waterfall.
This forms a prominent icefall in winter, **The Drool** (IV,4). **Flanker's
Route** (Very Difficult), takes the rocks right of the waterfall, skirting a
steep section which is climbed by **Vanguard** (HVS 5b).

CREAG AN DUBH-LOCH

(Map Ref 235 825)

Creag an Dubh-loch is a huge precipice overlooking the Dubh Loch,
set in a high secluded valley between the extensive White Mounth
plateau to the north and the cone-topped plateau of Broad Cairn
(998m) to the south. At more than a kilometre in length and 300m in
vertical height, it is the biggest cliff in The Cairngorms. With over 60
routes of VS and above, many of outstanding quality, Creag an
Dubh-loch has more to offer the hard climber than any other Scottish
mountain cliff; it is considered by many as Britain's finest. A high
standard has been set for stars and some routes will seem under-rated
compared to other cliffs.

  The rock is as good as any in the region, a very sound grey or pink
granite typified by a roof-tile formation of colossal glaciated slabs.
Progress is generally dependent on well defined crack lines with
tenuous slabby linkages where these fade out. The earlier routes took
the major faults of the cliff in the more broken and vegetated areas
between the open faces. Few of these are worthwhile summer climbs,
and there are better cliffs in the Cairngorms for lower grade routes.

  Creag an Dubh-loch faces north-east and several days of dry
weather are needed for it to dry out after a long wet spell (although
some of the steeper routes dry faster). During a good summer,
individual days of rain may have little effect on the drainage and the
cliff can dry quickly. The cliff catches the sun until about mid-day, so
an early start is worth the effort.

Creag an Dubh-loch is a lonely and intimidating place in winter, the cliffs taking on an impressive scale. There are some very fine and serious climbs, but with the cliff base at about 700m, it is less frequently in condition than the higher winter cliffs. Certainly, Lochnagar is a much more reliable choice when conditions are doubtful. In prime conditions however, the cliff is one of the best and iciest in the Cairngorms. Prediction of prime conditions has perplexed even the closest observers. A spell of very cold weather freezes the springs at source and even a day's thaw can strip the cliffs bare. Deep powder in the valley is usually an indicator of poor conditions. The Hanging Garden area is more reliable and the best conditions can form later in the season, after heavy snow followed by thawing and freezing.

If conditions are poor, Eagles Rock is higher and often draped with fine icefalls. These give entertaining pure ice climbs and can provide an alternative to disappointing conditions on the big cliff.

Access
1. From the Spittal of Glenmuick
The end of the public road is 15km from Ballater. In winter, the last 5km across the moor can be blocked. From the car park, follow a private unsurfaced road past where the Lochnagar road breaks off to the right and continue straight on towards the south-east side of Loch Muick, ignoring the left fork to Glen Clova *via* the Capel Mount path. Just before the loch, a small path leaves the road on the right and follows the shore to the north-western side. Cross the river and gain the road on the north-west shore and follow it to Glas-Allt-Shiel. On bicycle (highly recommended), follow the Lochnagar path to the building before the woods, then take the track along the north-west side of the loch. From the head of the loch, continue up the pleasant birch-strewn valley on a good path to the outflow from the Dubh Loch. The halfway point is marked by the Stulin, a waterfall tumbling down from the hidden Loch Buidhe. The loch has small paths on either side. This is the easiest way in (8km); the walking can be reduced to 3½km by using bicycles as far as Glas-Allt-Shiel.
2. From Callater (the Braemar approach)
Leave the Perth-Braemar road 3km south of Braemar and follow a private rough road for 5km to Callater Lodge. A path starts up the hillside just before the lodge, slants over the slopes of Creag an Loch and contours the southern shoulder of Carn an t-Sagairt Mor. Continue down to Allt an Dubh-loch (11km).

3. From Glen Clova

This is sometimes used as an approach from the south. From the road end at Braedownie, continue up the glen to the woods at Bachnagairn in Upper Glen Esk. Cross a footbridge over the falls and climb a zigzag path to the plateau and follow the path to two shacks known as the Sandy Hillock Huts. Follow a bulldozed track until it peters out under the summit cone of Broad Cairn, then break right to contour between the summit slabs and the lower outcrops to the Dubh Loch. In bad weather it is best to make for the head of Corrie Chash. Leave the path here and go north-west over the shoulder to Allt an Dubh-loch. The outcrops are easily passed (8km).

Accommodation

In summer it is possible to camp at the Dubh Loch; there are good sites at both ends. There is also a fine howff in the boulders under the Central Slabs.

Layout

The cliff is a straight face split into two main sections by Central Gully. The eastern, left-hand section contains the very steep Broad Terrace Wall high on the left and the great sweep of the Central Slabs on the right. These are separated by the prominent couloir of Labyrinth Groove which snakes up past the high amphitheatre of the Hanging Garden.

The western, right-hand section is dominated by the big slabby face of Central Gully Wall. Its top right extension is the steep, tilting False Gully Wall which forms the left flank of the broken North-West Buttress curving round to the right. At opposite ends of the entire face are South-East and North-West Gullies, with their smaller terminal buttresses.

Descents

Summer: Central Gully is the usual toe-crushing descent. When snow-filled in early summer, Central Gully Buttress is a useful alternative. Go down the easy crest and cut down left into lower Central Gully; this ends at an obvious slabby ramp. This is often greasy and there is an easier line 10m higher, a small ledge leading horizontally left to a short wall of blocks at the bottom, not obvious on first acquaintance. The north-west end of the cliff can also be descended; this is easy but care must be taken to go beyond the last outcrops. On the left of the cliff, the descent is down the easy hollow well beyond South-East Buttress (or the buttress itself).

CREAG AN DUBH-LOCH

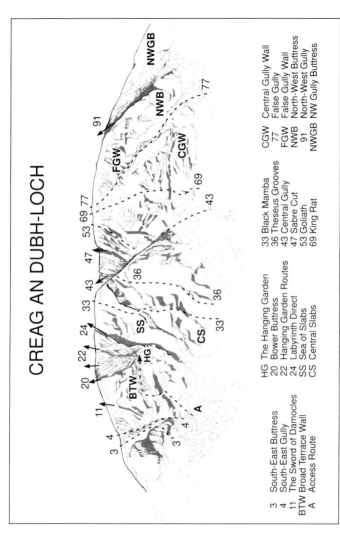

3   South-East Buttress
4   South-East Gully
11 The Sword of Damocles
BTW Broad Terrace Wall
A   Access Route

HG The Hanging Garden
20 Bower Buttress
22 Hanging Garden Routes
24 Labyrinth Direct
SS Sea of Slabs
CS Central Slabs

33 Black Mamba
36 Theseus Grooves
43 Central Gully
47 Sabre Cut
53 Goliath
69 King Rat

CGW Central Gully Wall
77 False Gully
FGW False Gully Wall
NWB North-West Buttress
91 North-West Gully
NWGB NW Gully Buttress

Winter: Central Gully is the usual descent and the best in poor visibility. The cornice is usually avoidable on the right (looking down). A little easier but longer, one can descend at either end of the cliff, giving the outcrops a wide berth. When there is a good build-up of snow, South-East Gully gives an interesting descent usually with a steepening near the bottom.

SOUTH-EAST BUTTRESS

This is the broken buttress at the left end of the cliff. The ordinary route goes up the easy right-hand side overlooking South-East Gully. The obvious discontinuous snow ramp trending left to right up the left side of the buttress is **Eastern Ramp**, Grade II. The most obvious feature of the frontal face is a big roofed diedre taken by Dogleg. The steep grooved wall just to the left of the diedre is **Rock Island Line** (VS 5a). Just left of Rock Island Line is a vague corner system which gives **Eastern Groove** (IV,4).

1 Friends Essential 30m E2 6a   (1983)
An obscure wee crack on the slabby wall on the left-hand side of the buttress, well left of Eastern Ramp where the wall is highest. The crack is prominent and stepped and the difficulty eases with height.

2 Dogleg 150m HVS   (1977)
This route takes the big roofed diedre. Start below and left of the line of a shallow chimney forming the back of the diedre at a pair of cracks, a boulder ledge and a spike belay.
1. 25m 5a Climb the cracks to a slabby ramp winding right to the mouth of the chimney.
2. 25m 4b Climb the chimney until close to the roof, then traverse right, including a short descent, to a blaeberry stance.
3. 25m 5a Work right into a groove right of the roof, then follow the groove to a branch leading left over blocks to a big ledge.
4. and 5. 75m Tackle the wall behind the belay on the right, cross over a slot and slant right up a slabby ramp to the top.
Winter: V,7   (1992)
Follow the summer route except, on the first pitch use the turf on the right and, on the third pitch, gain the system of steep cracks direct from the blaeberry ledge by stepping down right.

3 South-East Buttress 200m Moderate   (1930)
The crest overlooking the gully is mostly a grassy scramble, with a
slabby corner pitch at the start on the gully side of the crest. A start
not far to the left can also be made (this is the best line in descent).
Winter: II   (1948)
A pleasant route which should always be climbable, easy after the first
pitch. The left-hand start is the least awkward in soft snow.

4 South-East Gully 200m I **   (1947)
A popular climb, sometimes the only one in condition on the cliff. Grade
II in lean conditions, but an ice pitch near the bottom banks out after
mid-season to leave a steeper section. A disintegrating Difficult in
summer.

BROAD TERRACE WALL

This is the dark menacing crag high on the left side of the cliff. It is set
at a savage angle, particularly in the centre where a smooth wall leans
out over The Grass Balcony, a long ledge unvisited until 1982. To the
right, the face sustains a fierce angle until the boundary edge of Bower
Buttress. Climbs on this section follow parallel crack lines. Despite its
forbidding appearance, the rock here is more amenable with numerous
blocks, flakes and deep cracks, although mossy in places. All the
climbs on this face are memorable, particularly for their exposure.
Bounding the left side is the huge fault of The Sword of Damocles,
conspicuous even from the head of Loch Muick. Further left the face
is more slabby and curves round before petering out in the hanging
jungle above South-East Gully. Here lies the lesser fault of The Last
Oasis, with three routes on the slabs to its left.
    The wall was left alone until 1967, when Culloden was forced up
the frontal face. Since then, it has been less frequented than the
Central Slabs or Central Gully Wall, partly due to its atmosphere but
also because it is the last part of the cliff to dry; a band of snow at its
top usually forms seeps until July. The section from The Sword of
Damocles leftwards is particularly slow drying.
    Access is *via* Broad Terrace, the grassy promenade under the frontal
face. To reach it, zigzag up the left side of the broken lower crags by
luxuriant vegetation, starting near the foot of South-East Gully. This is
also the start for the left-hand routes, because the wall dropping into
the gully is repulsive and overhanging.

5 The Snow Desert 300m V,4   (1977)
A natural and exposed winter line working up the broken rocks overlooking South-East Gully; the more ice the better. Start by the zigzag approach to Broad Terrace and traverse left to the foot of the left-hand of two faults, The Last Oasis. Above and to the left is a hanging snow field. Climb a pitch up The Last Oasis and traverse left over a ramp. At the left end of the snowfield is an obvious broken chimney. Climb this to an exit left, then make a difficult horizontal traverse to easier ground and the plateau.

High on the left side of Broad Terrace Wall, above South-East Gully, is beautiful clean waterwashed rock which is bounded on its right by the fault of The Last Oasis. The connoisseur of technical climbing on perfect granite in a fine position will enjoy this wall. Unfortunately, near drought conditions are required, particularly after a snowy winter.

6 The Eye of Allah 90m E3 *   (1991)
The line is based on twin crack lines high on the left side of the wall.
1. 20m Start up The Last Oasis and follow the fault easily to below a steepening.
2. 30m 5b Climb the corner above, then step left onto a rib and follow a thin crack left to a ramp. Follow the ramp easily to its left end.
3. 25m 5c Climb a finger crack to a shelf, use a good flange to traverse right and pull into a little corner. Exit right to a ledge below a slanting corner.
4. 15m 5b Climb the exposed hanging slab on the left and finish up blocks above.

7 Alice Springs 95m E2 ***   (1983)
A superb route on perfect rock based on the crack line in the centre of the wall.
1. 20m Start up The Last Oasis and climb the fault easily to below the steepening. Alternatively, continue for another 10m to belay above the steepening.
2. 40m 5c Climb the corner above (as for The Last Oasis), then step left onto the rib and follow a thin crack left to ledges. Climb the prominent finger crack above to a ledge.
3. 35m 5b Move up to the base of a corner, step right to a rib and reach a crack line on the right. Follow this and a groove to the top.

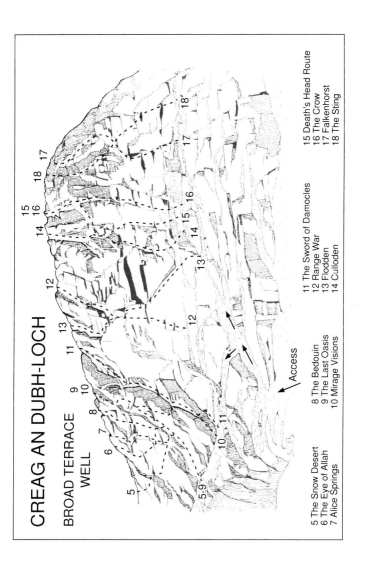

CREAG AN DUBH-LOCH

BROAD TERRACE
WELL

5 The Snow Desert
6 The Eye of Allah
7 Alice Springs

8 The Bedouin
9 The Last Oasis
10 Mirage Visions

11 The Sword of Damocles
12 Range War
13 Flodden
14 Culloden

15 Death's Head Route
16 The Crow
17 Falkenhorst
18 The Sting

Access

8 The Bedouin 95m E4   (1989)
The fine left-facing corner between Alice Springs and The Last Oasis.
1. 35m 4b Climb The Last Oasis to the top of the second steep step.
2. 45m 6a Step left onto the edge and go up to enter the left-facing corner. Climb this to a small overlap. Climb the bulge (crux), and move up to an undercling. Use the short corner on the left to gain the next break and follow the twin grooves to a ledge. Zigzag up the walls above, finishing through a steep slot to ledges. A fine sustained pitch.
3. 15m Easy blocks lead to the top.

9 The Last Oasis 100m VS *   (1971)
This is the less prominent left-hand of the twin faults; a major watercourse. When dry, however, it provides a good climb for its grade in impressive surroundings. The friction is still good in the wet. Follow the pink fault, with occasional diversions to the right, for about 80m. Move right at the top below bulges to belay under a short pale groove beyond a detached block (4b). The groove is taken by Mirage. Instead, climb up left over a bulge to ledges (4c). The big precarious blocks above can be climbed direct or turned by a 5m left traverse, then by going back right above them. Finish up the left-slanting groove.
*Winter: VI,6 ****   (1980)
Occasionally this forms a tremendous icefall, but it is susceptible to morning sun. The finish may be 10m of vertical ice, which on the first ascent was turned by the summer line on the left (1 peg and 1 nut for aid).

10 Mirage Variations 100m HVS *   (1976/1981)
Mirage itself takes a line between the faults of The Last Oasis and The Sword of Damocles, starting up the rib left of the latter. This variation is a natural but composite line with excellent sustained climbing.
1. 35m 5a Climb the steep wall left of the easy chimney of The Sword of Damocles by a series of small ledges and a crack leading directly to the base of the big corner. Climb this to a large ledge on the left.
2. 20m 5a Climb directly up the edge overlooking The Sword of Damocles to a good flake crack. Traverse this leftwards, then go up a prominent corner crack to a ledge.
3. 45m 4c Finish up The Last Oasis. Move left, pull over a bulge and return right as soon as possible onto the wall above. Mirage Original continues by the short pale groove to join The Sword of Damocles; instead, go left over the bulges and so to the top.

Polyphemus Gully, Lochnagar (Climber, Jane Naismith)

11 The Sword of Damocles 100m E2   (1970)

The right-hand fault above South-East Gully is a huge corner system, the most obvious line on the whole wall. It gives a strenuous climb of great character, but the top chimney is very slow to dry and repulsive when wet. Start at an easy chimney next to a steep wall.

1. 35m 5a Climb the chimney, then traverse left along the wall to a ledge at the base of the big corner. Alternatively, start up the first pitch of Mirage Variations. Climb this fine corner to the ledge on the left.

2. 20m 4c Go up the corner above to a large flake below the hanging chimney (or solo the initial chimney, then combine pitches 1 and 2).

3. 15m 5b Climb the very sustained chimney to big ledges at the top.

4. 30m 5a Move right and go up a short corner to a white slab. Climb the chimney on the right (hard and mossy), or left (as for Mirage), or go further right if damp. Finish up giant steps and broken ground.

Variation:

This is useful when the top chimney is wet. From below the hanging chimney, climb the first bulge until past the first old bolt. Traverse the left wall to the edge, move up the arete and traverse left to the short pale groove of Mirage. Go up this to the big ledge above the chimney.

12 Range War 110m E4 *   (1983)

This and the following route climb the appallingly steep wall between The Sword of Damocles and Culloden, crossing at The Pinnacle, the obvious feature at mid-height which links the lower part of the face with the steep upper section. A superb climb with a strenuous but well protected crux section. Start by scrambling up the big corner right of The Sword of Damocles, then traverse right and go up a short wall (Severe) to reach a short corner midway between The Sword of Damocles and Culloden (about 15 metres left of Flodden). Pitch 1 regains its vegetation quickly.

1. 45m 5c Climb the short corner to a roof, pull over and continue up and left to an obvious jammed blocky spike. Continue up and left to The Grass Balcony. Climb to the top of The Pinnacle on the right.

2. 35m 6a Launch up cracks in the leaning wall above to reach a niche below a roof; a good point to contemplate the exposure. Traverse right under the roof and pull into the corner above. Follow the corner to a recess, pull out left and continue up the corner until the angle eases.

3. 30m 4c Continue in the same line to the plateau.

The Shetlander, Creag an Dubh-loch (Climber, Wilson Moir)

13 Flodden 135m E5 ** (1983)

A stunning diagonal line, crossing the previous route and finishing up an obvious ramp line cutting left from The Pinnacle. Despite few repetitions, the route was still quite clean in 1994. It is high in the grade. Scramble up left, then traverse up right to a point 15 metres left of Culloden below an obvious long left-leaning corner.

1. 40m 6b Climb the corner to where it leans, then climb a flake with more difficulty to a resting place. Step up and move left across the wall to gain a crack, then climb to below a large roof.

2. 15m 6a Gain the crack round the left side of the roof, then climb it to a ledge above. Traverse this rightwards to a faint crack, then climb it and the scoop above to the right end of The Grass Balcony. Traverse left to belay in a corner.

3. 10m 5a Traverse left round a corner and climb a crack to the top of The Pinnacle (common with Range War).

4. 25m 6b Traverse left off the top of The Pinnacle and move up to a position under the left end of a roof. Step left and follow a ramp, passing a flake to step down from its top to a poor resting place (optional belay here before the crux, particularly if the rope drags). Climb the slim groove above and move left across a slab to gain a corner; follow this to a belay.

5. 45m 5a Climb the corner behind, then move left and follow the easiest line to the top.

14 Culloden 125m E2 * (1967)

A superbly positioned climb but a little mossy. To the right end of the smooth impending wall are two big roofs, one above the other. Culloden takes the first line to the right of these, a distinctive feature being a big V-groove halfway up. The highest ledge of Broad Terrace has some piled blocks at the highest point; start down left from these. Climb up left to a big obvious platform to belay.

1. 45m 5a Continue straight up grooves, cracks and a flaky wall to move right to the top of a monster flake.

2. 35m 5c Climb the overhanging crack and the big hanging groove to ledges. Go straight up the shallow grooves above to belay below a bulge.

3. 45m 5b Move left and climb a shallow corner, then return right above the bulge. Continue up a groove and short walls to finish up easy ground.

15 Death's Head Route 155m E3 *   (1976)
This and the following route take the twin parallel crack lines right of
Culloden, passing to either side of a black rectangular roof over
halfway up the wall. Sustained at 5a with breathtaking exposure and
a short crux section, the climb would arguably be better as an E1 with
2 pegs for aid. Start at the piled blocks on the upper ledge of Broad
Terrace.
1. 20m 4b Traverse left along the wall left of the blocks and go up to a
ledge. Climb the crack line direct to a ledge under a long corner crack.
2. 30m 4c Climb the corner and the overhang above to a ledge with
a peculiar block weathered like a man's face. Climb up this and the
wide crack above to move out right and go up big flakes to reach the
right end of the monster Culloden flake.
3. 35m 6a Move up right to a short overhanging corner (crux) in the
barrier wall, then gain the steep hanging corner running up to the black
roof. Move up the corner to just below an old peg, then swing left and
climb the rib to a horizontal flake crack. Hand traverse this left to a slab
at the top of the big groove of Culloden. Step left over the groove to
ledges.
4. 15m 5a Here Culloden goes straight up. Return awkwardly up right
and go easily along slabs to the top of a huge grass-topped block.
5. and 6. 55m Climb the short wall above (5b), then zigzag up big
blocks to reach another big block on the left. Drop down left and finish
up stepped walls.

16 The Crow 145m E2   (1976)
Another high quality but mossy route. Start at the same point as
Death's Head Route at the piled blocks on the upper ledge.
1. 15m 5b Climb straight up the steep wall immediately left of the
blocks, then go up easier ground to below a wide crack.
2. 30m 5b Gain the crack using a big flake on the left and go up it for
a few metres to reach for a flake handrail on the right. Go up a flake
and an overhang to step right and climb another flake to its top. This
is just right of the monster Culloden flake.
3. 10m 5b Move up over a bulge under the barrier wall. Climb a shallow
corner forming the right side of a scoop, then swing up right to follow
the left side of a prominent jutting flake to a ledge tucked under a big
jutting rib, a prominent feature of the line.

4. 35m 5c From the left end of the ledge, climb the wall above until it is possible to traverse right to a slab topping the rib. Step back left and go up a bulging wall past the right edge of a black roof. Go up the black corner above and swing left to the edge. Climb the bulging crack above to grass and the huge block on Death's Head Route.
5. and 6. 55m 5b Finish up Death's Head Route.

17 Falkenhorst 140m E1   (1973)
Right of The Crow is another crack line which peters out. This route takes the next crack system in the pink rocks to the right. Start at a short left-trending ramp left of the pinkest rock.
1. 40m 5a Go easily up a short steep slab, then move back left to a short overhanging groove. Climb the groove and go straight up then horizontally right along a narrow ledge to a corner. Climb the corner and escape left. Traverse left, then go up a corner to a large platform on the left. Belay at a big flake beside the upper ledge.
2. 15m 5b Move back right and climb a thin crack in a pink wall and continue to a ledge on the crest. Traverse right and climb to a niche formed by a huge detached flake, crux.
3. 10m 5b Move back down and climb an overhang on the right. Continue right and up beyond a poised block to a good ledge.
4. 30m Easier ground on the right edge now presents a choice of line. Go up a short way to a rock shelf below a wet corner. Climb two short walls on the right of the corner to a grass ledge. Go right and back left to a large grass platform directly above the corner.
5. 45m Trend left up an obvious fault over some huge blocks, then go straight up to the top. A more direct line can be made up the finish of The Sting.

18 The Sting 130m HVS   (1975)
This is the rightmost of the prominent crack systems. The rock on the first pitch is waterwashed and distinctly pink, but beyond it becomes increasingly mossy. Start right of Falkenhorst under a prominent triangular overhanging groove.
1. 25m 5a Climb the groove at the right-hand side, taking an overlap to reach the apex of the groove. Climb the overhang and continue up the crack above to a sloping grassy ledge, then continue to another ledge immediately above.
2. 35m 4c Follow the main groove to a ledge on the left, climb over huge blocks, then continue up the groove to a larger ledge. Climb a deep crack at the left corner of the ledge to another ledge.

3. and 4. 70m 4c Easy ground is now visible on the right (junction with Falkenhorst). Traverse horizontally left to a shallow mossy groove and climb this to easier blocky ground. Climb short cracks and huge blocks slanting left; many variations are possible.

Winter: VII,6 (1994)

A very steep and sustained icefall can form near The Sting. The icefall continues up to finish on the very brink of the vertical section of wall.

THE HANGING GARDEN

This lofty basin on the right of Broad Terrace Wall is bounded on the right by the big curving couloir of Labyrinth Direct. The couloir is blocked by a formidable *cul de sac* just above the level of The Hanging Garden, a grass slope surrounded by steep walls some 120m high. The rock climbing is wet and sometimes vegetatious and loose, so none of the routes are described in full. In full winter conditions however, The Hanging Garden comes into its own; an exposed snow field with ice-plastered walls. The winter climbs are difficult and serious with unique situations and scenery. Belay cracks can be hard to find so ice screws are invaluable. Retreat down Broad Terrace would be awkward in the dark.

Starting by the zigzag rakes near the foot of South-East Gully, the traverse of Broad Terrace provides an intricate but easy approach into The Hanging Garden. In good conditions, the lower half of Labyrinth Direct gives a better and more direct approach, Grade III.

19 The Aqueduct 120m V,4 (1975)

In favourable conditions, a steep icefall flows from The Hanging Garden directly over the tiered rocks below to provide a hard and poorly protected entry. Very Difficult and a watercourse in summer.

Ariadne (VS 4c) takes the rocks between The Aqueduct and The Labyrinth, heading for the prominent groove high up.

20 Bower Buttress 150m V,5 (1970)

A prominent edge forms the border between the left wall of The Hanging Garden and the vertical rocks of Broad Terrace Wall. This is the general line of the climb. A fine route on ice in its best condition, but it is also good and only a little more technical under powder. The exact line is open to variation. Climb grooves in the crest slanting left

to a big ledge, The Gallery. Follow ice-choked cracks trending slightly
right to enter a shallow gully which leads to snow slopes under the
cornice (avoided on the left). A harder line further left can be taken
above The Gallery, finishing up the final part of The Sting, on the brink
of Broad Terrace Wall. In summer the route is Very Difficult, taking the
leftmost of the two lines of weakness close to the edge.

21 Yeti 140m V,4 **   (1975)
Between Bower Buttress and the prominent gully of Hanging Garden
Route is an impressive set of slabby ramps. These form a major
drainage line in summer and can become sheathed in ice to give an
exposed and serious route. In the lower section, the icefall may split in
two; either branch can be climbed.

22 Hanging Garden Route 300m V,4 **   (1957/1977)
An excellent climb, usually the first of the big routes to come into
condition. The left fork is a classic, being the more obvious line of ice
with superb situations. The summer route, Very Difficult, takes the line
of the Right Fork, usually very wet. The Left Fork is worse, Severe.
Follow the initial couloir of Labyrinth and move left to enter The
Hanging Garden, then climb the gully at the top of The Garden to an
imposing triangular buttress which splits the route into its two forks.
Belay underneath and just left of the point of the triangular buttress.
Left Fork:
Go up the groove above until a steep wall forces a left traverse across
an exposed iced slab to reach snow under the cornice (avoidable on
the left).
Right Fork:
From the pedestal, move down and right to gain a stepped icy fault
which leads up and right to a difficult (occasionally impassable)
cornice, climbed on the right. An alternative line from The Garden is
the fault just right of the gully. Although a more logical start to the Right
Fork, it is poorer quality.

Between Hanging Garden Route (Right Fork) and Labyrinth Left-
Hand is a vegetated buttress cut low down by two shallow faults. The
left-hand one is the start of **Labyrinth Buttress** (V,6), which finishes
close to the Right Fork. The right one is the line of **Labyrinth Route**
(Hard Severe) which finishes up the rib left of the big corner of
Labyrinth Left-Hand (variation).

23 Labyrinth Left-Hand 300m V,5 *   (1979)
A fine climb. Climb the lower Labyrinth couloir and go left towards The
Hanging Garden. On the left side of the Direct, a big roofed slab is
usually sheathed in ice; from this slab an icefall forms towards the right
edge of the Garden. The exact line depends on the length of this icefall;
its base is reached from the left. The slab can be gained even without
ice by a short, very hard, overhanging cleft (1 nut for aid). Once
established, climb the slab up right to enter the easy upper reaches of
the Direct.
Variation:
A better finish if conditions allow. About 20m up the slab a big corner
runs up left to the top. Follow this in two long pitches to the cornice.

24 Labyrinth Direct 300m VII,6 ***   (1972)
This hard ice climb, one of the most demanding in the Cairngorms and
with negligible protection, follows The Labyrinth couloir directly
throughout. After the initial ice pitch, easy snow leads to the upper
section. Follow a steep groove to the *cul de sac*; a good belay can be
found on its right side if rock is visible (40m). Pass the *cul de sac* on
the left by 10m of vertical ice (crux). A steep groove continues for
another 30m before the angle eases for the final 40m to the plateau.

THE CENTRAL SLABS

This huge sweep of granite in the centre of the cliff presents over 300m
of cracked and overlapping slabs. The angle is just too steep for friction
climbing, so the routes must follow natural lines. Nevertheless, the
style is delicate and enjoyable, with the overlaps providing variety. The
continuity of the climbs is broken by a terrace system at mid-height,
effectively dividing the routes into two distinct halves. Routes are
interchangeable at this point and it is possible to traverse off right to
Central Gully Buttress. This escape makes the slab climbs less serious
than the more committing routes on Central Gully Wall.

   The Central Slabs have a very complex system of shallow cracks,
grooves and overlaps. It is possible to cross from one route to another
at some places and the original routes often took fairly devious lines.
The climbs now described have been rationalised on the lower slabs
to follow the most natural and direct lines. The routes are slightly
contrived, but they give superb climbing on perfect rock. Route-finding
above The Terrace is more difficult than on the lower slabs.

25 Labyrinth Edge 300m Severe   (1951)
Taking the left edge of the slabs, the line is irreproachable with fine situations but with much vegetation, this route has little to recommend it. Start at the foot of Labyrinth Couloir. Work up right by a grassy fault line for 20m to below big corners. Traverse right 10m and return left to a fern-filled bay above the corners. Alternatively, reach the bay by climbing the grassy right bank of the Labyrinth Couloir for a short way (the winter line). Continue by an easy grassy line up right until an exit to the left leads to a big groove. Go up this to a platform. Continue up right to emerge on the left side of the Sea of Slabs. Climb straight up these by a ribbon of grass-choked crack (or the crack to the right, VS) to exit by a cleft in a line of overhangs at the top. Jump down to a ledge on the left, then either continue left and climb straight up the steep Lower Tower, or bypass it by the short awkward wall on the right. Continue up to The Fang, an upstanding rock tooth on the edge. Turn this on the left wall overlooking Labyrinth Direct. The Upper Tower lies above; traverse along a ledge to a hidden chimney round the right side. Climb out by its right wall and finish up broken ground.
Winter: IV,5   (1959)
A good climb, possible in most conditions. The summer route is generally followed passing The Lower Tower on the right. The Upper Tower is normally the crux and can be climbed on either the right side, as in summer, or on the left flank; more direct but harder.

Mammoth (360m, IV,4) takes a diagonal line from the foot of the Labyrinth Couloir *via* the Dinosaur Gully to the halfway terrace, then it goes away right to finish on Central Gully Buttress.

26 Dinosaur/Pink Elephant 320m HVS **   (1964/1969)
The lower part of Dinosaur and the upper section of Pink Elephant provides the best route on the left side of the main slabs; unfortunately the big upper groove (crux) is slow to dry. Start at the lowest rocks.
1. 25m Climb broken cracks to a grass rake. Alternatively, scramble up the rake from right to left.
2. 40m 4b Follow the main crack system above (5m left of a thinner crack, Dragon Slayer) to a stance 5m below the long lower overlap.
3. 40m 4c Surmount the overlap above and go up the slab over an awkward bulge. Go up slightly higher and follow a toe traverse left (it is a mistake to go too high here). Step up left, then go slightly down left into the obvious shallow corner. Climb this using the left rib to the top of a big flake.

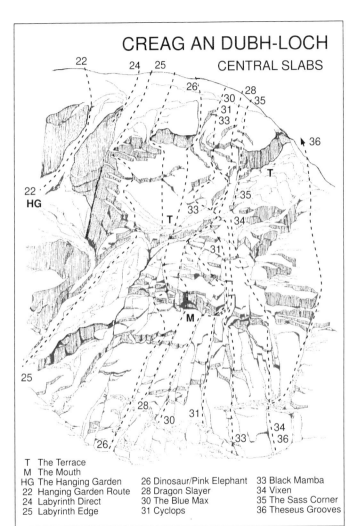

CREAG AN DUBH-LOCH

CENTRAL SLABS

T   The Terrace
M   The Mouth
HG The Hanging Garden
22 Hanging Garden Route
24 Labyrinth Direct
25 Labyrinth Edge

26 Dinosaur/Pink Elephant
28 Dragon Slayer
30 The Blue Max
31 Cyclops

33 Black Mamba
34 Vixen
35 The Sass Corner
36 Theseus Grooves

4. and 5. 80m 4c Dinosaur now goes left into Dinosaur Gully and finishes up Labyrinth Edge (or *via* a direct finish). Instead, switch to Pink Elephant and go up to a grassy niche and climb the bulging corner above. Break right over the big left-slanting overlap to reach slabs, then follow the obvious line up into Dinosaur Gully and follow its right branch to The Terrace.

6. 20m 4b There is an obvious corner on the right side of the Sea of Slabs; climb this to under bulges.

7. 45m 4b Continue up grooves above, go through the overhang by a short bulging slot and continue up slabs.

8. 25m 5a Climb a tapering slab leading up left to the right end of a big grass ledge below the upper overhangs. Traverse right to a slabby knife edge, then drop into the big upper groove.

9. 45m 5a Climb the groove, negotiating a steep step by the left wall, then regain the groove. Finish up the groove or by the rocks on its left side.

27 The White Elephant 320m VII,6 **   (1980)
A winter ascent based on Pink Elephant. The upper tier, *via* the big groove, is more often in condition than the fickle lower section. The line described gives a magnificent route taking a thin icefall emanating from the big groove and occasionally reaching the bottom of the cliff (VI,5 if well formed). Climb directly up the lower section and go over the overlap to enter Dinosaur Gully. Follow this *via* the right branch, or take ice on the slabs on the right to the Sea of Slabs. The continuation line of ice flows from the big upper groove directly into the corner of the summer line at the right side of the Sea of Slabs. Follow ice to the top.

Upper Tier Variation: V,4
It is common for the Upper Tier to be attractively icy while the lower slabs are bare. The upper icefall can be reached by starting up Labyrinth Edge and moving right to The Terrace. In good conditions, the Sea of Slabs may be iced over and can be climbed directly, followed by a traverse right to enter the big groove (IV,4).

An esoteric traverse, **Trunk Line** (IV,5) has been made from The Hanging Garden down into Labyrinth Couloir, out over its right wall (crux) to the base of the Sea of Slabs. These were climbed on ice and a finish up the big groove of White Elephant was taken.

28 Dragon Slayer 310m E4   (1972)
This route takes the most direct line on the lower slabs, with a disproportionately hard 10m through the main overlap. Above The Terrace, it follows either of two obvious corners round the right edge of the upper slabs. The mouth section on the lower slabs is slow to dry. Start by scrambling up the grass rake past a large block.
1. 40m 4c Climb the crack line 5 metres left of the more obvious Dinosaur crack system to a tiny ledge under the lower overlap.
2. 30m 4c Surmount the overlap directly above and continue straight up the crack line to under the great V-mouth in the main overlap.
3. 25m 6b Climb over a small overlap into the mouth, ascend the groove at the back, then go out across the left wall. Climb the slabs above to a poor stance below the next overlap.
4. 35m 4c Go up left, then climb a bulging crack to slabs. Go right up these to a ledge.
5. and 6. 110m Follow the obvious line to The Terrace, then scramble up the right edge of the upper slabs.
7. 40m 5a Round the edge is an obvious long corner, below and left of a great pink diedre (The Sass Corner, a good alternative). Climb the corner direct to a sloping ledge below a layback corner. Turn this on the left, then go up slabs to belay 10m higher.
8. 30m 5b Above are two V-grooves (the quartz corner of The Blue Max just on the left); climb the right-hand groove, then slant right to easier ground.

29 Groanmaker 335m E5   (1986)
This long hard route with a bold crux surmounts the main overlaps between Dragon Slayer and The Blue Max. On the upper slabs it goes between Pink Elephant and Black Mamba.
1. 35m 5b Climb the brown corner left of the twin cracks of Cyclops for some 5m, then pull out left onto the edge. Go up this to step right over the top of the corner, then go straight up the crack line, over an overlap and into a right-facing corner.
2. 15m 5a Move up to a small overlap and move right into a subsidiary right-facing corner. Move up flakes in the slab just left of this, then go back left into the crack line and climb it to ledges on The Blue Max.
3. 35m 6b Continue straight up in the same line and climb the 'steps' in the main overlap to a poor blade runner. Climb past this to the top of the overlap (peg runner). Climb the overlap direct, then go up a thin crack in a bare slab to belay 5m below the next big overlap.

4. 20m 5c Climb the overhang at the right side, then go straight up to the belay ledge of The Blue Max.

5. 40m Follow The Blue Max to the terrace.

6. 45m Scramble up and left to the upper ledges close to the corner of Pink Elephant.

7. 45m 5a Climb the pink rib right of the corner, then veer slightly right up pink cracks to join Black Mamba below its belay.

8. 40m 5b Continue straight up the corner line, then go up the right side of a huge down-pointing flake. Break out left onto the wall below a niche and pull over onto pink slabs. Climb these to a grassy notch, then pull up the right wall to a stance.

9. 30m 5b Climb the big 10m curving corner above, or a line to its left if wet. Continue up a bulging slab to a prominent bulging crack and climb this with a detour out right to grassy ground above.

10. 30m 6a Climb a subsidiary corner right of Pink Elephant, with awkward moves round the right side of the capping roof, then move up left to the plateau past loose blocks.

30 The Blue Max 295m E1 **   (1967)
This route gives very fine and sustained climbing, but the crux section is contrived. It breaks through the main overlap at a distinctive rockfall scar. Scramble up the grass rake to a large block.

1. 40m 5a Climb the crack line straight above the block over a difficult bulge. Continue up cracks and move right into a long corner.

2. 35m 5a Climb the corner to small ledges and go up to make a thin traverse right over a smooth slab to a belay under the main overlap.

3. 25m 4c Break through the overlap by a right traverse across the wall immediately above the rockfall scar, then go up cracks to belay.

4. 40m 5b This is the line of Cyclops, so leave it by a left traverse to below a huge diamond-shaped block in the next overlap. Climb the block by its right side to the upper bulge, step right and go over the bulge by a crack which twists back into the groove. Continue up the groove to belay on the rib; a superb well protected pitch.

5. 40m Continue up the rib, then go straight up the succeeding crack and corner to a roof. Turn the roof on the right by cracks leading to a small ledge. Go up walls on the left for 10m to a good ledge. Now scramble up to the right edge of the upper slabs.

6. 40m 4c   Near the right edge the most obvious feature is a big crescent-shaped groove with a crack in the back (Cyclops). Turn it on the right by a smaller groove (or a wide V-groove round the right edge) to a union below short twin grooves. Climb the left-hand groove and continue slightly left by a short cleft and cracks to a grass stance below an obvious nose.

7. 25m 4b   Climb up just right of the nose, then go left over a slab to the base of the Quartz Corner.

8. 25m 4c   Climb the corner for 5m and exit right to the rib. Continue up the rib to gain and climb grassy grooves.

9. 25m   Finish up the big groove on the right, traversing the right wall to reach broken ground.

31 Cyclops 275m HVS ***   (1973)
This fine direct route takes a straight line of cracks up the lower slabs, using the wall of The Blue Max to pierce the main overlap. Start at the top of a tongue of slab encircled by a ring of grass, which lies at the foot of the grass rake of Dinosaur.

1. 30m 5a   Climb the left-hand of twin parallel cracks right of a brown corner to pull on to a hanging flake from the right side. Go up the edge to under a small overlap (crux).

2. 35m 4c   Climb the bulge above, then follow the obvious crack to a scoop with a constricted groove above. Climb the groove over a grass plug and continue to a stance.

3. 35m 4c   Go straight up through the overlap by traversing right across the wall immediately above the rockfall scar (The Blue Max), then continue up the crack line to the second overlap.

4. 30m 4b   Follow the continuation fault to a point level with the large pointed block of Black Mamba to the right.

5. 30m   Climb directly up cracks in pink water-washed rock to The Terrace.

6. 40m 5a   The route now takes the big obvious crescent-shaped groove near the right edge of the upper slabs, entered direct by a short chimney groove, to join The Blue Max. Climb the groove on the left and continue left by a short cleft and cracks above to a grass stance below an obvious nose.

7. etc. 75m 4b,4c   Finish as for The Blue Max, pitches 7 to 9.

32 Slithy Tove 65m E3 *   (1986)
A short route between Cyclops and Black Mamba, but without an independent finish. Either abseil 50m from a peg on Black Mamba or continue up The Blue Max.
1. 25m 6a Climb the right-hand twin of the Cyclops crack for about 10m, then make a thin traverse right from the last runners and go up to a big hold. Continue up a crack line to a ledge close to Black Mamba.
2. 40m 5b Climb the crack above and slightly left into a corner. Move out left and pull up a bulge to gain a deep curving crack. Climb this and the bulge at the top, then continue easily to Black Mamba.

33 Black Mamba 310m VS ***   (1969)
The classic of the slabs. To the right of the grass ring of Cyclops is a ledge 20m up the slabs. Start from grass at a low point in the slabs.
1. 20m 4c Climb a delicate shallow crack line to reach the left end of the grass ledge (technical crux).
2. 45m 4b Climb directly up the crack system above to gain a long corner. Climb this and pull out left to a stance under the main overlap.
3. and 4. 90m 4b Climb the overlap using the cracked groove on the right and follow cracks to ledges. Step round a big flake and go up cracked slabs to a shallow gully containing a large pointed block. Continue up easy slabs leftwards to The Terrace.
5. 20m Scramble up to the right edge of the upper slabs.
6. 40m 4b The obvious crescent-shaped groove is taken by Cyclops. Climb up and diagonally left under small bulges left of this groove to gain a pink rib and slabs close to Pink Elephant.
7. 45m 4b Traverse back right to gain the crack line of The Blue Max, which leads to the grass stance under the obvious nose. Climb up just right of the nose, then go left to the base of the Quartz Corner.
8. and 9. 50m 4c Finish up The Blue Max, pitches 9 and 10.
Winter: VII,7   (1984)
This long and arduous route, with the crux right at the top, was unrepeated at the time of publication. On the first ascent, the first two pitches held good snow, but the snow above was only partially consolidated. The summer route was followed to The Terrace. Above, the White Elephant icefall was climbed to below a large overhang (40m). A traverse right led to a corner-groove and capping bulge on Groanmaker, then slabs were taken to the Quartz Corner (30m). This was climbed to its top (1 peg for aid at the final overhang), then ice led to easier ground on the right (45m).

34 Vixen 140m E1   (1977)
This line of grooves and cracks near the right edge of the lower slabs
is best combined with the top section of Dragon Slayer. Start about 15
metres right of Black Mamba.
1. 20m Climb a shallow pink corner to the middle of the first grass
ledge of Black Mamba.
2. 40m 5b Go up the obvious deep groove above, then move slightly
right into a smooth left-facing corner. Climb it until forced onto its right
rib, then continue to below a wall, the extension of the main overlap.
3. 30m 5b Climb the wall directly and go up the walls above to below
slabs which steepen to wall angle on the right.
4. 25m 5b A series of crack lines lie above; take the left one which
slants right and steepens at the top. Exit left and go up a short slab
and a small square corner (a good landmark from the ground).
5. 25m Climb straight up the slab above to broken ground.

35 The Sass Corner 40m E3 5c *   (1983)
This fine sustained route above The Terrace is unfortunately very rarely
dry. Climb the great pink diedre, situated right of Dragon Slayer's upper
tier.
Winter: V,5 *   (1993)
The diedre can fill with ice.

A low level girdle of the slabs below the main overlap has been
made at HVS (2 pegs for aid). An early route, **Yakaboo** (240m VS)
starts up Dinosaur, goes right to The Blue Max, then follows Black
Mamba to the Terrace. Finish up Theseus Grooves.

36 Theseus Grooves 300m III *   (1969)
A good winter line. Bordering the slabs on the right is a line of grassy
grooves and snow basins which trend right to Central Gully Buttress.
The first 10m is slabby but this is usually iced or banked out. The rest
is a fine narrow ice runnel or tedious wading in deep ferns (select one).
Minimal rock protection. Very Difficult and grassy in summer.

The large section of cliff right of the slabs and Theseus Grooves is
scrappy and tiered, but it contains some routes which all trend together
on the crest of Central Gully Buttress.

37 Nemesis 180m VS 4c   (1973)
The lowest point of the continuous section of cliff is riven by cracks and
grooves. Start 5 metres right of a big obvious boulder at pink rocks.
Climb directly up cracks and grooves in two pitches to a big grass
recess. Above, climb a chimney crack in the steep upper wall to easier
ground. Finish up the chimney of Minotaur.
Winter: VI,7   (1987)
Follow the summer line.

38 The Titan 300m V,6   (1991)
The ramp and corner system right of Nemesis, starting at the same
place but taking the right-slanting vegetatious ramp.
1. 30m Follow the ramp to a flake.
2. 30m Continue steeply up the ramp to a shallow corner. Go up this
to ledges below a wide obvious corner on the right of a large wall.
3. 25m Follow the wide corner to below a steepening.
4. 40m Continue up the corner, swing left to easy ground, then go up
to the foot of a corner just right of the Minotaur chimney.
5. 40m Climb the corner for 10m past a large hollow flake, then swing
out right to easier ground and grooves leading to a flake.
6. etc. 135m Follow the crest to the top.

39 Minotaur 180m Severe   (1956)
A disappointing route apart from the final chimney. Start at a prominent
rock pedestal up right from the big boulder of Nemesis. Climb the
pedestal, best on the right side, then go up steeply and veer left to
below a steep chimney. Climb the chimney and the slabs above to a
recess. Move down and right, then go up to a steep rib. Climb the rib
and grooves to open ground. Take the obvious line to a deep hidden
chimney and climb this to the top.

40 The Golden Thread 300m IV,4   (1991)
A winter line based on Minotaur. Start 5 metres right of the summer
start beneath a vegetated groove.
1. 45m Climb the groove to a stance in a recess.
2. 30m Continue up the steep right-facing corner above and move left
at its top to gain the summer line.
3. 50m Climb the groove system on the left to a terrace. Move left
beyond the summer chimney (taken by Nemesis in winter) to the left
edge of the upper buttress.

4. 30m Above is a short steep gully in the wall to the right of the final corner of Centaur; this leads to easy ground. Finish up the top section of Central Gully Buttress.

41 Centaur 300m III   (1970)
The chimney and ledge system which slants left below the crest of Central Gully Buttress. Start in a bay 30 metres from the corner of Central Gully. Climb either of two wide grooves and continue to the bay at the top of the fault. Above is the steep icefall of the direct finish. The original route goes diagonally left from the bay and follows obvious ledges below a deep chimney (Minotaur) to a wide corner. Climb this and exit left, then return right to the crest of Central Gully Buttress.
Direct Variation: 60m IV,5   (1975)
Directly above the bay is a steep groove that can form a prominent icefall. Climb this, then slant right up a slabby corner to the crest of the buttress.

42 Central Gully Buttress 300m II   (1955)
The easy-angled ridge bordering the left side of Central Gully. The crest is straightforward, but the first pitch starting at the base of Central Gully can be tricky unless there is a good build-up. Difficult in summer.

43 Central Gully 300m Easy
This is the corridor running through the cliff, remarkable for its scale and spectacular right wall. It is not a climb, barely a scramble, but large blocks choking the bed make the ascent quite agreeable.
Winter: I ***   (1933)
Entertaining and low-angled for the grade. The cornice is usually avoidable on the left.

CENTRAL GULLY WALL

This is the great convex face forming the right side of Central Gully. Magnificent in its monstrous bulk, it is a wall to rank alongside any in Britain.

There are two major facets, the 250m frontal slab face and the shorter but forbiddingly steep wall impending over the gully. At the bend in the face between the two facets is a transitional zone, a maze of roofs and hanging slabs taken by routes like the classic Cougar. These extend over a tremendous overlapping wall guarding the mouth of the gully and contain some of the most impressive granite routes in the country. Climbs on the frontal face tend to be easier and generally follow big raking crack lines, while the gully wall is cleaved by three great corner systems.

The climbing is of uniformly high quality and climbers should not be disappointed, even on the less well known routes. At the top of most of the climbs there is a scrambly finish up a chaotic region of blocks and greenery below the rim. After prolonged rain, weeps continue to ooze down from this area for several days; if a line has wet streaks it is usually a waste of time embarking on it. The section from the Naked Ape to Vampire is the quickest to dry; Mousetrap and The Wicker Man also dry quickly.

At the top of Central Gully is a short but very steep wall arrayed with sharp hanging aretes. This section is separated from the main wall by the fault of Sabre Cut.

44 Four Corners Route 70m VI,7   (1987)
Start at a corner right of a 10m corner containing blocks, which is about 35 metres left of Sabre Cut, and left of Treeline Groove.
1. 20m Climb the corner until a step left can be made into a higher corner. Climb this and move left to a small pinnacle belay.
2. 10m Descend a ramp on the left to below a third corner.
3. 20m Climb the corner past a platform at halfway, then traverse right and return left above.
4. 20m A short crack on the left leads directly to the base of the fourth corner. Climb this directly to the top (crux).

In summer, the route starts up the 10m corner and is VS with 1 point of aid in the first corner. **The Om**, VS and A1 on the first pitch, starts on the right of this route but there may be some coincidence higher up.

45 Treeline Groove 90m IV,5   (1985)
Climb the second groove left of Sabre Edge, then traverse right from the top ledge to the arete and finish as for Sabre Edge.

46 Sabre Edge 85m Hard Severe   (1952)
The arete left of Sabre Cut. Start just right of a long bald slab and go up steep rock to a stance near the slab edge; unpleasant and loose (35m). Continue up to the base of the pinnacle and climb the crevasse to its top. Use a shoulder to cross the gap, then go over a bulge to a

small grass shelf (much harder without the shoulder). Move left and climb a steep groove to easier ground and a platform below the final overhanging wall. Traverse a slab rightwards to a notch in the arete and turn the last overhang on the right.

Winter: V,6   (1987)
Follow the summer route, including the combined tactics at the pinnacle (a good pitch to lead!).

47 Sabre Cut 80m IV,5   (1957)
The obvious fault is short but steep. The cornice is often big and can pose a serious problem. Severe in summer.

48 Idol Threat 40m E3 6a   (1987)
This route takes the left-hand crack line in the wall left of The Wicker Man, starting from a niche directly below the line. Climb a crack, move across and go up right to holds which lead back up left to a shallow niche at the start of the crack. Climb the crack to the niche just below the top, then gain the grass shelf above (unstable but useful block in the niche). Follow the shelf up right over a slabby rock step to join and finish up The Wicker Man, or abseil off.

49 The Wicker Man 150m E3 *   (1982)
Below the fault of Sabre Cut is the corner system of Vertigo Wall. This fine route, with a sustained but safe crux pitch, takes the conspicuous crack line in the centre of the wall left of Vertigo Wall. The finish is disappointing, and it is arguably better to abseil off. Start as for Vertigo Wall.
1. 30m 5a Climb to a grassy bay below a left-trending groove. Follow the left wall and rib of the groove to a ledge and a large perched block.
2. 35m 6a Step right and climb thin cracks in a faint groove to a ledge below a small square-cut overhang. Climb the thin right-hand crack into the sentry box, then go up the wall above to a ledge. Climb the obvious corner crack to a belay on the right.
3. 25m 5a Continue up the corner and the slabby groove above, exiting right at the top. Go up grass ledges to a large embedded flake.
4. 30m Move left around the corner and follow easy ledges left and back diagonally right to below the bulging headwall.
5. 30m 5b Move up right to a glacis and climb the overhang at its narrowest point to reach a right-slanting groove. Climb a crack on its right to the top.

50 Vertigo Wall 160m VS   (1954)
This is the huge recessed scoop below Sabre Cut, easily recognised
by the scar of a big rockfall. A climb of considerable character and well
named. Start at a big block in the gully up from the true line of the
corner where a grassy shelf leads right onto the face.
1. 25m From near the left end of the shelf, climb straight up to gain a
traverse line which leads right to a grassy recess below an obvious
crack.
2. 40m Climb the crack to a platform, then move up right to a big
detached block. Traverse right, then pull over blocks on the left to gain
a shelf. Continue right up stepped slabs to under a black chimney.
3. 30m 4c The chimney is usually wet and slimy; if so, use a nut for
aid. Above this an overhang forces a detour right for some 10m, then
go up and back left into the true line of the corner. It is unwise to belay
below the creaking flake, so climb up left to a poor ledge.
4. 25m 4b Climb the slab above to the impending headwall and
traverse right along the alarmingly creaking flake into a shallow corner.
Move up and across the wall on the right, then finish with a pull-up to
the top.
5. 40m Easier climbing leads to the plateau.
Winter: VI,7 ***   (1977)
An outstanding truly mixed route, with turf, rock and ice, near the
summer line. Only the third pitch requires ice, and it often holds
enough. In the second half of the season the top wall receives sun and
is stripped of snow.

51 Bombadillo 125m E4 *   (1982)
This bold route, with good sustained climbing, follows an improbable
line of grooves in the nose of the buttress between Vertigo Wall and
Goliath. Start as for Goliath by traversing 15 metres right across slabs
to a grass ledge and peg belay.
1. 50m 5c Step down and right, then go up to gain the slab above.
Climb this and a shallow groove to exit left by a rock scar to ledges.
Move right and climb a slab rightwards, then go up a hidden flake crack
to a niche. Move left and pull up into a prominent V-groove; climb this
and continue to a large ledge. Belay uncomfortably 5 metres right
along the ledge.
2. 40m 6a Climb the broken wall rightwards to a ledge below an
overhanging groove. Hand traverse left across a steep wall, then pull
up to the slab above (poor peg runner). Traverse delicately back right

to the groove and a welcome peg runner, then climb the groove to where the angle eases (crux). Follow an obvious left-slanting ramp to the arete, move left to a crack, then go up to a ledge.
3. 35m 5b Climb a vague crack above for 5m, then traverse right to an obvious thin crack. Follow this until a good ledge leads right to the arete, climb this to the top. Scrambling remains to the plateau.

52 The Israelite 125m E4 *   (1982)
The smooth waterworn groove above the initial traverse slab of Goliath provides a long and particularly fine pitch, but it is slow to dry. In the opinion of some, the true grade is more like E5.
1. 25m Start as for Goliath; traverse right across slabs to a small stance and peg belay below the groove line.
2. 45m 6a Climb the slab above, then slightly left until a traverse right can be made to a crack leading up to an overlap. Climb the overlap to enter the main groove and follow it direct to where the angle eases. Traverse back right to the belay of Goliath.
3. 20m 5a Go up the obvious thin crack in the centre of the slab to a large ledge below the huge corner.
4. 35m 5b Climb the corner directly to the top. Scrambling remains to the plateau.

53 Goliath 150m HVS *   (1969)
This varied route breaks through the guarding walls and slabs between the great corners of The Giant and Vertigo to finish up the big diagonal slabby corner in the upper cliff. The climbing is mainly slabby, but in an impressive position. Further up the gully from The Giant is a vertical wall with a vast wedged block. Start up and left from the block.
1. 40m 4b Climb diagonally right, then traverse right across slabs to below a small corner in the steep wall.
2. 40m 5a Climb the steep corner and move up to a shelf (crux); step left and continue up the fault line to a belay on the right.
3. 40m 4b Go across the slab on the left, then climb to a ledge leading left to a huge slab. Climb the slab for 10m and continue to a stance about halfway up the great corner.
4. 30m Traverse right to finish up fine cracks splitting the slab. Scramble to the plateau.
Direct Start: 35m E2
A good start with a unique pitch past the vast wedged block. Start 10 metres left of the block.

1. 20m 5b Traverse right on a grass ledge (or gain this from below on the right). Hand traverse right and mantelshelf onto the block. Chimney up the back to the top.

2. 15m 4c Go left up a flake and pull over a bulge to gain slabs near the start of the second pitch of the normal route.

The Shelf Variation: 30m HVS 5a

After the 10m corner of pitch 2, continue right up the slabby shelf to a wall at the top. Climb this to the stance on the parent route.

Winter: VII,7   (1980)

A superb exposed route, mostly on ice, but it does not often come into condition. The route followed will depend on the ice, but it will always take the Goliath Icicle as the first pitch. Climb the initial slab and a steep finger of ice, the Goliath Icicle, which forms in the groove of the Israelite. Traverse right to meet the summer route and follow this up and back left to the stance halfway up the great corner. Traverse horizontally (peg to start) across the slab below the summer cracks, with a short descent to pass under an overlap, then a short rise to reach easy ground. Continue to above the slab, then follow easy ground to the top. A tempting line right of the big upper slab may be a dead-end without ice high up.

54 Goliath Eliminate 130m E2 **

Sustained high quality climbing, low in the grade. Climb the Direct Start to Goliath (5b,4c) and the crux of the normal route (5a). Take the Shelf Variation (5a) but go up and right to the final corner of The Giant (this is reversing part of The Catwalk). Climb the final big corner of The Giant (5b).

55 The Giant 100m E3 **   (1965)

A climb of great character taking the lowest of the three great corners systems, an impressive slash in the fiercest section of the wall. The short but desperate crux is slow to dry, and the seriousness depends on the state of the protection peg. This was replaced in 1992, but the sling to aid clipping rapidly degenerates in the wind. Start by climbing easily right up a sloping ramp to belay at the foot of the first corner.

1. 20m 5c Climb cracks to the base of two parallel grooves. Swing up to a flake in the left-hand groove and climb this to a ledge.

3. 20m 6a Above is another set of twin grooves; the crux. Climb the left one, using the peg in the right one for protection. Above the grooves, go left and climb a vertical flake crack to a big ledge.

4. 30m 5a Climb over blocks in a groove with a steep slab on the left. At the top of the groove, below an impending wall, move left to a slab and go up and left to a grass ledge. Traverse back right to step onto an overhanging nose. Climb the crack above, go left, then climb to a big platform below the impressive final corner.
5. 30m 5b Climb the fine corner, then easier ground leads to a grass ledge. Scramble to the plateau.

56 The Naked Ape 130m E5 ***   (1982)
This magnificent route, which finds a line up the big arete right of The Giant, offers bold climbing in an impressive situation. Start below a groove leading directly up to the main corner system of The Giant.
1. 35m 5b Climb the groove and, where it forks, keep right up a flake-crack to reach a ledge at the top of the initial ramp of The Giant.
2. 30m 6b Above is a smooth groove right of The Giant. Boldly climb its left hand rib (crux), then step across it to a peg runner at 10m. Move up right on to the steep slab, traverse right to the arete and step up to a peg runner. Continue traversing right along an obvious foot ledge, then step up to a good ledge (junction with Ascent of Man and Voyage of the Beagle). The pegs were reported to be in a very poor state in 1993.
3. 25m 6a Follow the left-slanting slabby corner to a niche below a roof and place a runner in the lip. Climb delicately down left to a good foothold near the arete. Step up left and climb a break in the overhang to gain a sloping ledge. Climb a short steep wall, peg runner, to a ledge in a niche.
4. 40m 5b Climb the overhanging crack above to a large ledge, then step up right and climb cracks to enter a groove system. Follow this to a grassy terrace at its top. Scramble up right to the plateau.

57 The Ascent of Man 130m E5 **   (1982)
An extremely fine natural line up the obvious groove and crack line in the huge steep wall between The Giant and Cougar. Sustained and strenuous. Start below the line.
1. 30m 6b Climb a short crack, then traverse right along a ledge to gain the lower groove. Follow this up and traverse left across a slab to regain the crack. Climb this to a break in the roof (peg runner), pull into the groove, then follow it to a hanging peg belay.
2. 30m 6a Step up and move across right to gain a subsidiary groove (if wet, climb the arete on its left, and return to the main groove as soon

as possible, 6a, unprotected). Climb this and move left to climb a crack which leads to a leaning wall. Step up left to a ledge and belays at the top of pitch 2 of The Naked Ape.

3. 10m 6a Climb the short crack above and hand traverse right into a groove and go up this to its top.

4. 35m 5b Climb the short corner above to the traverse line of The Prowl, then follow this up left along a slab and down into a recess with a large detached block (junction with The Naked Ape).

5. 35m 5a Step back up right and climb cracks to enter a groove which leads to a grassy terrace. Scramble off right.

58 Perilous Journey 125m E5 *   (1983)

This route climbs the face not far right of The Ascent of Man to gain an obvious hanging crack leading up to Cougar below its last pitch. Below The Ascent of Man is a big overhanging alcove; start up a break in the bulge just up the gully from this.

1. 20m 6a Swing up right to a jug on top of a peculiar boss of rock, then surmount the bulge. Move up right and climb a crack to easier slabs. Climb an overlap and go up to a detached block in an open corner; climb this to a thread belay.

2. 20m 6b Climb the slabby wall directly above to a slabby shelf (the last runners for the hard section are here, but protection can be improved by making a detour left along a creaking flake and moving up to a jug where more runners can be arranged, then return to the original line). Make a hard mantelshelf move above the shelf onto a smaller shelf. Go left and step up delicately to reach good flake holds leading to a peg belay on the big slab.

3. 30m 6b Step down left and traverse the lip of the slab to an evil sloping perch at the end. Swing left round the overhanging nose and make hard moves across left and up past a peg runner. Climb up and step right to follow a vague groove system, then hard twin cracks lead up a wall to a peg belay (good nut up on arete on left). There is an abseil spike here for escape, which can also be used from Ascent of Man and Voyage of the Beagle.

4. 25m 5b Move up left round the arete into the groove of The Ascent of Man. Go up this a short way, then continue to make an awkward move across a slab on the right to reach the hanging crack. Climb the crack and go up to the top of the great blocks of Cougar.

5. 30m 5b Climb a shallow recessed corner, as for Cougar, then go left up a shelf, as for The Prowl. Climb a bulging nose past a spike and go slightly right then left to join the left traverse of Cougar just below

the rounded spike. Finish as for Cougar, traversing left along a bulge, then moving up to easy ground.

59 The Web of Weird 80m E6   (1987/1994/1995)
The big overhanging alcove is nearly always a little wet, but was dry in 1995. The Original Start avoids the wet bit, but it is less direct.
1. 35m 6b Climb the groove past a peg runner to a rest where the groove starts to impend. Avoiding the wet flakes on the right wall, climb the groove *via* a hard undercut move (crux) to better (but wet) holds in the vertical groove above. Continue up the easing groove (the Perilous Journey belay is on the left if the rope drags), to another vertical section (the Bluebell Groove). Climb this (peg runner) to a slab.
2. 10m 6c Move left and delicately gain a higher slab under the big overlap. Gain holds on the lip to the right and make wild moves over the bulge. Step left and go up a delicate groove to belay as for Voyage of the Beagle.
3. 10m 6b Move up left onto a slab beneath an overhanging wall. Follow the weakness leftwards (poor protection) to a higher slab and belay as for Perilous Journey; a nasty pitch. A less independent but pleasant option is follow Voyage of the Beagle to the Perilous Journey cracks and climb them to the belay.
4. 25m 6a Move back right past stacked blocks, then hand traverse right (peg runner) into a niche in the overhanging wall. Pull round the corner onto a shelf at the base of an overhanging crack. Finish up the crack (which is to the right of the flake crack on pitch 4 of Perilous Journey).
Original Start: 30m 5c
Start up Cannibal, but keep to the left-hand crack, veering up and left to the groove above the alcove. Climb the slab to below Bluebell Groove, and traverse across to the left edge to belay on Perilous Journey.

60 Cannibal 140m E6 ***   (1984)
Another hard climb with increasingly hard pitches, all of high quality. Start at a prominent arete approximately 10m down from Perilous Journey and 15m up from Voyage of the Beagle. This is just right of the large overhung recess.
1. 30m 5c Climb the crack just left of the arete until moves can be made round the arete into another crack. Climb this until it fades, then step left to gain a crack on the crest. Climb this steeply to a stance on the slab above.

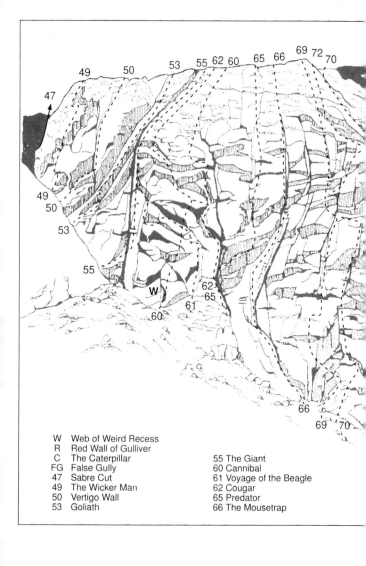

W	Web of Weird Recess		
R	Red Wall of Gulliver		
C	The Caterpillar		
FG	False Gully	55	The Giant
47	Sabre Cut	60	Cannibal
49	The Wicker Man	61	Voyage of the Beagle
50	Vertigo Wall	62	Cougar
53	Goliath	65	Predator
		66	The Mousetrap

CREAG AN DUBH-LOCH

CENTRAL GULLY WALL

R

FG

C

69 King Rat
70 Waterkelpie Wall
72 Gulliver
73 Cayman
76 Sous les Toits

80 Masque
81 The Snake
84 Slartibartfast
85 Sans Fer
87 Falseface

2. 10m 6a Move up left and gain holds which lead to a peg runner below the roof. Pull out right until a crack above the roof leads to a stance and peg belay on the higher slab.

3. 30m 6b Move up to a left-slanting corner and climb this to a roof. Traverse left and pull into the recess above, peg runner, then pull over its right wall onto the Cougar Slab; belay as for Cougar at the right end of the slab.

4. 40m 6b Above and slightly right is a stepped corner. Climb the first step, then swing right to the arete and move up until the corner can be regained. Continue up the corner and pull out right below a steep nose. Climb the wall right of the nose to gain a short crack, then pull onto a block on top of the nose. Follow a slab left below a roof to a stance.

5. 30m 5a Climb the crack above, then scramble to the top.

61 Voyage of the Beagle 160m E4 ***   (1983)
This superb, sustained and exposed route takes the very prominent line under Cougar to link with the top pitches of The Naked Ape. It offers slabbier climbing than other routes on this part of the wall. Start 5 metres left of Cougar at a groove.

1. 25m 5c Climb a flake crack on the right to gain the groove. Follow the groove, initially with difficulty, then more easily up the continuation to a small square-cut ledge (the belay is optional; less rope drag on the subsequent technical crux, but a direct fall onto the belay).

2. 15m 6a Move left across the wall, then regain the corner. Step down left and gain a crack leading back into the fault, which leads to a belay on the start of the slab.

3. 15m 4c Climb across the slab to an old peg belay.

4. 40m 6a Move across left to place runners on the upper slab, then return and step down to gain a lower slab. Cross the slab to the arete, step sensationally left round this and climb straight up to enter a groove (on The Ascent of Man). Climb this to its top; to protect the second it is advisable to split the ropes and return right on the upper slab to place runner. Move left to gain a groove leading to the stance on The Naked Ape at the end of its second pitch. A bold lead; take care with rope drag.

5. and 6. 65m 6a,5c Follow The Naked Ape to the top.

62 Cougar 135m E3 ***   (1968)
The Central Gully Wall below The Giant soars up for about 100m in a series of monolithic slabs and roofs. This magnificent climb takes a

curving line of diedres near the right end of the wall, then cuts in over the main section by the huge hanging Cougar Slab to thread the maze of roofs above. The climbing is exposed, very sustained and intimidating despite good protection (although spaced on pitch 4). Start at the foot of Central Gully on top of a mound with embedded blocks, common with Vampire and Predator.

1. 30m 4c Make a short right traverse into the initial corner and climb it (often wet) into a notch. Continue up left and work up to a good ledge under an overhang (common with Vampire).

2. 40m 5c Follow cracks leading up left over a bulge and go up the steep corner line above to the Cougar Slab.

3. 35m 5c Traverse the slab left by a crack and step down into a recess below a short overhanging corner crack. Climb this strenuously, then continue left by great flakes to under a short impending recessed wall.

4. 30m 5c Climb the wall to gain the girdling slab (The Prowl) under the final bulging band. Move right and mantelshelf onto a block. Above is a crack with a protruding stone; climb it to reach an overlap. It is possible to climb straight up at 5c, but better to make a left traverse under the overlap bridging a slight gap. Continue traversing left to reach a good rounded spike and from this make a step up and traverse left under a bulge until it is possible to move up then left to a good ledge under a roof. Scrambling remains to the plateau.

In the case of retreat, a 45m abseil from the base of the overhanging crack (Cougar Slab) will just reach the gully bed (50m abseil from the top of the crack).

63 Vampire 225m E2 **   (1972)

A fine sustained route, although slightly dirty in places. Start as for Cougar.

1. 30m 4c Climb the first pitch of Cougar.

2. 40m 5a On the right, the bulge is split by an overhanging crack with a jammed flake at its base. From the jammed flake, pull right round the bulge and climb the corner above to a grass ledge with a good stance just above.

3. 40m 5b Step back down, then go up to a slab on the right. Go diagonally right up slabs and a bulge to reach a ledge after 20m. Make a toe traverse left across a tiny dwindling ledge, go up a corner to bulges, then break out left by a short wall and slab to a grass stance (poor protection).

4. 25m 5b Move left up a slab and climb a short recessed corner. Climb the slot above and go up a slab to exit right. (Alternatively, move right and climb a steep crack to the same point, 5c; or start up the crack and move left above the slot, 5b).

5. and 6. 90m 4c It is now easy to move left to broken ground then right to the plateau, but better climbing is possible by continuing to trend right and following the final two pitches of Raptor to easy ground.
Variation: E3 5c
Climb the big corner directly above the stance at the end of pitch 2; dirty.

64 Raptor 215m E1   (1981)
An eliminate line between Vampire and Predator which dries very quickly and gives good continuous climbing.
1. 25m 5b Start up the Direct Start of Predator to belay under the short wall.
2. 30m 5b Climb the wall, go up the slab (as for Predator), then traverse left over the top of the slab below a steeper slab. Climb up the centre of the slab until a horizontal traverse right leads to the block-strewn ledge of Predator (crux).
3. 35m 5b Return up left across a slab and climb the slabby wall above by a crack leading to a slab. Move up left to join Vampire at the bulge of its slab section. Go diagonally right as for Vampire to belay before the traverse.
4. 35m 5b Continue directly up the groove above to reach another blaeberry stance. Move up slabs and go straight up a bulging wall section of a big overlap to a ledge. Layback directly over the overlap above and climb slabs to a ledge.
5. and 6. 90m 4c Move left round cracked blocks and work fairly directly to easy ground, climbing not far left of a grass-choked groove.

65 Predator 180m HVS *   (1970)
The obvious black corner system right of Vampire, the leftmost of the big frontal crack systems, gives a sustained route in a fine position but occasionally mossy. Start at the top of the mound, the first 10m being common with Cougar and Vampire.
1. 35m 4b Make a short right traverse into the corner and climb it (often wet) to a ledge on the right. Climb the short vertical crack above to gain a shelf leading away up right to a grass ledge.

2. 30m 5a Climb the short wall above and go up a slab to the foot of an overhanging crack in a red wall. Traverse right to breach the wall by a shorter overhanging crack and gain the corner above (often wet). Climb the corner and swing out left and across a slab to a block-strewn platform.

3. 30m 5a Climb the bulging crack above, then move right to a slab. Continue up through the roof and climb the crack line to above the left end of the prominent bow-shaped roof of The Catwalk.

4. 40m 4c Follow cracks to below roofs, climb a smooth scooped corner and move right across a slab to a recess.

5. 45m Climb cracks through another overlap and continue to easy ground.

Direct Start: 25m HVS 5b

Start up a break in the wall down right from the ordinary start to gain a shelf, then a higher shelf. (These shelves lead right towards the Mousetrap recess, the higher being the line of the winter ascent of The Mousetrap.) Climb twin cracks in the vertical wall above to gain the normal route.

66 The Mousetrap 180m VS **   (1959)

This fine natural line, giving the easiest way up the frontal face, is well protected and fairly quick to dry. It uses the obvious grassy recess right of the grassy mound above the foot of Central Gully, which leads up to the big crack system right of the black Predator crack line. At the lowest point of the frontal face is the big King Rat recess; start up left from this at a deep easy groove leading to an array of cracks.

1. 35m 4a Climb the groove, traverse left over a slab, then go up to belay below and left of the main crack.

2. 45m 4c Move up right and climb the wide crack (crux), or use the rib on the right before moving back left, and so to the recess above. Continue up the recess to belay near the top.

3. 25m 4c Climb the steep flake corner on the left, move up to cracks and follow these to a stance.

4. and 5. 75m 4c,4b Continue up the crack line to easier ground.

Winter: VII,8   (1980)

Climb the first short corner of Predator (technical 8), then traverse right round a shelf under the twin cracks of Predator Direct Start. Continue right, then go up to the grassy recess of The Mousetrap and continue up the summer route; sustained and thin, but ice high up will help.

The Kraken (HVS 5a) starts up The Mousetrap, climbs wide cracks to the right of The Mousetrap crux and exits out of the top right side of the recess to join Dubh Loch Monster.

67 Dubh Loch Monster   200m E1 *   (1970)
The line of the thin solitary crack to the right of The Mousetrap-Kraken cracks, some way left of the King Rat system, gives excellent pitches although escape on to The Mousetrap is possible. Very sustained at 5a with one move of 5c. Start just below and right of the easy groove of The Mousetrap.
1. 30m 4b Climb cracked slabs to under a chimney break.
2. 40m 5c Climb the chimney (crux), then continue up an awkward wall and follow the crack line to under a big overhanging notch.
3. 10m 5a Move left and climb the arete, returning right to a big ledge.
4. 25m 5a Follow cracks to above a double bulge; climb the first bulge, move right 2m and climb the second with difficulty. Go up slabs to under a short wall.
5. 45m 5a Move left to a break (junction with The Kraken) and climb this to gain the slab above. Move left 2m and pull over a short wall into a corner. Follow the corner for 5m, then the rib on the right over two bulges, the second being turned on the left, then move right to a ledge.
6. 50m Climb slabs diagonally right to a crack at the right end of an overlap. Go up the crack, then climb a steepening corner. Follow the crack above to easier ground.
Variation to pitch 6:
The Kraken finish. Climb up and slightly left to gain a corner which leads to a ledge going left to below an overhanging groove. Go up the groove, then move left to awkward cracks which lead to a belay. Climb the cracked slab above to easier ground.

68 The Rattrap   350m VIII,8   (1986)
A voyage of determination, taking the line of least resistance and most vegetation on the right side of the front face of Central Gully Wall. Climb Dubh Loch Monster to above the summer crux, then traverse right above the roof system of King Rat to reach the Red Wall of Gulliver. Pass it by the diagonal fault on its left to join Gulliver. Follow the Gulliver crack line, 3 pegs for aid, then take the iciest line to the top.

Voyage of the Beagle, Creag an Dubh-loch (Climber, Murray Hamilton)

69 King Rat 220m E1 **   (1968)
This is the very fine crack running straight up from the frontal face.
From below, the route is dominated by a big roof 50m up. Climbed with
2 points of aid, the route is VS. Start close to the left wall of the big
recess at the lowest point of the face, directly below the big roof.
1. 40m 4b Climb steep rocks at the back of the recess for some 15m,
then traverse the left wall using flakes to a ledge on the open face (a
more direct line continues straight up the recess to the slabs below the
roof, 5a). Climb straight up the crack line to a big grass ledge.
2. 20m 5c Move right from the ledge and go up cracked slabs to a
shallow cave under the roof. Move awkwardly up left into a corner and
climb this to a ledge.
3. and 4. 50m 4b Now follow the general line of the cracked ribs above,
until under a short vertical wall. Go left up slabs to below the short
leaning corner of Waterkelpie Wall.
5. 10m 4b Climb the corner to ledges.
6. 30m 4c The obvious right-trending line is Waterkelpie Wall. Climb
a short wall to gain a slab under the roof, surmount the bulge some
3m left of the roof, then traverse a narrow slab right above the roof and
go up to ledges.
7. and 8. 70m Move into the upper crack system and follow it in to
grass ledges. Scramble away left and up to the plateau.

70 Waterkelpie Wall 250m E1   (1958/(1964)
A meandering route up the centre of the frontal face, but it has some
good pitches. In the middle of the face, the Red Wall of Gulliver
overlooks the left end of The Caterpillar, a long grass ledge. The lower
section takes a vague line straight up to the left end of the ledge
system. A circuitous line left then right leads to the continuation of the
Red Wall cracks. Start at the right side of the King Rat recess.
1. 45m 5a Climb a rather unpleasant grassy fault to a rockfall scar.
Move left under the scar and over alarmingly hollow flakes, then go up
the second corner left of the scar to slabs. Climb the slabs to a vertical
corner immediately right of the King Rat roof. (The start to this pitch
can be avoided by going up King Rat to the left traverse, then
continuing straight up and slightly right to regain the route, 5a).
2. 10m 5b Climb the vertical corner to a ledge.

Cannibal, Creag an Dubh-loch (Climber, Murray Hamilton)

3. 35m 4c Climb up right to a terrace and go straight up cracks to the left end of The Caterpillar ledge system.

4. 15m 4b Work left over pink slabs, ignoring an obvious break. Go left and up a slab to below a short leaning corner (common with King Rat).

5. 20m 4b Climb this to ledges and follow the obvious line up right to a barrier bulge with prominent old pegs.

6. etc. 125m Climb the double bulge (5b) and traverse away right over slabs to gain the line of the chimney-crack above the Red Wall. Follow it to the top (4c). Left hand variations (better quality, but 5a) are possible if the crack is wet (as for Gulliver).

71 Chimera 220m E2   (1995)
A direct line through the steep walls and hanging corners left of the lower section of Gulliver. Start a few metres right of Gulliver at the lowest point of the face.

1. 35m 5a Climb straight up a shallow corner line to the bulge of Gulliver. Surmount this to reach the left end of a grass ledge, then step up and left to a pedestal stance.

2. 30m 5c Move 5m up and right to below a left-facing corner and pull onto the slab above. Trend up and slightly left and continue up a series of steep right-facing corners above to make a difficult exit (crux) onto the left end of the shelves at the end of Gulliver pitch 2. A sustained and intricate pitch which requires small wires and RPs.

3. 45m 5c Climb the steep wall directly behind the belay and exit right onto slabs. Follow these *via* a short corner to a terrace. Move left and climb the tier above by a crack. Continue up the cracked slabs on Waterkelpie Wall pitch 3 to the belay at the left end of the Red Wall of Gulliver.

4. 30m 5a Move up to the foot of the Rattrap groove left of the Red Wall and pull out left onto the arete. Follow this to below steep walls and step left to belay on the ledge below the barrier bulge of Waterkelpie Wall.

5. and 6. 80m 5b Continue up Waterkelpie Wall to the top.

72 Gulliver 235m E2   (1970)
A direct line right of Waterkelpie Wall, taking the steep Red Wall. This is sustained and strenuous, substantially harder than anything else on the route. Apart from the Red Wall, a little disappointing in quality, and slow to dry. Start directly below the Red Wall at the lowest point of

the face, just right of the King Rat recess and the grassy fault of Waterkelpie Wall.

1. 35m 5a Trend right up broken slabs and cracks, then go up an awkward bulge and the slab above. Traverse horizontally right to below a two-tiered corner.

2. 40m 5a Climb the two-tiered corner, then traverse left over detached blocks on the lip of the overhang to shelves.

3. 10m 5a Go right and up a bulging wall to ledges below tiered walls.

4. 45m 4b Climb the walls using the heathery break, then go up slabs to ledges under the Red Wall.

5. 20m 5b Climb parallel cracks in the Red Wall.

6. 40m 4c Continue up cracks above over a bulge to under the chimney-crack of Waterkelpie Wall.

7. 45m 5a Climb slabs and corners leftwards to easy ground. Alternatively, finish up the crack line of Waterkelpie Wall, the natural way when dry.

73 Cayman 270m E2 *   (1977/1984)
A direct line right of Gulliver, offering good climbing throughout its length. It reaches the left end of The Caterpillar, which is the grass runnel slanting left into the face towards the Red Wall of Gulliver. Above, it breaks through a long roof right of the Red Wall to follow an obvious crack system. The start is the Bower-Lang Route, HVS 5a, which can be used for access to False Gully Wall (see pitch 2), but there are other options. In the middle of the rocks below The Caterpillar is a big curving roof. The route starts with a rising traverse line above this roof. Start just right of the lowest part of the face, close to Gulliver.

1. 20m 4c Climb straight up cracked slabs, then go up and right into a shallow left-facing corner; exit out right to small ledges.

2. 20m 5a Traverse right and go up a shallow corner to exit right onto a slab. Make a thin 5m traverse right to a small ledge leading up into a short corner. (For False Gully Wall: Traverse right, go up and over a big jutting nose and move rightwards *via* short walls to grassy ground in The Caterpillar; two pitches, 4c).

3. 35m 5b The crux pitch? Traverse 5 metres right, climb the wall above, then trend left up slabs. Climb the right side of a big slabby plinth to gain the right end of a ledge. Climb the awkward recessed wall above and go up short walls.

4. 25m 4c Traverse right up the steep wall above using flakes and go left by two detached blocks to The Caterpillar.

5. 10m 5c Above is a roof; in the centre is a down-pointing flake shaped like an alligator's head. Climb left up big flakes into a corner, then move right and up over the roof using the alligator's head. Continue up the crack line above, surmounting a hard bulge at the top, then go up to a ledge on the right occupied by big flakes.

6. 20m 4c Go up through the obvious notch above and follow a groove to grassy ledges.

7. 20m 4c Continue up the pink groove above, alongside a big smooth slab.

8. 30m 4c Climb up right then left by slabby rocks to under a big steep chimney.

9. 40m 5a The line of False Gully has been joined, the original line of this taking the left arete of the big chimney, usually wet. Move right to the right arete of the chimney, passing a small spike. Continue up thin cracks to step right into a groove and move left to a ledge. Go up and right across a perched block to climb the right edge of a groove and its continuation; step right just below the top to a good ledge.

10. 50m Move up left and scramble to the top.

Variation: **The Croc Finish**

9a. 25m 5a Climb the big chimney, pass a steep bulge at the top on the right, then step left to a good ledge.

10a. 25m 5a Continue up a groove on the right to a steep exit.

74 Dragonfly 90m HVS   (1981)

This route goes up rightwards below the big curving roof of Cayman. Start about 10 metres right of Cayman, below and right of a rowan sapling.

1. 30m 4c Go up right over the first overlap, continue up right, then traverse left and break through short walls. Traverse right, then climb up and left to a spike below and just right of the left end of the curving roof.

2. 10m 4c Traverse horizontally right across a slab to a grass patch. Move further right, then go straight up to an overhang.

3. 50m 5a Continue traversing below the roof, then climb an obvious corner to a pedestal. Trend left and continue up to The Caterpillar.

75 The Fox Moth 90m E1   (1994)

A direct line cutting through Dragonfly. The first two pitches are worthwhile and would make a good direct start to Cayman. Start 25 metres right of Dragonfly below a conspicuous groove capped by a small overlap.

1. 25m 5b Climb the groove and overlap, then move up and left to a steep wall. Climb this on good holds to a stance below the left end of the big curving roof (shared with Dragonfly).

2. 25m 5c Pull straight over the roof directly above the belay (crux), then climb straight up for 10m (the ramp above the slabby plinth on Cayman pitch 3 goes left from here). Bear up and right, crossing the Bower-Lang Route, to belay below a left-facing corner cutting through a short steep wall.

3. 40m 5a Climb the corner and continue straight up *via* short walls and slabs to The Caterpillar.

The Caterpillar itself is mainly grass, but includes a short slab, VS 4c. In winter it is Grade IV with 4 points of aid.

76 Sous les Toits 110m E2   (1976)

This route weaves its way up the subsidiary buttress on the right of Caterpillar Crack. Good sustained climbing, which can also be used as an approach to False Gully Wall. Start in a grassy bay at the right side of the buttress.

1. 20m 6a Climb the obvious steep chimney, then take a traverse line leading horizontally to the belay (Friend 2½ or 3). Alternatively, continue up and left above the chimney for about 5m, then traverse left to a possible stance under a jutting nose and abseil to the stance (this reduces the grade to E1).

2. 30m 5b Traverse the slab to the far end, go round the corner and climb up left by a delicate slab under a bulge. Break out over the wall above on the right side of an overhang and move up right to a recess. Pull straight over the roof above to under more roofs.

3. 10m 5a Turn these on the right, then go up and left to the lip of the left-hand roof. Go up the slim ramp above and swing right to a stance below the final roof.

4. 40m 5a Turn this by a corner running up the right side, then go away up and left to grass under a short wall.

5. 10m Climb the wall to the grass of False Gully.

FALSE GULLY WALL

This is the tilting wall of the rounded North-West Buttress. It lies high on the right above the frontal face of Central Gully Wall and above False Gully, an intermittent terrace slanting left which peters out in the upper rocks.

The distinctive feature of the wall is a smooth and very steep central section containing the hardest routes. At the right side of the smooth area are the thin crack lines of Sans Fer and Iron in the Soul. The smooth area is bounded low down to the right by the very prominent leaning corner of Falseface, and on the left by the corner lines of Masque and The Snake.

The harder routes are often reached *via* False Gully, but the first pitch of either Sans Fer or Falseface can be recommended as an alternative. A route on the lower tier is recommended as an approach for the easier routes.

77 False Gully 200m VI,7   (1964/1995)
An interesting and unusual winter route. The crux is right at the top, from where retreat might be difficult. Follow the fault for several pitches until it peters out into a ledge. Continue by a prominent shallow chimney above (The Croc Finish to Cayman), exiting left at the top (25m). Move left into a left-facing corner (to the left of the groove taken by The Croc Finish) and climb its steep left wall to easier ground (35m). The original ascent tensioned left to the chimney's left arete (V,5), and a later ascent continued left on ice from the ledge below the chimney, but was forced to use tension (V,4). Hard Severe in summer.

78 Hotblack Desiato 45m HVS   (1986)
Above Masque is a large horizontal roof. Start below the left end of this in a shallow corner.
1. 20m 5b Climb the corner and pull over the roof. Step right to gain an obvious crack line and follow this to a stance.
2. 25m 4c Continue up to the big obvious corner, then follow this up and left to the top.

79 Heart of Gold 70m E3   (1989)
This route is based on the horizontal roof and corner left of Masque; it starts at the same point as Hotblack Desiato.
1. 15m 5c Climb up right to a short overlap below the main roof. Move right along the overlap, then go up to a peg runner. Climb up to the main roof and traverse right to the base of the big corner.
2. 35m 5b Climb the corner and cracks above to the base of another corner.
3. 20m Climb the corner, work right, then go straight up to finish.

80 Masque 60m E2 *   (1983)
This is the left-hand and deeper of the two corner lines which bound
the smooth section of the wall at its top (left) end. Start below the steep
leaning corner at the left end of a grassy terrace.
1. 20m 5c Climb the leaning corner to a roof, pull out left and climb a
crack to ledge.
2. 40m 5b Climb up the twin right-slanting cracks above to a roof. Step
right and climb a fault to enter a grassy groove which leads to the top.

81 The Snake 65m E4 *   (1984)
Another good line; it starts up the right hand and shallower of the two
corners.
1. 30m 6a Start up the corner, then move out slightly right and go up
to the top of a big flake. Step up past the flake and move right to flakes
on the arete (the left edge of the smooth wall). Climb the flakes to an
evil sloping shelf, step right to good protection and climb a bulging wall
to another shelf. Step right again and go up a short corner past a spike
to exit left at a roof to a ledge (peg 5m up on the right).
2. 35m 5b Go up past the belay peg, traverse left round the edge, then
traverse horizontally into a jam crack in the slabs. Climb this for 5m to
join the crack line of Masque and finish up this.

82 Fer de Lance 65m E6 *   (1987)
The wall crack just left of Improbability Drive is serious with no resting
places.
1. 30m 6b Climb the crack (peg runner) to gain the awkward shelf of
The Snake; follow this to the belay.
2. 35m 5c Climb up past the belay peg and go up diagonally right into
the corner of Slartibartfast. Climb this corner past the bulge above,
then step left along a shelf. Climb the bulging crack above, step left
and pull up onto a big flake. Move up left to easier ground and the final
grassy groove of Masque.

83 The Improbability Drive 60m E6 *   (1984)
The main pitch of this route, the wall left of Slartibartfast, is sustained
and fierce with limited protection. Start 10 metres left of Slartibartfast,
just right of an obvious crack.
1. 20m 6c Climb right up little foot shelves using diagonal cracks, then
go up the wall to a horizontal break. Go straight up the wall to a
semi-resting place at the next break. Climb the twin cracks directly

above, using mainly the left-hand crack (crux). Belay pegs are in place on the slab above (the left side of the Slartibartfast niche).

2. 10m 5c Climb directly up the bulge just left of the belay and go up slightly right to climb the third roof of Slartibartfast's second pitch. Belay here or on the ledge on the right rib.

3. 30m 5c Climb the obvious groove on the right rib, then veer slightly right and make awkward moves up a notch into the niche of Sans Fer. Stride across the black gunge usually flowing down here, and finish as for Sans Fer (if too wet, move back left below the notch and rejoin the final cracks of Slartibartfast).

84 Slartibartfast 80m E5 **   (1982)
This route takes the most prominent crack and groove line in the centre of the smooth wall, some 30 metres left of the obvious leaning corner of Falseface. High quality climbing taking a fine line but with a serious first pitch. Start from a slanting grass terrace, below a crack in the middle of the smooth wall.

1. 20m 6b A ledge on the wall, just right of the crack, leads to a small groove. Climb the groove until it peters out (crucial RP3, hard to place, up on the right), then go up and left across the wall to the crack. Follow the crack and a shallow corner, moving right at the top to sloping ledges.

2. 20m 6a Climb the obvious corner, containing three small overhangs, to the slab above.

3. 40m 5c Continue in the same line *via* steep cracks to the top.

85 Sans Fer 145m E4 **   (1979)
This route and Iron in the Soul offer good climbing but have interchangeable pitches and escapes are possible. The highlight is a fine crack in the smooth wall right of Slartibartfast. Start 10 metres left of the leaning corner of Falseface in the middle of the face.

1. 40m 5b Climb to a niche and slab, heading for a prominent finger crack; climb this to a sloping stance and belay as for Falseface.

2. 20m 6b Walk left 10m to the base of a crack and climb it.

3. 40m 6a Traverse 5m left to a groove and climb this to a rest under a bulge. Continue over the bulge, then go up grooves slightly right, then left to a ramp.

4. 45m 5c Traverse up left on the ramp to a niche and exit left through the roof. Traverse left, then go up into another niche. Continue straight up through a roof to easy ground and a block belay.

86 Iron in the Soul 80m E4 *   (1984)
Starting up the next crack right of Sans Fer's main crack, this route
shares the stance then goes up the continuation of this crack when
Sans Fer goes left. More sustained but not as well protected as that
route. Start up the first pitch of Sans Fer or walk along the terrace,
passing under Slartibartfast and Sans Fer.
1. 20m 5c Climb the crack directly to a shelf, then go up and left
negotiating two bulges. Traverse the slab left to Sans Fer's belay.
2. 30m 6a Climb the bulge above and go up cracks and a corner-crack
slightly left under the next bulge. Layback right and go over the bulge
to follow a flake crack curving up and left in a slab. Go on up a short
corner to the ramp of Sans Fer.
3. 30m 5a Above are mossy cracks; move left up the ramp and climb
a short cleaned crack. Step right and follow more cracks and blocks to
easy ground.

87 Falseface 90m E2 *   (1969)
A first class climb, often approached *via* a lower tier route. From a point
in False Gully below the big obvious corner, climb up and slightly
rightwards to a grass shelf leading into the corner, Very Difficult.
1. 20m 5c Climb the strenuous big leaning corner to a sloping ledge.
2. 35m 5b Climb the short wall above and move right into a hidden
chokestone chimney. Climb this to a ledge on the left below an overlap.
Gain a sloping ledge above, surmount the overlap (prominent old peg)
and traverse right across the overhung slab to good holds. Climb up
and back left to a series of grooves and follow them to a big ledge;
belay at the far end.
3. 35m 5a Move back left and climb into a big steep corner. Go up this
until near the top, then go along the right wall and climb a detached
flake to ledges and easier ground.
Variation Start:
The hidden chokestone chimney can be reached by a fault which
slants in from the right, but this misses out the best pitch (E1 overall).
Variation Finish:
Once easier ground is reached, an obvious ramp (joined by Sans Fer)
can be seen leading left; by following it, one can take in the last pitch
of Sans Fer (5b).

Well to the right of Falseface is a short line, starting in a prominent
slanting fault and following a corner and wall; **Coon's Yard**, E1 5b, 1
peg for aid in the wet.

NORTH-WEST BUTTRESS

This is the broad broken buttress at the right end of the cliff; its left side is False Gully and its right side borders North-West Gully. The left edge overlooking False Gully Wall is the disappointing **False Impression**, Very Difficult. It has a VS direct finish, which sticks more closely to the edge.

88 Mistral 200m IV,4   (1972)
This route follows an obvious line of grooves just right of the edge (False Impression). Start at the foot of False Gully and climb an easy snow ramp up right to the line of snow and ice grooves. The route was climbed in excellent conditions and might be harder when lean.

89 North-West Buttress 250m III   (1995)
A turfy central line. Start at the break on the left-hand side of the lower tier, just up and right from the shelf leading to False Gully. Climb up and left by a shallow groove, then go up right to the terrace. Cross this, move up right and follow snow on the left of North-West Gully Arete, then continue in grooves and chimneys, moving left to finish.

90 North-West Gully Arete 200m II   (1967)
The broken ridge on the left of North-West Gully is nearly always climbable in winter. The easiest way lies on the right side of the crest. Grassy and Moderate in summer.

91 North-West Gully 200m II *   (1952)
A classic winter gully, usually climbable but grade III in lean conditions. The entry slabs can form a big icefall, avoidable on the left but better climbed direct. Moderate in summer.

NORTH-WEST GULLY BUTTRESS

The rocks to the right of North-West Gully are very broken, but low down there is a pleasant plaque of pink slabs. This little buttress has some enjoyable climbs but they are unfortunately no quicker drying than the bigger routes.

92 Blizzard Nightmare 50m V,5   (1985)
Climb the icefall which forms on the left side of the buttress.

93 The Strumpet 60m VS   (1974)
This climb takes the deep crack splitting the big flake-whaleback on
the left. The buttress is undercut and the route starts at an arete on
the right, the lowest point of the buttress.
1. 20m Climb the arete for 5m, then traverse left to below an obvious
corner (Late Night Final).
2. 20m Work left to a groove which leads to a ledge under the
whaleback.
3. 20m 5a Climb a thin crack leading to the main crack on the crest,
and follow this to a good stance below easy ground.

94 Jezebel 50m E3   (1984)
A short direct line with a very hard friction start. Between The Strumpet
and Late Night Final is a smooth slab with twin parallel cracks. Start
immediately below these.
1. 25m 6b Climb the overhanging wall and go up across The Strumpet
to climb the left-hand of twin cracks, moving left into a scoop after 3m.
Climb this and the big corner above to below a wide crack.
2. 25m 5b Climb the crack and the corner above, then move left to
easy ground. Belay up on the right.

95 Late Night Final 60m Hard Severe   (1969)
A pleasant route; start as for The Strumpet.
1. 40m Follow the big corner to its top.
2. 20m Continue up cracks to an overhanging corner in a steep wall.
Go up this to a grassy niche, then move right and go up to the top.
Winter: VI,7   (1987)
Follow the summer line up the big corner (1 peg for aid), then finish up
a slabby corner right of the steep summer crack.

GIRDLE TRAVERSES

There are two girdle traverses of the Central Gully Wall. Unlike many
other Cairngorm girdles, they follow natural lines and give good
climbing, but are recommended only to those familiar with the cliff.

Catwalk 400m HVS   (1969)
Most of the climbing is about Mild VS, but there is one hard but well
protected section. Climb The Caterpillar and traverse to its left end
under the Red Wall. Continue along pink slabs and go up to the short
leaning corner of Waterkelpie Wall. Traverse left to a break in a leaning

wall (common with Kraken and Dubh Loch Monster). Go up this and move left along a narrow slab to a crack line on Mousetrap. Climb the crack for a short way to a slab stance above. Traverse left below the prominent bow-shaped roof (5b), then go up to a good stance (Predator). Climb the cracks and corner above for 20m, then move left to a stance beside a small curved roof. Move left round cracked blocks, then go along the lip of the roof. Go up cracks to grassy ledges (escape to the plateau apparent here). Follow the ledges left to belay by a large block level with the base of the final corner of The Giant. Traverse left under the corner and descend a groove to traverse left again into Goliath. Finish up Goliath.

The Prowl 420m E2   (1978)
A very sustained girdle, at a lower level than Catwalk, with increasingly impressive situations and a memorable pitch leading into The Giant. Go up Caterpillar Crack to a bare slab. Step left and work up, then down and away across sustained pink slabs to belay on the jutting nose of Dragonfly/Bower-Lang Route (5b). Continue at the same level below an overlap and go up a short groove on the right side of a slabby plinth (Cayman) to a belay ledge (4c). Go left along the ledge and climb a bulge (Gulliver) to easy ledges. Go along these and down slightly left to a ledge 5m above the roof of King Rat. Go up King Rat for 5m, then go left by small ledges into the crack line of Dubh Loch Monster (4b). Go up this to the overhanging notch and exit left into The Mousetrap recess (4c). Go up The Mousetrap for 10m, then move down left into the overhanging cracks on the red wall of Predator. Climb Predator to a point some 5m above the break in the roof (5a). Traverse left (not obvious) to step down to a ledge on Vampire slab some 10m below the toe traverse (5a). Climb along the toe traverse, then go up and left to the next stance (5b). Traverse the big slab on the left, hand traverse a block and step down to the small girdling ledge of Cougar (5a). Go along this, joining The Ascent of Man, and go round a nose to belay on a hanging green slab (4c). Move up the slab and climb a bulging wall to gain a higher slab tucked under the roof. Go left along this, then climb down a little arete to gain a huge recess occupied by a big detached block (5a, common with The Ascent of Man). Swing up the arete on the far side and move left to an airy belay perch (5a). A fine 10m flake crack leads sensationally into The Giant corner (4c). Climb left to an old peg in a slab, then surmount the overhang above and step left to Goliath's Shelf Variation (5a). Finish up Goliath.

BROAD CAIRN BLUFFS
(Map Ref 248 818)

The bluffs come into view on the left about 1km before the Dubh Loch on the approach from Loch Muick. They form the 60m left wall of an open green shoot (or easy-angled snow gully in winter), going up to the last step in the flat ridge of Broad Cairn before the rise to its summit.

The obvious narrow gash is **Coffin Chimney** (Difficult and Grade III), and the buttress on its right is **Rake's Rib** (Difficult and Grade III). The front of the buttress facing the valley gives **Yoo-Hoo Buttress** (Grade III), a pleasant climb when icy, and a good indicator of conditions on Creag an Dubh-loch.

Funeral Fall 50m IV,4 **   (1974)
Above Rake's Rib, a very prominent icefall forms which catches the eye from the last stretch of the path before the Dubh Loch. Good for a short day, bad weather, or a change of plan.

THE DIAMOND SLAB

Lower down the south side of the glen, about 1km up from Loch Muick, an intriguing, isolated, diamond-shaped slab is obvious from the Dubh Loch path and provides some shorter climbs which are very accessible.

The Only Game in Town 70m VS   (1994)
A disjointed route on the left flank. Start at the foot of the ramp just right of the rowan tree.
1. 50m 4a Climb the edge just left of the crack until vegetation leads up and right (back to the slope).
2. 20m 4b Climb the main crack in the side wall.
Variation Start: 5b
Near the top of the rib, move left and climb the bulge. This extends the clean rock section.

Solitaire 35m E2 **   (1983)
The obvious central line. Start at the toe of the buttress below the main slab.
1. 10m 5a Pull left over the initial overhang, then step right and climb the central shallow groove over a bulge. Go up past a block to below a steep cracked slab.
2. 25m 5b Climb the cracks up left, then move right and go straight up to the top. Limited protection.

Two's Company 40m E3 *   (1992)
A technical and serious route up the wall and arete right of Solitaire.
Start 3m up and right from the toe of the buttress, below a prominent
corner.
1. 15m 5a Bridge up the corner to a good jug on the right and continue
past the block to belay as for Solitaire.
2. 25m 5c The wall right of Solitaire is cut by a small discontinuous
crack system. Climb the crack past a poor peg to a good hold on the
right (crucial Rock 3 runner in the crack on the left). Continue to a small
niche, step right (crux) and climb the arete above on good but hidden
holds to the top.

*Information about the following routes was received just in time for
inclusion:*

THE CENTRAL SLABS

Howff Dweller 45m E3 6a   (1995)
About 50 metres right of Theseus Grooves there is a smooth slabby
wall at the base of the cliff. The route climbs a large left-facing corner
curving into an overlap above the wall.
1. 30m 6a Climb the corner and under the overlap to a semi-hanging
stance on the right.
2. 15m 4c Continue up the shallow right-facing corner and a crack in
the headwall.

CENTRAL GULLY WALL

The Shetlander 60m E6 6c   (1995)
This route climbs the crack line between Idol Threat and The Wicker
Man.
1. 15m 5b Climb a flaky crack line for 10m to gain a tufty break. Move
left along this to belay at the base of a right-slanting corner.
2. 30m 6c Climb the right-slanting corner, then go up a crack leading
into another corner. Continue up this to gain a resting place above.
Follow the steep crack line to a semi-rest at a flake. Climb the
desperate bulging groove to gain a peg and nut belay in the niche
above.
3. 15m 6a Move up from the belay until it is possible to step right. Go
up and right, then back left to climb a crack to the top.

Approximately 100 metres left of the last pitch of The Wicker Man is a steep slabby wall immediately below the plateau rim. The wall faces south-east and is reached by abseiling to the blaeberry balcony beneath it. Its best feature is a right-slanting diagonal crack up the centre which gives the following route:

Billy Nomates 20m E4 6a   (1995)
Start just right of the crack. Gain the crack and climb it with an excursion on the left wall to gain a horizontal break. Move back right along this and continue up the crack line to the plateau.

FALSE GULLY WALL

Below and to the right of Falseface there is an obvious wall split by numerous cracks. The rightmost line of stepped corners gives the following route:

DD's Recurring Dreams 40m E3 5c   (1995)
Start just right of the toe of the buttress and continue up a slabby ramp to climb the second corner. The third corner is avoided by climbing the chokestone crack round its left rib. This leads to another corner leading to easier climbing. Finish up a short crack to gain an abseil point.

The Gathering 30m E3 6a   (1995)
This route ascends the most prominent right-slanting crack on the wall. Start up a steep pink ramp to gain a ledge. Continue steeply up excellent steep cracks above, easing towards the abseil point (or belay) of the previous route.

The Quickening 30m E4 6b   (1995)
Climb the initial ramp-crack of The Gathering to the first ledge. Move left onto pink-streaked rock to reach and climb the leftmost diagonal crack line running up to a ledge. Continue by the thin crack above to reach the abseil point (belay) common to the other two routes described above.

Glen Clova

Glen Clova is the long narrow valley of the River South Esk which penetrates into the south-east Cairngorms. In this area, south of the Lochnagar — Broad Cairn range, schist and gneiss replace granite, grass replaces heather and the character of the mountains changes. The cliffs become rather vegetated and the rock climbing generally deteriorates, the exception being at Red Craig, a line of Lakeland-like outcrops on the east side of Glen Clova overlooking the public road shortly before it terminates at Braedownie.

Red Craig is fully described in the *Northeast Outcrops* Climbers' Guide (SMT, 1994) and is not duplicated here. However, the higher corries, such as Corrie Fee and Winter Corrie, give good winter climbing particularly in the lower grades, and these crags have always been popular due to the relative ease of access from Dundee and Angus. They are also a good option when bad weather discourages the higher hills.

BASSIES

822m (Map Ref 294 734)

The large gully directly behind Whitehaugh Bothy (Map Ref 300 743) is **Whitehaugh Gully**, Grade I/II. About 1½km south-east of the Winter Corrie of Driesh is a stream which joins the River South Esk at Map Ref 296 745. Midway up the open hillside of Bassies, this stream issues from **Hogmanay Gully**, Grade III.

The corrie between this hillside and Winter Corrie is Corrie Farchal. The gully in the middle of the craggy back wall is **Farchal Gully**, Grade II/III.

BOUSTIE LEY

876m (Map Ref 323 761)

Corrie Bonhard lies south-west of this minor summit on the north side of the road. The obvious wide gully on the left side of small buttresses gives **Chokestone Gully** (150m, Grade II/III). The chokestone can present difficulties. The short icefall on the extreme right of the corrie, beyond a deep gully, gives a 60m Grade III climb. **Left Edge Route**, also Grade III, takes the vague grooves left of the icefall.

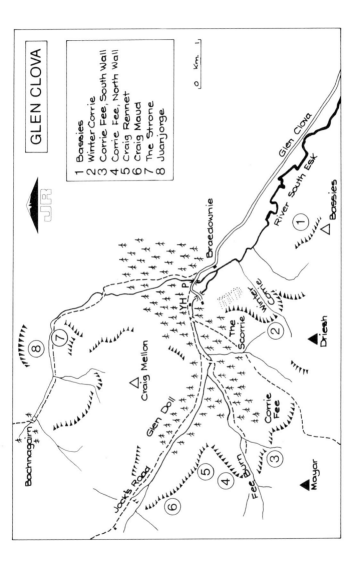

GLEN CLOVA

1 Bassies
2 Winter Corrie
3 Corrie Fee, South Wall
4 Corrie Fee, North Wall
5 Craig Rennet
6 Craig Maud
7 The Strone
8 Juanjorge

0 Km. 1

Bachnagairn

The Strone

Craig Mellon

Glen Doll

Jock's Road

Braedownie

YH P

Winter Corrie

The Scorrie

Corrie Fee

Fee Burn

Bassies

River South Esk

Glen Clova

Driesh

Mayar

DRIESH
947m (Map Ref 271 736)

Winter Corrie is the high cupped corrie on the left side of the glen opposite Braedownie. On its right side lies a conical outlying buttress, The Scorrie. The rocks in the corrie are very broken, offering little in the way of good rock climbing, though the back wall rises for almost 250m. In winter, however, there are several gullies which offer fair ice climbing. As they are mainly watercourses, ice may form here as early as November and as this corrie is higher than Corrie Fee, the routes come into condition more quickly.

1 The Waterfall 60m II/III *
Climb the icefall (waterfall) high on the left side of the face. On the left of the corrie below The Waterfall, there sometimes forms a fine two-pitch icefall, Grade IV.

2 Central Gully, Left Branch 50m II/III
Where Central Gully bends right, there is sometimes a large icefall on the left.

3 Central Gully 120m II
The obvious deep gully right of The Waterfall, in the centre of the corrie.

4 Easy Gully 120m I
The prominent straight gully gives a straightforward snow climb and a good approach to Driesh.

5 Easy Gully, Right Branch 45m II
Climb up right below the obvious cracked buttress right of Easy Gully.

To the right of Easy Gully is the highest section of cliff. The most prominent feature is Diagonal Gully, which cuts centrally through the steep lower section of the face (Main Buttress) and opens out at mid-height into a grass or snow slope, The Basin.

6 Backdoor Chimney 200m II/III
Left of Main Buttress is the wide Backdoor Gully. From the back wall where this bends right, the deep chimney gives the line of the route.

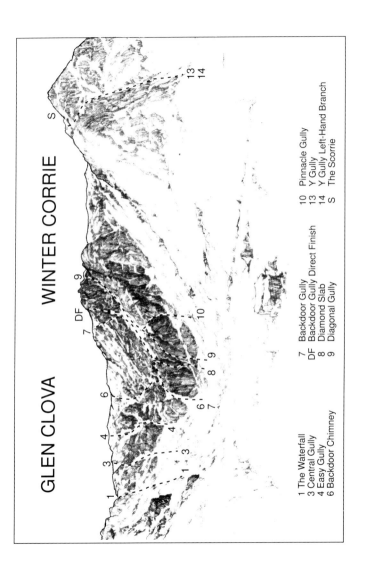

GLEN CLOVA   WINTER CORRIE

1 The Waterfall
3 Central Gully
4 Easy Gully
6 Backdoor Chimney

7 Backdoor Gully
DF Backdoor Gully Direct Finish
8 Diamond Slab
9 Diagonal Gully

10 Pinnacle Gully
13 Y Gully
14 Y Gully Left-Hand Branch
S The Scorrie

7 Backdoor Gully 200m II *

This gully cuts deeply behind Main Buttress to emerge at the left side of The Basin. Either move left as soon as possible to reach easier ground or, usually easier, cross The Basin to its top right corner and finish up a gully on the right (near the finish of Diagonal Gully). An icefall on the left of the gully (Grade III/IV) may be similar to the following variation.

Direct Finish: 80m IV,4   (1988)
Above the top left of The Basin, climb directly up ice steepenings to below a deep crack. Traverse right, then go back left to climb the wall right of the crack. Continue slightly right to finish at the apparent summit. The deep crack itself is an obvious feature of a summer route.

8 Diamond Slab 70m III,4   (1980)

The chimney and steep slab to the left of Diagonal Gully give a good climb. It is easily combined with Backdoor Gully Direct Finish.

The rock rib between Diamond Slab and Diagonal Gully has also been climbed (60m, Grade IV).

9 Diagonal Gully 200m III **

The best climb in the corrie. In the centre of Main Buttress is a 30m icefall coming from a right-sloping chimney. Climb the icefall and chimney to The Basin. From its top right-hand corner, climb an icefall and continue until forced right to belay at a block. Continue more easily to the top. Backdoor Gully Direct Finish is a good alternative.

Variation:
A tricky option, rarely with ice. Starting 5 metres right of the icefall, climb a chokestone chimney behind a pinnacle. Follow the snow slope on the left to the top.

10 Pinnacle Gully 120m II

The first deep gully right of Diagonal Gully leads into The Basin. The logical finish is to go out right at the top of The Basin.

11 Wiggle 220m III *   (1991)

Climb heathery grooves to the right of Pinnacle Gully, then traverse left and go up to a steep wall. Climb a narrow chimney (crux) on the left to easier ground, then move up a broad ridge to finish.

12 The Shute 120m I
The obvious wide snow gully at the right side of the cliff.

The Scorrie, which was climbed as a difficult scramble in 1931, is the conical-shaped outlier on the right of Winter Corrie. Two routes have been recorded but, being low, they require a severe winter for worthwhile conditions.

13 Y Gully 250m I/II
The obvious Y-shaped gully.

14 Y Gully, Left-Hand Branch 250m II/III
The deep, well defined gully on the left.

MAYAR
928m (Map Ref 241 738)
The plateau surrounding this rounded peak presents a steep scarp to the north and north-east, along which a variety of climbs can be found.

CORRIE FEE
This corrie is the finest feature of the district for scenery and mountain atmosphere, but although its cliffs are high (200m) and most of the rocks steep, its buttresses are too vegetated to provide continuous climbing in summer. Under snow, however, this area gives the longest and finest winter routes in this area.
  The corrie has two walls meeting at the Fee Burn waterfall at its head. The South Wall, which is the finest, extends south-east from the waterfall to the Shank of Drumfollow, while the North Wall extends to the headland of Craig Rennet.
  For descent, A and D Gullies are often used. In severe weather or white-out, follow a new fence from the top of B Gully Chimney round to the Shank of Drumfollow, then go down the Kilbo path into the forest.

SOUTH WALL
From left to right there are five gullies: A, B, Look C, D and E. All except Look C are well defined.

15 A Gully Buttress 200m I/II   (1972)
Left of A Gully is a large triangular buttress which provides the route.
Start just right of steep rocks at the base of the buttress and traverse
diagonally left to the crest.

16 A Gully 200m I
The gully on the left corner of the cliffs provides uniform snow slopes.

17 A-B Integrate 200m II
On the right of A Gully there is an easy-angled 100m corner which
contains ice early in the season.

18 A-B Intermediate 200m II/III
This lies midway between A and B Gullies. Start at an obvious ice pitch,
then climb a shallow gully and small pitches right to the Upper
Chimney, exiting near the top of B Gully Chimney.

The deep-cut B Gully is the best defined of the gullies. About 60m
up B Gully, B Gully Chimney breaches the left wall. B Gully Buttress
is formed between the two, culminating high up in a pinnacle with a
great flake on the left shoulder at the top. The left branch of B Gully
runs up to a col behind this pinnacle.

19 Central Route 250m II   (1975)
Start at A-B Intermediate. Climb an ice pitch then the groove above to
a large snow basin. Climb the groove on the right for two pitches until
forced to descend into B Gully Chimney.

20 Shelf Route 165m III
Start in B Gully 30m below and left of B Gully Chimney. Traverse left,
climb a shelf parallel to B Gully, cross B Gully Chimney and go up to
join B Gully Buttress below the pinnacle.

21 B Gully Chimney 150m III,4 ***   (1962)
A good and recommended ice climb, following the chimney which
breaks left out of B Gully. Some pitches bank out under heavy snow. It
can be combined with Look C Gully, as described below. Difficult in
summer.

GLEN CLOVA, CORRIE FEE
SOUTH FACE

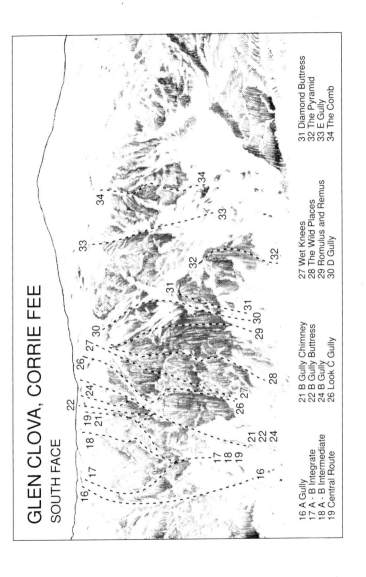

16 A Gully
17 A - B Integrate
18 A - B Intermediate
19 Central Route

21 B Gully Chimney
22 B Gully Buttress
24 B Gully
26 Look C Gully

27 Wet Knees
28 The Wild Places
29 Romulus and Remus
30 D Gully

31 Diamond Buttress
32 The Pyramid
33 E Gully
34 The Comb

22 B Gully Buttress 150m III * (1915)
Climb the buttress direct from its base at the bottom of B Gully Chimney. Moderate in summer.

23 Alphabet Arete 120m IV,5 (1995)
This route follows the right edge of B Gully Buttress. Start just right of B Gully Chimney and climb a scooped left-facing groove to the crest. Follow cracks up the crest to a sapling, then continue past two steep sections and an arete to finish as for B Gully Buttress.

24 B Gully 200m II * (1915)
This generally contains at least one ice pitch, although it can be avoided by climbing up right. The left branch, the obvious deep chimney high up which contains several chokestones, is recommended. The easier right branch, starting opposite B Gully Chimney, is rarely climbed.

25 Crestal Clear 240m V,6 (1988)
This route takes the line of grooves up the crest of B-C Buttress overlooking Look C Gully. The first pitch up a groove to a small hidden gully is poorly protected at the crux. After the gully, either climb direct or *via* a ramp and the right-hand of parallel grooves to easier ground.

26 Look C Gully 200m IV,4 *** (1953)
Probably the best route in the corrie, low in its grade. It requires a good freeze to come into condition and takes the steep shallow gully in the left section of the largest mass of rock, Central Buttress.
1. Climb the left side up tiered ice to belay above a short chimney.
2. Climb the left-hand gully line to a basin, then follow the rib on the right to belay below the main icefall.
3. 35m Climb the icefall direct, a classic pitch.
4. Continue up short ice pitches to the gully bifurcation.

The upper section of Look C Gully is easy-angled and uninteresting. By climbing the left fork and descending a small gully into B Gully, this route can be combined with B Gully Chimney to give over 200m of excellent and continuous climbing.

27 Wet Knees 200m IV,4 * (1972)
This route follows a direct but discontinuous line of chimneys which breach the steep rock bands immediately right of Look C Gully. Start up an ice smear at the base of Look C. The optional last chimney is the best.

28 The Wild Places 200m IV,4 * (1980)
A line of ice grooves lead to the obvious overhung niche in the centre of the face between Look C Gully and Romulus and Remus. Start directly below the niche in a right-slanting ice groove. Hooker's Joy, Moderate, is a herbaceous summer route following a similar line.

29 Romulus and Remus 250m IV,5 (1985)
A scrappy and escapable route comprising two sections on the right of Central Buttress. Very Difficult in summer.

30 D Gully 200m I *
A straightforward snow climb up the right side of Central Buttress.

31 Diamond Buttress 60m Severe
On the right of D Gully are two pyramids; the upper and leftmost gives probably the best rock route in the corrie.
Winter: V,7 (1985)
Technical climbing following the summer line. Start at an alcove on the right and climb a flake crack and a slab to a rib. Above, take a groove to the top.

32 The Pyramid 60m IV,5 ** (1975)
The lower of the two pyramids. Very Difficult in summer.

33 E Gully I
A short open runnel high up at the end of the face.

34 The Comb 60m IV,4 * (1973)
This is the small isolated buttress high up on the extreme right of the face, just right of E Gully and some 300 metres left of the waterfall. Difficult in summer.

A left to right girdle traverse has been climbed, starting in B Gully (Grade III, 1970).

NORTH WALL

There can be good climbing here but it faces south and needs a hard winter for worthwhile conditions. The dark rift of **Slanting Gully**, which lies well inside the corrie near the waterfall, is only seen when one is close under it on the approach from the north side of the corrie. This is Grade III if the first pitch is avoided, the standard route, but Grade IV if climbed direct. **Slanting Left Face**, Grade III, climbs the open 'gully' left of Slanting Gully. It can have a fine 30m initial ice pitch. The main wall has been climbed direct in good conditions: **North Wall Direct** (IV,4) starts from a 15m icefall at a right-trending ramp, then goes through a snow and ice filled depression to a large steep icefall on the upper buttress; this was avoided on the right.

GLEN DOLL

Glen Doll carries the southern headstream of the River South Esk and leads to the Clova — Callater watershed. The path going up the glen is known as Jock's Road.

CRAIG RENNET (Map Ref 251 757)

Craig Rennet is below Spot Height 745m at the northern tip of Corrie Fee; the prow is a fine impressive feature, Grade II. The first shallow gully inside Glen Doll from the prow is **North Gully**, Grade I. Further right is the deep-set **Glen Doll Gully**, which generally gives one good ice pitch, Grade II.

G-Force 170m VI,5   (1986)
This fierce ice problem is reluctant to form and takes the central line on the deceptively steep buttress on the south side of Craig Rennet. Start at a tree by a prominent icicle. Climb the icicle and a bulge to a good flake. Follow the groove and traverse right on a ledge, then go up to below a steep wall. Work back left, then climb directly up easier ground to the top.

CRAIG MAUD (Map Ref 239 768)

Between Glen Doll and Craig Maud is the Dounalt escarpment, which offers little climbing. Craig Maud is a rambling 200m buttress flanked by **Curving Gully**, Grade I, on the left and **North Gully**, Grade I, to the right. Right of Curving Gully is a crag with a rocky gully in its centre. Left of this is a triangular slab with a big slabby buttress above and behind. The following route starts in a grassy corner between these.

Trouble with Lichen 70m E2   (1987)
1. 30m 5b Climb the corner until a dirty crack leads to a slab on the left, then traverse 6m left below a roof.
2. 10m 5c Move up and left to a niche, then traverse round the arete under a roof *via* a lichenous niche.
3. 30m 5a Climb the obvious corner-ramp above.

   On the north side of Glen Doll, opposite Craig Maud and just short of the point where Jock's Road rises more steeply to the plateau, there is a crag immediately on the right after leaving the forest. The obvious feature is **Maud Buttress**, Very Difficult in summer, IV,5 in winter.

THE UPPER SOUTH ESK VALLEY

The following crags lie in the right-hand branch of Glen Clova, where it divides at the carpark before Glen Doll Lodge. This valley is rather quieter and more secluded than Glen Doll.

THE STRONE (Map Ref 275 788)

This is the group of buttresses on the left where the valley turns westwards. The prominent gully on the left of the upper leftmost of the buttresses is **Roofed Gully** (110m, Grade III). The roofs can be avoided by climbing ice on the slabby left wall.

JUANJORGE (Map Ref 265 795)

This most curiously-named cliff lies above the main northerly head-waters of the South Esk. It lies on the flank of Sandy Hillocks, about 5km from Braedownie and 1½km short of the gorge, waterfall and larches of Bachnagairn. As seen from the glen, the rocks rise steeply in smooth slabs on the right of a small hanging corrie, at the back of which the rocks are even steeper. The principal mass is on the left of the corrie and is hemmed in on the left by the scree-filled West Gully.

   Low on the left of the crag is a steep 30m wall of excellent granite. Four good routes have been recorded (for full descriptions, see the *Northeast Outcrops* guide); **Rhiannon** (E3 6a) takes the obvious corner line in the centre of the face; **Granite Heids** (E1 5b) follows the left of two grooves left of it. Right of Rhiannon, **Roslin Riviera** (E3 6a) climbs a groove in the toe of the wall, then the prominent left-slanting crack above. **Ladies of the Canyon** (E3 6a) takes scoops in the wall 5 metres right of Roslin Riviera.

Gimcrack Gully 200m II   (1950s)
The obvious gully on the left side of Juanjorge, nearer Bachnagairn, starts low down and has several chokestones. Difficult in summer.

West Gully 200m II
The gully just on the left side of the crag has two sections; the second has an alternative steeper finish up ice on the right.

Diagonal Crack 70m VI,8   (1994)
A short technical climb, Very Severe and lichenous in summer. Start 50m up West Gully on a platform on its right wall below a prominent wide and very steep right-trending crack. The first pitch is the crux, but the second is technically harder.
1. 30m Climb the steep, sustained and awkward crack (Hex 11, Friend 4 and other large pieces are useful).
2. 25m The crack line continues rightwards across the front face of the buttress but the route stays on the gully wall. Move easily up to a small tree, then pull over a bulge on the left onto a slab. Move left around an exposed edge to a ledge, then climb up and back right to a stance directly above the previous belay.
3. 15m Step left and continue easily to the top.

   Also starting up West Gully is **The Good Ship Venus** (100m, V,5), which takes the prominent corner on the slabby face left of the Amphitheatre (3 pegs for aid).

CRAIG OF GOWAL (Map Ref 235 805)

This retiring hill lies 1½km south-west of Broad Cairn. The climbing is on the east face which lies above the Burn of Gowal, a tributary of the River South Esk (upstream of Juanjorge). The rock is granite and must be very close to the southern frontier of the Lochnagar intrusion. The climbing is best reached by the pleasant walk up from Glen Clova.

The face is mostly broken and vegetated but there is a cleaner strip of slab near the centre, taken by The Gowk. Left of this strip, an obvious gully slants up left, Grade II. Left again is a smaller buttress which gives **Slipup** (IV,4), starting by the prominent steep icefall in its lower rocks (crux). Further up the burn is another crag; **Lucky Jim** (Grade II/III) takes the vague groove-gully just left of centre.

The Gowk 200m HVS   (1968)
A pleasant route, but the band of clean rock is narrow and the cliff remote. Start at the lowest rocks. Find a way up the slabs for 60m to reach a prominent overhang barring the whole slab. Break through this on good holds and follow a slab and whaleback to a ledge and block belay. Traverse down left to a small ledge below a small overlap, then continue delicately left (5a) to another ledge. Climb the short wall and slab above to a belay. Climb the crack in the broken wall to the left, then go directly up the slab to a small overlap. Traverse right and break through the overlap *via* a rounded flake. Continue by a short wall and slabs to belay below the huge terminal overhangs. Traverse right under these and climb a damp corner to a 5m crack. Go right across sloping ledges on the wall, then climb a short slab to the top.
Winter: IV,4   (1979)
When sheathed in ice, the slabs give a fine sustained climb near the summer line.

The Skiver 200m III   (1975)
This takes the shallow recess immediately right of The Gowk slab, starting at almost the same point. Climb to a snow basin, then go up a shallow gully leading to a large rock wall. Climb this directly, or detour to the left depending on build-up.

HUNT HILL *(Map Ref 385 805)*

Although it lies in Glen Esk, some way north of Glen Clova, this hill is included here because both forks of Glen Esk are initially approached from the Dundee to Aberdeen road.
    An icefall forms on the left side of Eagles Crag, above the Falls of Unich. This is **Eagles Fall** (90m, IV,4).

SOUTHERN OUTLYING AREAS

The following minor crags and routes are most easily approached from various points along the Spittal of Glenshee to Braemar road.

CARN AN TUIRC

1019m (Map Ref 174 805)

The fine little Coire Kander is easily approached from Glen Callater and lies about 3km beyond the head of Loch Callater. It can also be reached from the Glen Shee road (A93) by skirting Carn an Tuirc on its north side. The corrie contains an inky lochan dominated by grassy crags of schist. These are too broken for summer climbing, but they provide good Grade I snow routes over 200m long. There is little scope for harder routes, but high on the left flank an obvious curving recess gives a Grade III route with several good but avoidable ice pitches.

On the north-east spur of Carn an Tuirc, running out from Coire Kander and facing down towards the head of Loch Callater, there is a burn running through a small gorge. This produces an icefall, **Snip-snip** (150m, Grade III), which has some fine ice scenery.

CREAG AN FHLEISDEIR

(Map Ref 197 828)

This little crag is wrongly marked on the OS map as Creag an Fhir-shaighde; its local name (and that used on old maps) is Creag an Fhleisdeir. It lies on the north side of the glen about 1km beyond the head of Loch Callater. It is broken, but in the centre lies a compact slabby buttress. An obvious gully runs up the left side, which gives **Central Slabs Cleft** (Severe). This gives a climb early in the winter season (100m, Grade III). The crag terminates at its eastern end in a gully, which is Grade I. The vegetated grooves just left of Central Slabs Cleft can be climbed at Grade II.

About 2km beyond Creag an Fhleisdeir, on the same hillside, lies Creag Leachdach. It consists of broken slabs, but pleasant pitches can be found.

GLAS MAOL
1068m (Map Ref 167 766)

This rounded hill is more famous for its skiing, but some climbing has been recorded in the rather remote Caenlochan Glen at the head of Glen Isla. Access is usually through Glen Isla, although it may be quicker to come over the summit of Glas Maol. While steep in places, the crags are mostly broken and too vegetated for good rock climbing.

There are recorded climbs on the face below Druim Mor (961m), known locally as Craig Herrich (Map Ref 190 772), a top attached to Cairn of Claise. The cliff is seen high up on the north side of Caenlochan Glen, about 1½km above the junction of the streams. **Craig Herrich Buttress**, Difficult, follows a central rib just to the right of a scree fan and culminates in a notch halfway up the cliff.

Between Craig Herrich Buttress and Caderg to its right, a Y-shaped gully gives a winter route. Other easy winter climbs have been done in this area.

Almost 1km south-east of the summit of Glas Maol there is a corner of the Caenlochan Glen, just to the north-west of the ruined shack (Map Ref 175 761) on Little Glas Maol (973m). From this corner an easy gully rakes down beneath the undercut base of a north-facing buttress. The obvious weakness in the overhanging wall is a prominent ramp which slants right to reach a couloir between two large rock ridges. This is **The Ramp**, Grade II/III. The east-facing broken cliff on the left (facing down the easy gully; Map Ref 175 765) has several ice runnels and vegetated rock. Ice frequently forms here early in the season. **The Central Runnel** climbed directly is Grade II/III. **Blatant Theft** (150m, Grade III) takes a slender curving ramp in the broad buttress left of the icefall of The Central Runnel.

GLAS TULAICHEAN
1051m (Map Ref 052 760)

There is a slabby south-facing belt of rock some 80m high in the north corrie of the mountain. Six routes from Moderate to Very Difficult have been climbed here.

CARN BHINNEIN
917m (Map Ref 092 764)

Craig Dallaig lies on the south-west shoulder of this hill, above Gleann Taitneach (Map Ref 083 757). There is a small rock face with a pinnacle which was climbed by J.N.Collie in 1909. From its top, one can continue up a sharp arete to the top of the crag; loose and dangerous.

B Gully Chimney, Corrie Fee, Glen Clova (Climber, Doug Lang)

Beinn a' Bhuird

The huge massif of Beinn a' Bhuird (1196m, Map Ref 092 005) includes the highest summit of the Eastern Cairngorms, and it is one of the finest mountains in the country for snow and corrie scenery. It is a remote mountain of vast proportions with great corries walling an extensive plateau to the east. Only two corries, Coire na Ciche with its characteristic top, A' Chioch, and the expansive Coire nan Clach, can be seen from the Braemar approach. The grander Coire an Dubh Lochain, hidden by A' Chioch, and the remote Garbh Choire at the head of the Slochd Mor, reserve their charms for the climber and walker.

Accommodation
There are no recognised huts or bothies close to Beinn a' Bhuird, but there is a small howff at the foot of the Dividing Buttress. This is the Smith-Winram Bivouac (Map Ref 907 996), a built-up recess under the second largest boulder immediately below a short belt of pink glaciated slab. The accommodation is rough (capacity 2 to 3) but it is ideal as a base close to the crag. Many excellent camp sites are to be found on the approaches, especially in the Fairy Glen below the ruined Slugain Lodge.

Approaches
1. The recommended approach is from the A93 Braemar to Aberdeen road, starting from Invercauld Bridge. Leave the main road 100 metres east of the gates to Invercauld House (signposted Keiloch) and follow the upper road, bypassing the house (there is a locked gate just beyond the house). Continue past Alltdourie cottage and enter Glen Slugain through a conifer plantation.

  Alternatively, when running low, the River Dee may be forded at several points along a ½km stretch downstream from Braemar Castle. Once safely across, follow the right bank of the Slugain burn through woods to join the Slugain track at the end of the plantation. This is a considerable saving to the pedestrian approaching from Braemar, but the hazards of wading the Dee should not be taken lightly, especially in poor light or when carrying a heavy rucksack. It can only be recommended in summer.

Cumming-Crofton Route, Mitre Ridge, Beinn a' Bhuird (Climber, Geoff Cohen)

A good stalker's path goes through Glen Slugain, passes the ruined Slugain Lodge and arrives in Glen Quoich. For Coire na Ciche, cross the Quoich Water at the confluence of the stream issuing from the corrie. For Coire an Dubh Lochain and Coire nan Clach, keep to the path leading to a huge boulder called Clach a' Chleirich, breaking off before the final rise to the stone. For Garbh Choire, follow the stream past the stone to the Sneck between Ben Avon and Cnap a' Chleirich, then contour left avoiding rock ribs by descending. The distances from Invercauld gates are: 11km to Coire na Ciche; 13km to Coire an Dubh Lochain and Coire nan Clach; 15km to Garbh Choire.

2. The plateau of Beinn a' Bhuird may be attained relatively easily but not aesthetically by following the private landrover track from the Linn of Quoich (bicycle recommended). This track follows the Quoich Water to its confluence with the Dubh Ghleann stream, then strikes up the prominent shoulder of An Diollaid to reach the plateau close to the edge of Coire an Dubh Lochain. All the corries may be reached by an easy descent on their north side (11km from Linn of Quoich to Coire an Dubh Lochain.) This track may also be reached from Derry Lodge by following the Derry road south for 3km, then crossing the pass called Clais Fhearnaig.

3. The approach from the north is only really applicable for Garbh Choire. Gain Glen Avon either from Tomintoul or Glenmore and follow it to a bridge where a path runs up the broad shoulder on the west of the Slochd Mor. Follow the path, continue directly up to the plateau, then descend into the corrie. Alternatively, follow the stream into the corrie. Using a bicycle on the track from Tomintoul is the best way to make this approach practical.

COIRE NA CICHE

(Map Ref 098 985)

This is the symmetrical cup-shaped corrie so well seen from the public road at Invercauld. The north wall is dominated by A' Chioch, the great tor rising above the plateau. It is possible to scramble at will on this part of the corrie as the rock, although quite good, lacks continuity. However, most of the climbing is concentrated on the partially hidden south wall, which appears as a broad buttress when viewed from the Invercauld approach.

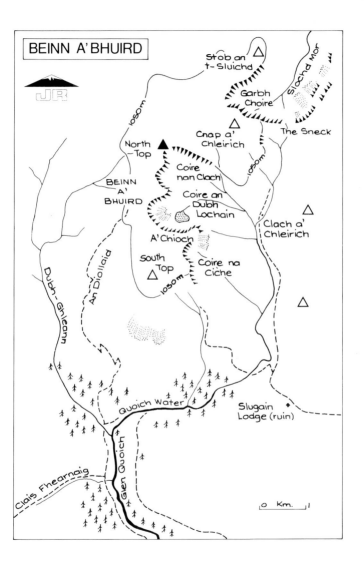

BEINN A'BHUIRD

Stob an
t-Sluichd

Garbh
Choire

Sloched Mor

The Sneck

North
Top

Cnap a'
Chleirich

BEINN
A'
BHUIRD

Coire
nan Clach

Coire an
Dubh
Lochain

Clach a'
Chleirich

A'Chioch

South
Top

Coire na
Ciche

1050m

Dubh-Ghleann

An Diollaid

Quoich Water

Slugain
Lodge (ruin)

Glen Quoich

Clais Fhearnaig

0 Km. 1

The extreme left of this visible section is a narrow rib. Trident is on the immediate right of this. Passing rightwards, there is a large area of slab to the right of a huge alcove set in a vertical blank wall. The Carpet goes up this slab; The Great Slab. The apparent crest on the right skyline is followed by Slugain Buttress. As one nears the entrance to the corrie, the whole of the South Wall comes into view. Twisting Gully, which has a right branch ending in a *cul de sac*, separates the triangular-based Slugain Buttress from the much steeper Hourglass Buttress. South Corner Gully, an open scree shoot terminating the main face, lies at the back of the corrie. Midway up South Corner Gully beyond a steep left branch is the Grey Tower. The back wall of the corrie, immediately right of South Corner Gully, comprises a huge area of glaciated slabs known as Slab Buttress.

The rock is generally sound and rough, and it dries relatively quickly. There is a little vegetation which tends to be mossy in nature and should be treated with caution.

Winter
Beinn a'Bhuird is an inhospitable place in winter and climbers are rarely seen. The relative accessibility and sunnier aspect of Coire na Ciche gives it a less austere atmosphere than the other corries. It is a good choice in arduous walking conditions or after a visit to the more committing Garbh Choire the previous day. Most of the climbs are short, steep and technical, there being only two major gullies, both easy. A large build-up of snow on the steep South Wall is unusual but Slab Buttress soon disappears and often carries a considerable depth.

Winter Descents
Gentle slopes well to the south of the corrie lead back to upper Glen Quoich. To return to the base of the cliff, it is better to descend the ridge below A' Choich. In good conditions, South Corner Gully is faster.

1 The Grinder 90m E1   (1982)
A slabby rib terminates the cliff at its southern end. Start immediately right of this by scrambling up a vegetated groove to below the lower of two steep corners which breach the left wall.
1. 40m 5b Climb the lower corner, go round a bulge and follow a crack to a small stance above the higher corner. Continue up the crack until it fades into slabs. Move left and climb a grassy corner to easy ground.
2. 50m Easy climbing leads to the plateau.

2 Trident 110m Severe   (1953)
This somewhat vegetated route ascends a line of weakness immediately to the right of the slabby rib containing The Grinder. Start up a
vegetated groove as for the previous climb. Climb the groove until very
steep rock forces a move right to a sloping platform. Surmount the 4m
wall ahead (crux), then follow a slab for 6m and traverse left to a flake
belay. Continue up the slab straight ahead or climb the obvious layback
crack just to the right. Avoid a vertical wall in front by traversing right,
then climb an easy slab to piled blocks. Scramble to the plateau.
Winter: IV,5   (1967)
Follow the summer route.

3 Neptune's Groove 100m IV,6   (1982)
To the right of Trident is a prominent 20m V-chimney with an overhung
top; a natural winter line. Climb the chimney and swing strenuously out
left at the top onto a strip of grass or ice in the slab above. Climb this
and the easy corner above, then move left into a larger corner (junction
with Trident). Follow Trident to the plateau.

4 The Carpet 110m VS   (1955)
Once a popular climb, but the best pitch on The Great Slab is now
somewhat overgrown. Start from the right-hand corner of a grassy
recess below and to the right of a huge alcove with a blank vertical left
wall.
1. 30m Climb a slabby depression up right to grass ledges below The
Great Slab.
2. 30m 4b Above the ledges a thin crack leads slightly right up the slab.
Climb the crack for about 10m until it is possible to move left. Continue
up a rock band to easy grass shelves below a short overhanging corner.
3. 4c Climb the overhanging corner. A short chimney and a traverse
to the right leads to a stance in a crevasse.
4. Go left to a slab and up a line of dimples on the right of a corner.
Winter: VI,5   (1970)
A serious route involving thin slab climbing but with adequate belays.
The Great Slab faces south-east and catches the sun, so thawing
conditions are often found. The Great Slab occasionally ices up, which
makes the climbing easier, but the route is equally fine under powder.
Above The Great Slab the natural winter line is an iced groove on the
left; under powder the left-hand of twin grooves is the easiest. The
overhanging corner (combined tactics) is the original winter line.

5 Homebrew 140m VS *   (1973)
A good slab climb taking the right-hand of two prominent cracks in the
large area of slab right of The Carpet. Start as for The Carpet. Climb
the first pitch of The Carpet and traverse right for 20m to the foot of the
crack. Climb the crack to a small stance at its end (5a). Traverse right
into Three Step, climb this for 20m, then go left up slabs, a 5m crack
and a chimney in the centre of an overhung bay.

6 High Step 155m E1   (1976)
Below and to the right of The Great Slab is an area of slabs and
overhangs resembling steps in a giant staircase. Two right-trending
lines of corners break through the overhangs. This is the upper line,
which has two great steps.
1. 30m Cross a large slab diagonally to below the first wall.
2. 20m 5b Climb a break in the wall trending left until stopped by loose
blocks (possibly dangerous). Gain the second slab and cross this to
below the second wall.
3. 45m Climb the corner crack and traverse a grass ramp; junction
with Three Step.
4. and 5. 60m 4c/4b Finish up Three Step, pitches 4 and 5.

7 Three Step 135m E1 **   (1964)
A fine, well protected climb following the three giant steps below and
right of High Step. Start on the lowest slab.
1. 10m Climb to below an overhanging corner.
2. 25m 5b Ascend the corner and traverse diagonally right across the
slab above to below a short wall.
3. 40m 5c Climb the wall and move right round the corner. Go straight
up a fault and a short wet corner on the right to a grass terrace; junction
with High Step.
4. 35m 4c Move left onto The Great Slab and climb directly to a
stance.
5. 25m 4b Move to the right edge of the slab, then climb a layback
crack and an exposed overhang on the skyline to reach the final slab
and the plateau.

8 Slugain Buttress 130m III *   (1957)
A popular winter climb. The buttress is well defined by a slanting groove
on the left which forms an apex halfway up the buttress. Start on the

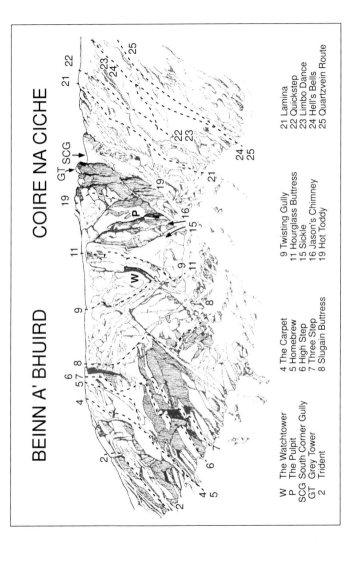

BEINN A' BHUIRD   COIRE NA CICHE

W	The Watchtower	4	The Carpet	9	Twisting Gully	21	Lamina
P	The Pulpit	5	Homebrew	11	Hourglass Buttress	22	Quickstep
SCG	South Corner Gully	6	High Step	15	Sickle	23	Limbo Dance
GT	Grey Tower	7	Three Step	16	Jason's Chimney	24	Hell's Bells
2	Trident	8	Slugain Buttress	19	Hot Toddy	25	Quartzvein Route

right of the buttress or by a chimney on the right. Below the apex, traverse left and climb a steep pitch to a huge semi-detached block (the apex). Easy climbing in the upper recess leads to the top. Difficult and grassy in summer.

9 Twisting Gully 130m II **   (1948)
The best of the lower grade winter routes. The gully twists to the left below a small buttress (The Watchtower) and ends in easy ground above Slugain Buttress. The lower 60m often contains ice but with a large build-up the pitches can bank out and become Grade I. Moderate in summer.

10 The Watchtower 80m VS 4c   (1968)
This climb ascends the small buttress left of the *cul de sac* in Twisting Gully and finishes beside the tower formation on the edge of The Hourglass. Start at a triangular block at the foot of the buttress.
1. 15m Cross the left edge of the buttress to gain a chimney. Climb this for a short way, then pull onto the edge and traverse right to a spike.
2. 25m Step left, then go straight up cracks to a broad ledge. Continue up a steep slab to the top of the buttress.
3. 40m Go up right over huge blocks to the edge of The Hourglass below a tower. Traverse right, then go up a crack to a mossy ledge. Swing left into a chimney on the right of the tower and continue to the top.
Winter: VI,6   (1986)
Approximates to the summer route. Climb the big groove on the left of the buttress, traverse right across the wall above it to a tiny ledge, then climb the wall above. Climb the big chimney, crossing two overhangs, to an exit on the left wall.

11 Hourglass Buttress 110m VS *   (1953)
A good steep route which dries quickly after rain. Above the neck the climbing is exposed and on excellent rock. Start at the foot of Twisting Gully.
1. 45m Climb a long fault to the neck or climb the lower buttress direct.
2. 10m From the neck, climb easily to a large block belay below a steep wall.
3. 35m 4b Go up the wall on good flake holds, traverse right and climb a deep crack to a rock ledge overlooking the chimney of Sickle. A thin crack leads out left to a large platform.

4. 20m 4c Climb the difficult wall above the platform at a left-slanting crack and move left to a perched block. Either climb straight up or continue left to finish up a short chimney.
Winter: V,6   (1970)
Follow the summer line.

12 Joker's Crack 50m E2   (1982)
A prominent corner-crack set into the right side of Hourglass Buttress, between it and Sickle. Climb up the broken ground of Sickle to below the crack.
1. 20m 5b Climb the steep crack until it eases, and continue to a belay.
2. 30m Finish in the same line.

13 Thief's Corner 120m VI,6   (1984)
This is the corner between Joker's Crack and Sickle, reached by taking Hourglass Corner to the neck, followed by a 6m right traverse.

To the right of Hourglass Buttress are three chimney lines. The leftmost, Sickle, is the most prominent; the rightmost, Sandy Crack, does not reach the base of the cliff and ends at the Pulpit which is passed on the right. Sandy Crack joins the central chimney, Jason's Chimney, 20m from the top. These three chimneys are tucked in the shade and remain in winter condition longer than other climbs in the corrie.

14 Dans Macabre 110m E3   (1986)
Start at the base of Jason's Chimney.
1. 40m Climb the left-hand rib to an obvious flake below a slab.
2. 30m 5c Climb direct to a grass ledge, move left below the slab, then climb an obvious right-slanting undercut flake. Where this peters out, move left onto the arete and climb this on the left to a peg runner. Go straight up (crux) to a ledge beneath an overhanging rib; dubious rock and poor protection.
3. 40m Finish leftwards up the obvious narrow chimney of Sickle.

15 Sickle 110m IV,5 *   (1959)
The prominent leftmost chimney, bounding Hourglass Buttress on the right. A fine line, sustained but easier than Jason's Chimney. Very Difficult in summer.

16 Jason's Chimney 100m IV,6 **   (1974)
The steep central chimney offers a traditional Cairngorm-style climb, very technical under powder but sustained and icy in mid to late season (and a compromise grade). Severe in summer, or Very Difficult by the variation using the rib on the left.

17 Sandy Crack 120m V,6   (1973)
The rightmost fault. Start directly in the line of the fault, climb out left, then return into the fault. After a steep step, take a rake leading right to the Pulpit. Reach a stance above the summer chimney *via* the edge on its right flank. A layback exit leads to the final chimney; climb this direct (1 nut for aid) to gain and finish by Jason's Chimney. Very Difficult and unpleasant in summer.

18 Pigs on the Wing 85m E2   (1985)
A line right of Sandy Crack and left of the obvious leaning corner high on the face. Start at a pronounced buttress 10m up the gully from Sandy Crack.
1. 25m 4c Climb the buttress by the obvious central crack.
2. 25m 5a Climb the rib above, heading for the big corner for 15m, then go out left under a broad hanging flake to reach a groove. Step left onto an edge and go up to a small ledge below a huge hollow flake.
3. 35m 5c Climb the blunt arete up right of the belay by way of an obvious leaning pillar, using a hidden crack on the right, to reach easier ground.

19 Hot Toddy 100m VS   (1977)
Rearing up from South Corner Gully on its south wall, between Sandy Crack and the fault of Little Tower Gully, is a well defined bulging headland. This route takes a fairly direct line starting on the right-hand side of an overhanging prow.
1. 25m Climb a shallow vertical fault tucked under the prow past a rock thread and gain a ledge on the right.
2. 25m 5a Step up and move left across an undercut wall to layback an obvious crack. Move up right and straddle across a rock bollard to a good stance below an overlap.
3. 25m Cross the slab on the right below the overlap and go up a short grass trough to a big ledge on the brow of the buttress.
4. 25m Climb the slab and groove directly ahead to easy ground.

20 South Corner Gully 120m I
A straightforward snow climb usually with a respectable cornice. The sporting exit is up the left-hand corner.

The narrow gully breaking the left wall of South Corner Gully is **Little Tower Gully**, Grade II. The very steep buttress on the left of Little Tower Gully is Hot Toddy (described above). The pinnacle on the right of Little Tower Gully is called the Grey Tower. **Grey Tower, Left-Hand Route** (Severe, IV,5) takes a line up the left side of the obvious pinnacle, while **Chimney Route** (Severe, IV,6) follows the right-hand side of the pinnacle.

SLAB BUTTRESS

This is the large area of slabs to the right of South Corner Gully. The rock is clean, although occasionally gritty on the surface. Five good routes are described, each open to variation. Protection is limited. On the left side of the slabs is a lush green gully which peters out into slabs. Lamina is on the left of this gully and Quickstep is immediately on its right.

In winter, Slab Buttress carries very large accumulations of snow and at peak periods all but the steepest sections of Quartzvein Route are buried. For this reason no winter routes have been described.

21 Lamina 180m VS *   (1965)
This sustained route lies on the left flank of Slab Buttress, adjacent to South Corner Gully. It gives good climbing on smooth clean slabs but with minimal protection. Start at the lowest rocks left of the gully.
1. 50m Climb easy slabs.
2. 45m 4a Trend right across smooth, clean, waterwashed slabs, then go up to a ledge just above and right of a large scoop.
3. 45m 4a Climb a very shallow groove left of obvious parallel right-slanting cracks. This leads into a vague crack line slanting right. Belay below an overlap.
4. 40m 4a Continue up the crack line to the top.

22 Quickstep 130m HVS *   (1982)
On the right side of the lush green gully is a prominent diamond-shaped block lying against the slab. This route climbs directly upwards from the

block, keeping to the cleanest rock but with very poor protection overall. Start on top of the block, at its right-hand end. Climb directly up slabs, hardest for the first 5m, to reach the left edge of a large shallow depression high up on the slabs (5a,4c). Continue up rippling slabs left of the depression to the top (4b).

Starting near the prominent block of Quickstep are two right-slanting shallow crack lines. The lower one starts below the block and is the line of **Vatican Steps** (VS 4c), which follows the crack line and traverses to join Hell's Bells. The upper crack line is the main feature of Limbo Dance.

23 Limbo Dance 125m HVS   (1983)
Start on top of the block as for Quickstep; the first 10m are common to both routes.
1. 45m 5a Climb to the start of the upper right-slanting crack line and follow this to its end.
2. 45m Climb obliquely right towards the left end of a large obvious overlap, go up through the break and continue to a large terrace.
3. 35m Climb a right-sloping ramp to the top, common with the last pitch of Hell's Bells.

24 Hell's Bells 185m VS 4c   (1970/1976)
A good but poorly protected direct route up the highest section of slabs. There is some gritty rock and no definite crux. Start at the foot of Quartzvein Route (15m left and up from the lowest rocks).
1. and 2. 60m Climb directly to a prominent short left-facing corner, midway between the diamond-shaped block of Quickstep and the extreme edge of the buttress on the right.
3. 25m Climb the corner, then slabs to a grassy ledge below an overlap.
4. 25m Surmount the overlap, and go up then left to a triangular niche at another overlap (junction with Vatican Steps). Climb this to a poor belay.
5. 40m Climb a bulge, go left then up through an obvious overlap break, then trend right past the right end of a long horizontal roof to a large grass ledge.
6. 35m Traverse left, then go up a ramp rightwards to the plateau.

25 Quartzvein Route 195m Very Difficult * (1953)

A pleasing route on good rock with ample holds. It follows a dyke containing a vein of quartz which trends slightly right up the highest section of Slab Buttress. In winter it is Grade III or IV depending on the build-up. Start about 15m up and left from the lowest rocks.

1. 45m Climb the vein over easy-angled slabs to a small flake belay.

2. and 3. 60m Continue up the vein to below a short vertical wall.

4. 15m Climb the wall and go up to ledges and a flake belay on the left below the steep upper nose.

5. 30m A grass-lined groove leads up right. Follow the groove and regain the vein which continues as an exposed rightwards traverse to a spike belay.

6. 45m Continue on the traverse, then go up left over slabs to the top.

COIRE AN DUBH LOCHAIN

(Map Ref 090 993)

Despite being one of the most attractive corries in the Cairngorms, tucked in behind A' Chioch with its lochan nestling in the bottom, this corrie tends to be neglected by climbers. The rock is limited, but there is enough to justify a weekend in beautiful and remote surroundings.

The sweep of clean pink slabs at the back of the corrie, Glaucous Buttress, receives much sun and provides a contrast with the steep Bloodhound Buttress high up on the left. The two buttresses are separated by a prominent diagonal shelf – the Main Rake. The routes dry more slowly than those in Coire na Ciche.

In winter, the corrie bites into the Beinn a' Bhuird plateau and receives a lot of drifting snow. At peak conditions, only Bloodhound Buttress and the final 100m of Glaucous Buttress remain unsubmerged. In general, the corrie is a big disappointment in winter, although early in the season good ice climbing may be had on the slabs of Glaucous Buttress.

The large area of broken cliff to the left of Bloodhound Buttress gives straightforward snow climbing up to Grade II standard. In the extreme south-west corner of the corrie, right of Glaucous Buttress, a huge snowfield known as the Avalanche Slope forms. This gives a long easy snow climb.

Descent
The quickest summer descent is by the Main Rake. This is also true in winter but the cornice may be a problem. A longer but easy alternative is the ridge of A' Chioch between Coire an Dubh Lochain and Coire na Ciche; this is the best way back to upper Glen Quoich.

BLOODHOUND BUTTRESS

The south side of the corrie left of Bloodhound Buttress is composed of short slabby buttresses and broken rock. Two shallow gullies run the full height of the face. These are **A Gully** on the left and **B Gully** on the right. Both give Grade I winter climbs with possible cornice difficulties, while the rib between them is **Central Rib**, Grade II.

In its upper reaches, the right wall of B Gully has a short belt of steep slabs leading across to the overhanging prow of Bloodhound Buttress. From the top of the main rake, the prow bears some resemblance to the head of a bloodhound. Towards the left side of these slabs is a section of slabby ribs and corners, the line of **Tail-end Slabs**, Grade III. Below the slabs, at the bottom left of the buttress, is a band of overhangs above a prominent incut slab (there is a second incut slab, less obvious, just below and to the right). These overhangs have only been breached using aid. **Hooker's Route** (HVS 4c) climbs the incut slab and penetrates the overhangs above by lassoing a hook *in situ*. The following route climbs the buttress passing just to the right of this band of overhangs.

1 The Scent 125m HVS **   (1978)
This fine steep route, perhaps the best in the corrie, is very sustained but poorly protected on the middle pitch. The intention is to gain the large hanging slab directly underneath the nose of the buttress. Start on the Main Rake about 50m below Tantalus Gully.
1. 50m Climb up and slightly left, heading for a short left-facing corner which leads up from the left end of a small rectangular roof. Pass a good ledge and belay beside the small roof.
2. 40m 4c Climb the corner and step right to reach the base of an undercut diedre (this has been climbed using 1 nut for aid to start; 5b). Traverse right to slabs until it is possible to move up and back left to overlook the diedre. An awkward ramp on the right leads to the slab.
3. 35m 4c Climb the corner at the left side of the slab (the right side is easier but leads nowhere) and step out to the rib on the left, finishing by a series of blocks and steep cracks.

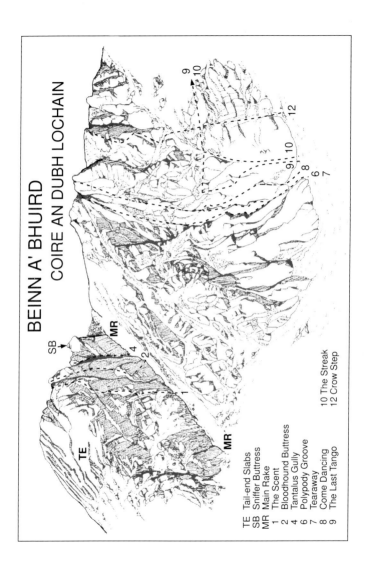

BEINN A' BHUIRD
COIRE AN DUBH LOCHAIN

TE   Tail-end Slabs
SB   Sniffer Buttress
MR   Main Rake
1   The Scent
2   Bloodhound Buttress
4   Tantalus Gully
6   Polypody Groove
7   Tearaway
8   Come Dancing
9   The Last Tango

10   The Streak
12   Crow Step

2 Bloodhound Buttress 90m VS   (1964)
This route follows a line just to the right of the overhanging nose of the
buttress and is located by a precarious arch of jammed blocks on the
first pitch. Start 20m below Tantalus Gully.
1. 30m Work up left past the arch of jammed blocks and continue to a
steep crack.
2. 15m 4c Climb the crack to a small ledge. Move right across a smooth
slab to a comfortable platform.
3. 15m 4c Move round to a crack on the right and climb it to easy
ground.
3. 30m Finish up the prominent depression, almost a gully, right of the
overhangs (loose rock).
Winter: VI,7 *   (1975)
A good technical route, mostly climbing turfy cracks. Follow the summer
line closely, but climb the crack above the comfortable platform directly.

3 Desolation Crack 70m E1   (1989)
The prominent crack on the left wall of Tantalus Gully. Scramble to
below the first pitch of Tantalus Gully and traverse left to a small wedged
flake.
1. 20m 5b Go up left to a grass ledge. Climb the steepening groove
and make an awkward move right into a slabby recess. Continue to the
foot of the crack.
2. 25m 5a Climb the crack to a ledge; an excellent pitch.
3. 25m 4c Finish up the fault with a tight squeeze at the overhanging
slot.

4 Tantalus Gully 80m III *   (1957)
A good short climb and accessible from the plateau by descending the
Main Rake. It can be combined with a route in Coire na Ciche. This is
the first break in the wall right of Bloodhound Buttress, about midway
up the Main Rake. The lower section forms a steep ice pitch, up to 15m,
which may be fairly hard. Higher up, the gully cuts deep into the cliff but
the climbing is straightforward. Severe in summer with the crux at the
start.

   The small buttress on the right of Tantalus Gully, **Sniffer Buttress**,
has an attractive shape from the corrie floor but the climbing does not
match its appearance: HVS 5b, by a loose line near Tantalus Gully.

5 Main Rake I *   (1911)
An uncomplicated snow ramp, and the cornice is often easy. A useful means of descent.

GLAUCOUS BUTTRESS

This buttress has two distinct features, a lower apron of clean slabs and grooves and an upper rampart consisting of a series of small ribs divided vertically by thin converging chimneys. The lower slabs have different aspects on each side of a long vertical break. On the left side there are a number of easy-angled pillars with their attendant grooves. The right side is a smooth 80m sweep of smooth clean slab, with a watercourse running down its right side — the Waterslide.

There are five fine climbs on the slabs. The upper buttress is disappointing and only hortophiliacs may wish to continue to the plateau. Descent is possible by traversing right or left above the slabs. The descriptions assume that no snow is obscuring the start of the routes.

High up to the right of the main mass there are a number of subsidiary buttresses and chimneys. The broad crescent-shaped rib bounding the Main Rake is **May Day Route** (Difficult, Grade II).

6 Polypody Groove 200m Severe *   (1949)
A good and popular climb, though marred by vegetatious scrambling in the middle section. It follows a large corner separating the pillared section from the slab section of the lower buttress. A large snow bed lingers late into the summer and much of the good climbing may be obscured until July. Even once this has gone, the route is slow to dry but some or all of the Rib Variation can be followed. Climb the groove in 3 pitches to the terrace. Follow a line slightly right to the deepest and most obvious chimney in the upper ramparts. Climb the chimney, exit right across a slab, then follow easy ground to the plateau.
Rib Variation: 100m Very Difficult
This faster drying and easier alternative can also be joined after 2 pitches of the groove, reducing the standard of the normal route to Very Difficult. Start immediately left of the normal route and climb the slab, never far from the left arete of the groove, to the terrace.
Winter: III   (1969)
An extremely variable climb, only recommended in early season when it offers sustained climbing in the iced groove which may be IV,3. In

middle and late season the lower slab can be completely banked out. Under these conditions Polypody Groove as such does not exist and it is best to climb the lower part of May Day Route and traverse in below the upper cliff. On the upper cliff follow the deep-set chimney on the summer line. The chimney immediately right of the tapered rib of Tearaway often contains ice and has also been climbed.

7 Tearaway 200m VS *   (1965)
This route follows the shallow corner system right of Polypody Groove on the slabby section of the lower buttress. In the upper part it merges into a tapering rib. The lower section provides good climbing on clean rock. Climb Polypody Groove for approximately 15m, move right into the base of the corner system and climb straight up to a small niche (40m). Continue up the corner to a flake on the rib left of the small first overhang in the corner. Follow cracks in the rib until it is possible to traverse a thin horizontal crack back to the corner immediately above the second larger overhang (4b). Continue up the corner until it meets the tapering rib and follow this to the top.

8 Come Dancing 200m VS *   (1977)
Harder and as good as Tearaway, this route follows the left of two thin cracks on the slabs right of Tearaway. Start at the base of Polypody Groove.
1. 5m Go diagonally right up pink slabs to the left end of a long narrow ledge.
2. 50m 4b From the left end of the ledge, move up to the base of the thin crack. Follow a groove on the right of the crack initially, then climb the crack itself and a slab to reach the first small roof in the Tearaway corner (this is avoided on the left by Tearaway).
3. 40m 5a Follow the corner round the roof, climb a second roof and continue up the corner (junction with Tearaway) to grass ledges.
4. etc. 105m Either follow the tapering rib of Tearaway to the top or traverse left across grass to descend by May Day Route.

9 The Last Tango 80m VS   (1982)
This pleasant but artificial route follows the right-hand of the thin cracks on the slab.
1. 40m 4b Gain the ledge at 5m either by the start of Come Dancing or, if dry, The Streak. From the centre of the ledge, climb straight up the slab to the start of the crack. Follow the crack, or the groove on its right to a ledge (escape to the right is possible here).

2. 40m 4b Above is a vegetated groove. Traverse left 10m onto the face and climb shallow grooves about 5m right of Come Dancing to vegetated ground above the slabs. To descend, traverse rightwards off the buttress.

10 The Streak 50m VS 4c *   (1981)
After a spell of dry weather, the Waterslide dries to a pink streak of delightfully clean rock on the slabs right of Polypody Groove. This catches the sun in the morning and gives a fine solo preamble to one of the harder routes (there are no runners). The first 5m is the crux; thereafter climb the streak directly on emerging holds. Descend on the right by the lower slabs of Crow Step Route, Moderate.

11 Faux Pas 200m III   (1972)
This is the short right-facing corner gully in the upper buttress directly above the Waterslide. It has a pronounced square tower formation on its left (the square tower is just right of the upper rib of Tearaway) and the upper buttress of Crow Step Route on its right. Follow the line of the Waterslide, ice or banked out, directly up to the gully. The initial 30m corner of the gully is the crux.

The upper buttress right of Faux Pas contains other routes. **Crow Step Route** (Very Difficult, Grade III; route 12 on the diagram) starts up stepped slabs right of the Waterslide, crosses grass and climbs the upper buttress right of Faux Pas. The next two routes are 60m in length and take obvious chimney lines right of Crow Step Route. **The Vital Spark** (Grade II/III) climbs the leftmost corner-chimney, while **Birthday Route** (Severe, IV,5) is the third chimney right of the upper buttress of Crow Step Route, immediately left of a pointed buttress which breaks the skyline.

THE DIVIDING BUTTRESS (Map Ref 096 996)

When approaching from upper Quoich Water *via* the Dubh Lochan burn, the view is dominated by a bold triangular headland. This is the Dividing Buttress, separating Coire an Dubh Lochain on the left and the more extensive Coire nan Clach on the right. The left skyline of this huge buttress is the ridge of **Slab and Arete** (Moderate, Grade II under powder), which gives a pleasant romp amid grand scenery in either season.

The right skyline is Sentinel Route. Between these routes there is an expanse of slabs containing the large right-facing corner of the Jewell-Kammer Route. **The Fringe** (VS 4b) climbs cracks in the slabs left of the big corner. Streaker's Root follows the groove line some 10 metres right of the big corner. **Parkie's Route** (HVS 5a) is a further 10 metres right; climb slabs, then a corner, then move right over a rib into a niche and finish back left.

Jewell-Kammer Route 80m VS   (1974)
The right-facing corner mentioned above. Bypass the first part of the corner on the right by a slab and wall (4c), which leads up to the right-hand end of a big roof. Follow the corner which curves right thereafter.

Streaker's Root 115m HVS *   (1982)
A lovely route, pity about the name, with sustained climbing on excellent rock. It takes a series of left-facing corners some 10 metres right of the big corner of the Jewell-Kammer Route. A grassy rake runs up the left side of the lower slabs, passing below the start of Jewell-Kammer Route. Start in this at the foot of the lowest tongue of slab.
1. 35m 4b Climb the tongue and the first steepening by a corner. Step out left at the top of the corner and climb slabs to enter a shallow corner which leads to a ledge below the main groove.
2. 30m 5a Climb a slab to reach the groove, then follow it over a bulge to a tiny ledge beneath a steep wall.
3. 25m From the left end of the wall climb the direct continuation corner.
4. 25m Scramble up right, then away left.

Moving into Coire nan Clach from the Smith-Winram Bivouac, it will be seen that Dividing Buttress ends abruptly with a short very steep wall dropping into and overhanging a slanting corner gully; this is **The Ramp**, Grade II. A rib, broad at its base and tapering towards a grassy glacis at mid-height, separates The Ramp from **Sentinel Gully** (Grade II/III) on the left. **Sentinel Route** (Difficult, Grade III) ascends the rocks to the immediate left of Sentinel Gully.

GABLE WALL

This is the short north-facing wall dropping into and accessed from The Ramp (Difficult from below or scrambling from the plateau). The main features of the wall are a pair of steep parallel cracks and a huge detached flake on the immediate right of the right-hand crack. Right of the huge flake the wall presents a small slabby face.

Sawfly 40m VS   (1990)
Below and right of the huge flake is another flake (grass topped). Start down and right of this lower flake where good holds permit entry through the overhang.
1. 25m 4b Pull up left and climb the slab up and left to gain the grass ledge on top of the flake. Move left and climb straight up, left of a vertical caterpillar, to a square-cut roof. Move right and go up to belay below the headwall.
2. 15m Move left, climb a crack, then go up and right *via* a slanting crack to gain a platform and easy ground.

Weevil's Way 35m E1 5b   (1991)
Start as for Sawfly. Move left through the overhang, then climb straight up the slab to a small bulge. Pull over this, move delicately left, then go up to a flange just left of a thin vertical crack. Climb the crack and continue up slightly left to finish by a steep crack in the headwall.

The Gnat 40m VS 4c   (1990)
At the right side of the slabby face, a pod-like ramp leads up left to a grass ledge below two prominent overhanging cracks. Start at the right edge of the slabby wall. Go up past a detached flake, then move left and climb a ramp. Exit by the right-hand crack to the platform of Sawfly. Finish by an optional crack on the right.

COIRE NAN CLACH
(Map Ref 093 000)

Though containing limited rock of interest to the climber, Coire nan Clach with its extensive floor and chaos of boulders, may attract a visit through its beauty and air of seclusion. At the back of the corrie a rock promontory contains two short easy climbs. In winter the corrie is ringed by a continuous cornice and gives good straightforward climbing, especially on the wall running west from Dividing Buttress. Four gullies of up to 200m run up through the small upper buttress. Of these, the rightmost (**Crocus Gully**) is better and more defined. All are Grade I climbs.

There is a small south-west facing outcrop situated below the plateau rim approximately 400 metres ESE of the North Top (Map Ref 097 004). This is called Black Crag and, although the climbing is good, it is rumoured to be the furthest outcrop from the road in the Cairngorms (more than 3 hours). It can be visited from the plateau after climbing in any of the other corries. The obvious line is the fierce diagonal crack of Twisted Sister.

Bete Noir 30m E3 6a   (1990)
Left of Chocolate Girl there is a recess which forms a leaning corner at its top. This strenuous and sustained climb starts 10m up the recess at a pedestal and avoids the impasse above by taking the uppermost of three left-slanting crack lines. Climb the fingery crack to a hanging corner. Continue up this to a bulge and surmount this awkwardly on the right.

Chocolate Girl 35m E1 5b *   (1988)
Start just left of Twister and climb the crack line slanting out left to an arete. Climb the arete and the jamming crack above to the top.

Twister 30m E1 5b *   (1984)
Start at a small recess below a large rectangular overhang at the top of the crag and climb the wall left of the diagonal crack line of Twisted Sister. From two large flakes go up left following shallow cracks until a thin move right gives access to a line of flakes leading up into a big bay below the final overhangs. Finish up left of the capping chokestone.

Twisted Sister 35m E2 5c *   (1988)
The fierce diagonal crack line. Start down and right of the corner crack and climb the thin crack to enter the corner which leads up and left to the big bay of Twister. Finish as for Twister.

Abdel Wahab 35m HVS 5a   (1990)
The obvious corner crack right of Twisted Sister. Gain the corner from the left on jugs. Make an awkward move on a slab to gain the main crack (dirty). Move left and up on a flake crack to the base of a bulge, then surmount this on the right to gain easy ground.

GARBH CHOIRE
(Map Ref 107 015)

For climbers who seek remote seclusion, there can be few finer places
in this country than the lonely Garbh Choire of Beinn a' Bhuird. Hidden
on the northern slopes of this complex mountain at the head of Slochd
Mor, the corrie reveals its secrets only to the determined few. In recent
years, the quality of its climbing is becoming recognised and one can
no longer expect to be alone in the corrie in summer.

The main area of crag, averaging 200m in height, extends north-
westwards from the Sneck for about 400m. Two superb buttresses are
situated at each end of this main face; Squareface and Mitre Ridge.
Between them, a stretch of cliff of lesser character contains many
gullies. One of these, The Flume, encloses a large stream which is a
landmark in thick weather. To the right of the main face the continuity
of the cliffs is interrupted by a wide gravely depression, beyond which
a series of miniature aretes run up to the backbone of Stob an
t-Sluichd.

The best rock climbing is to be found on the clean rough granite of
Squareface and Mitre Ridge. The west face of Mitre Ridge is impressive and has several fine HVS routes on good steep rock.

Winter
A combination of its magnificent isolation and the shortness of a
winter's day combine to make this a serious place in which to climb.
Nevertheless, it is one of the finest winter corries in the Cairngorms.
The seriousness of climbing in such a remote place cannot be over-
emphasised but, with a bit of luck, those prepared to make the effort
will be well rewarded. In common with the other corries on Beinn a'
Bhuird, good snow and ice conditions can occur any time from
November to April. The most reliable time is probably the second half
of the season when the days are longer, the build-up is well established
and there is less chance of deep powder on the approach. A continuous cornice can form for the full length of the main face and well around
the extreme north-west corner. The safest approach from the south is
via the Sneck.

Descent in Winter
The quickest route off the plateau in wild weather is to follow the corrie
edge back to the Sneck. Keep well up the slope from the cliff edge and

take care to avoid a small slabby outcrop on the east-facing slope of
Cnap a' Chleirich about 400 metres south of the Sneck. In better
weather, and especially when there is powder in the valleys, it is easier
to go to the summit of Cnap a' Chleirich and follow the blunt ridge back
to Clach a' Chleirich (the edge of Coire nan Clach on the right is usually
corniced).

SQUAREFACE BUTTRESS

A fascinating buttress, with two sharply contrasting faces; the slabby
west face high up contains one of the best Very Difficult routes in the
Cairngorms, and contrasts with the formidable north face.

Going westwards from the Sneck, a series of ill-defined ribs and
buttresses lead up to the north face, which has a short lower tier
separated from the huge wall above by a prominent terrace. On the
left of the face, the rock is appalling, crumbling and vegetated. Here
is the Crucible, a large basin high up. As one moves right the rock
steepens to a smooth, clean face, capped by a blank gritty band of
rock which has ended all attempts to date. The magnificent flake crack
slanting right into the centre of the face has been climbed to its top,
about 10m from the plateau (HVS), but a free finish appears problem-
atical. Further right, beyond a loose overhanging fault, the cliff is split
by a ledge which leads left from the west face and passes under two
intriguing cracks. These are overhanging and the rock has a crumbly
surface.

The name Squareface is derived from the 100m rectangular west
face which overlooks a large grassy amphitheatre, the High Bay. The
route Squareface lies on this slabby west face and is hidden from
below.

1 Alchemist's Route 230m III   (1980)
This route lies towards the left end of the north face. The main feature
is the zigzag ramp which bypasses the obvious chimney halfway up
the face. Start at the foot of an obvious ice gully (taken by Crucible
Route), but slant up left to gain a snow slope. Climb this until an obvious
branch leads right across the bounding rocks, then go up to the
chimney. Follow a ramp on the left wall, then climb to the top of the
chimney. Climb the shallow gully above, which gives out onto steepish
snow slopes. The cornice on this face is notorious, both for its height
and its continuity leftwards almost to the Sneck. To pass it, traverse
right into Crucible and exit up right.

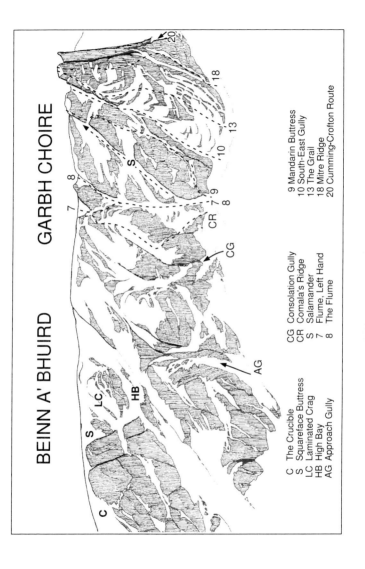

BEINN A' BHUIRD   GARBH CHOIRE

C   The Crucible
S   Squareface Buttress
LC Laminated Crag
HB High Bay
AG Approach Gully

CG Consolation Gully
CR Comala's Ridge
S   Salamander
7   Flume, Left Hand
8   The Flume

9   Mandarin Buttress
10 South-East Gully
13 The Grail
18 Mitre Ridge
20 Cumming-Crofton Route

2 Gold Coast 190m VI,5 *   (1982)
High up on the face, just left of the very steep part of the upper buttress,
is a snow basin (the Crucible) usually capped by an enormous cornice.
Below the basin, a snout of rock splits the drainage into twin icefalls,
the left-hand usually containing more ice. This fine but serious route
climbs steeply into the Crucible by the left-hand icefall. Climb a short
ice gully below the Crucible, then go up to steep ground. The left icefall
flows down a very steep wall to a slab. Climb up and follow rightwards
a shallow corner which is formed by the junction of the slab and the
wall, crossing the icefall to gain a large block, almost a pinnacle (belay).
Go diagonally left, heading for the icefall above its steepest section.
The line ends on a grass ledge just right of the icefall. Use a poor low
peg to reach grass beside the icefall. Follow the icefall and the left side
of the snout to reach the cornice, avoided on the right. A truly direct
ascent of the icefall would be very worthwhile but the required amount
of ice does not form readily.

3 Crucible Route 210m V,4   (1978)
An alternative line into the Crucible, based on the right-hand icefall,
which can be climbed in conditions of little ice. Climb the short ice gully
as before but move right until under the line of the right-hand icefall.
Go slightly left, then go right across the icefall by a ramp. Climb steeply
up and back into the line of the icefall. Gain a pedestal on the snout to
the left, then traverse left (tension may be required) to gain the
left-hand icefall near its top. Enter the Crucible and exit on the right.
    A similar line has been climbed in summer. All the unpleasant
features of the face were encountered – **Rocky Horror Mountain
Show**, Hard Severe.

4 Squareface 90m Very Difficult ***   (1953)
This excellent route ascends the steep slabby face of the west wall of
Squareface Buttress. It combines continuously exposed climbing with
impressive situations and is remarkable for its low technical standard.
The face dries quickly after rain. Access from either the plateau or the
corrie floor is *via* a wide easy rake which slants right from the lowest
rocks into the High Bay and continues to the plateau. The left side of
this face is a stepped arete bordering the north face. Start just round
the crest of the arete, near the foot of Back Bay Gully.
1. 35m Climb cracks and grooves to a large platform, then follow the
arete to belay below an overhang.

2. 25m Launch out on to the wall by a 10m traverse, past the first obvious vertical crack, then climb straight up and return left to a platform on the edge.
3. 30m Return to the face and follow cracks up right for 10m to a short horizontal crack. Just to the right a deep fissure cleaves the final section. Either climb the fissure (Severe), or layback a flake on the right for 4m, then leave it for a shelf on the right, thence gain the top by an awkward traverse.

5 Angel's Edgeway 65m VS *   (1959/1989)
This independent variation offers fine exposed situations.
1. 30m 4a A vertical crack leads directly to the stance below the overhang at the top of pitch 1 of Squareface. Start in Back Bay Gully and climb slabs left of the corner formed by the crack. Where these steepen, move right and follow the crack through a bulge to belay on Squareface.
2. 15m 4b Climb close to the edge and belay on the platform (as for Squareface).
3. 20m 4a Follow Squareface to the short horizontal crack. Move left and layback a hollow flake to the top.

Squareface has been ascended in winter (Grade IV), in unusually banked-up conditions. The route will always be hard due to its slabby nature and lack of vegetation.

6 Rhombus 60m Severe *   (1981)
Start in the gully bed at a point directly below the deep fissure in the top pitch of Squareface.
1 30m Climb up and slightly left to join the second pitch of Squareface at the end of the 10m traverse. Follow Squareface to a small ledge in the middle of the face.
2. 15m Climb diagonally right, step round a rib into a shallow groove and follow this up and right to a small stance below the obvious finishing crack.
3. 15m Climb the crack to the top (the lower section may be varied by an airy excursion on to the right edge *via* the obvious horizontal crack).

Back Bay Gully (Difficult, Grade II) is the narrow gully ascending to the plateau from the High Bay close under the west wall of Squareface. The left branch is steeper but the cornice will provide less of a problem. The squat crag right of Back Bay Gully gives **Laminated Crag**, Very Difficult. Both the gully and the crag appear dangerously loose in summer.

Between the rake leading to High Bay and The Flume is a big area of scrappy cliff. A steep lower section is crowned by a belt of vegetation. Above, a margin of broken rock forms a frieze under the plateau. The lower section is split by two defined gullies; the left-hand is **Approach Gully** (Grade II), which leads into High Bay, and the right-hand one is **Consolation Gully** (Grade II). A right-slanting ramp starting at the bottom of Consolation Gully is **Nomad's Gully** (Grade II), and the broad rib between it and The Flume is **Comala's Ridge** (Grade II).

7 Flume Left-Hand 200m IV,4   (1987)
Left of Flume Direct a two-tiered icefall flows down from a snow bowl below the plateau into the easy lower couloir of The Flume; climb the icefall.

8 The Flume 200m II **   (1954)
This is the channel gouged in the cliff by the Allt an t-Sluichd, already a lusty stream on the plateau before it drops over the edge. The gully ends under the plateau in a huge waterfall which freezes in winter. The easiest line, which is very icy, threads its way between the Direct icefall and Flume Left-Hand. There is often a massive cornice, usually avoidable on the left.
Variation: **The Flume Direct** IV,4 **   (1974)
Climb the icefall directly. Both lines are recommended.

Salamander (Grade III) starts up The Flume, then exits right and goes left of the crest of Mandarin Buttress.

9 Mandarin Buttress 200m III   (1959)
This is the large buttress between The Flume and South-East Gully of Mitre Ridge. The steep lower section may be quite difficult if the build-up is poor. Thereafter, the upper ridge gives fine exposed climbing. The buttress is not a safe alternative in avalanche conditions as a cornice forms at the top which can sweep the buttress. Difficult in summer.

There is an area of surprisingly good rock on the lower section of Mandarin Buttress. There are two obvious large slabs, one on each side of the buttress. The left-hand slab is climbed by **Surgeon's Slab**, Severe. A second route, of good quality, climbs a triangular section of rock between Surgeon's Slab and the slab further right. This is **Witch Doctor** (VS 4b), which follows an obvious crack line, avoiding the bulge at the apex of the triangle on the right.

MITRE RIDGE

This is one of the finest pieces of rock architecture in the Cairngorms. It thrusts out boldly between its gullies, 200m from the scree to the plateau in two walls meeting at an acute angle and topped by three towers. The west wall is nearly vertical with good rock, while the east is less steep but slabby and somewhat vegetated, designed for winter climbing.

10 South-East Gully 200m V,4 *   (1959)
The shallow gully bounding Mitre Ridge on the left gives a superb climb in good conditions, but it often has unconsolidated snow and becomes very serious, as rock protection is minimal. The crux is a steep narrow section just above half-height. The cornice is seldom troublesome. Severe and dangerous in summer.

11 Black Danube 190m V,5   (1988)
This climb takes the wall left of East Wall Direct, following a vague fault in the upper buttress. Climb South-East Gully for a pitch, then break out right and climb directly up a shallow groove line to a large snowfield. Continue to the upper buttress. Climb a steep thin slab to a deep groove, which leads to a short right traverse into a parallel groove. Follow this to a snow bay. Exit the bay on the left by a steep slab and continue to a short wall, above which is easier ground.

12 East Wall Direct 220m IV,5 *   (1974)
A fine climb with sustained difficulties from start to finish. Start about 20 metres left of the lowest point of the slab apron on the east wall. After 30m, a short thin ice traverse left leads to a long chimney system. Above mid-height, a set of stepped ramps lead underneath an imposing vertical wall to reach an ice couloir. Climb the ice couloir to its top, then exit left of overhangs ringing the top and follow an easy gully to the final col of Mitre Ridge. It is possible to reach the ice couloir from just below the depression of South-East Gully. The route is Severe and vegetated in summer.

13 The Grail 250m V,5 **   (1984)
A direct and natural winter line up the centre of the east wall. The grade
assumes the initial wall is banked up. Start just left of the lowest rocks
and about 15 metres right of East Wall Direct. Climb very directly up a
vegetated fault in three pitches to the terrace left of The Shoulder. Go
up to the steep wall above and traverse left over a small rib to the base
of a ramp overlooking the couloir of East Wall Direct. Climb the ramp
to the col between the First and Second Towers (two pitches, crux).

14 The Bishop 200m HVS   (1978)
A direct line to the right of East Wall Direct and left of and parallel to
Mitre Ridge. The climbing is good in the lower part, although more
vegetated than the West Wall routes. Start at the lowest point of the
apron of slabs, about 15 metres left of the big groove of Mitre Ridge.
1. 5a Climb a crack to a bulge, then move left and continue more easily
to the foot of a grass tongue.
2. 35m 4b Move up right into a corner and climb slabs and grooves
up right to a turf ledge below and left of a pink rock scar.
3. 30m 4b Go up left and climb the leftmost of three cracks. Continue
right to a steeper wall.
4. 4c Climb the wall to exit beside a loose block. Scramble across
broken ground to belay below an impending wall, level with the
shoulder on Mitre Ridge.
5. 20m 5b From a flake on the left, climb a groove to gain a thin crack
which leads to a ledge on the left edge. Go up right through a slot to a
large ledge.
6. Follow a deep fissure and continue straight up the edge overlooking
the East Wall meadows. Scramble up the crest to the col below the
Second Tower on Mitre Ridge.

15 The Actress 250m VI,7   (1984)
A hard winter route starting near Mitre Ridge Direct and finishing by
The Bishop. Start just left of the big groove of Mitre Ridge. Climb
straight up a shallow corner-fault line for 70m. From here an inviting
ramp (Helter Skelter) slopes up right, joined higher by The Cardinal.
Traverse left and slightly down for 10m to gain a small ramp leading
up and back right to the base of a steep right-facing corner. Climb this
(1 peg for aid) and a chimney above to reach the terrace left of The
Shoulder. The steep wall above is cleft by twin narrow chimneys. Climb
the left one (desperate start) to the slab above. Traverse easily left and
follow the edge of The Bishop, overlooking the ramp of The Grail, to
the col between the First and Second Towers.

16 Mitre Ridge Direct 200m HVS   (1975)
A mountaineering route taking a classic line, including a spectacular
crux pitch up the crest of the First Tower. The pitch grades are unknown,
probably 4c or less (except for the crux), with vegetation on easier
ground. Start 5 metres left of the big groove of the normal route.
1. 45m Move left onto a rib and climb cracks and grooves to a poor
stance below twin breaks in an overlap.
2. 45m Climb the overlap and continue to below an obvious notch in
a steep wall.
3. 45m Traverse slightly right, climb a steep corner, go up cracks on
the edge of the buttress to an obvious poised flake, then continue to
the shoulder of the ridge.
4. 30m Traverse right, then go up to a steep wall on the normal route.
5. 10m 5b Traverse right across a slab to make an awkward mantelshelf onto a sloping shelf below an overhanging wall. Make a delicate
traverse back left to gain the leftmost of twin cracks. Climb the crack
up a gently overhanging wall to easier ground.
6. 25m Continue to the top of the tower and scramble along an arete
(friable rock) to the foot of the second tower. Finish by Bell's Variation
on the right.

17 The Cardinal 250m VIII,8   (1995)
This direct line up the crest of the buttress is loosely based on the
summer line of Mitre Ridge Direct.
1. 50m Climb a series of grooves and overlaps just left of the edge
overlooking the big starting groove of Mitre Ridge. Belay beneath a
prominent V-groove.
2. 25m Enter the groove with difficulty from the right, and climb to its
top beneath a steep wall.
3. 30m Step left and move up to the foot of twin shallow chimneys.
Climb the left-hand chimney (first crux), then move up and right across
a ramp to the buttress edge. Climb the wall above (second crux, bold)
and continue up a groove to near the top of the shoulder.
4. 50m From the col behind the shoulder, climb the crux wall of Mitre
Ridge, then continue straight up to the foot of the right-facing inset
corner below the headwall of the First Tower. Climb this to a stance.
5. 25m Continue up the awkward left-facing corner system on the left
flank of the tower to its top.
6. and 7. 70m Drop into the col between the First and Second Towers
and climb up and left as for Mitre Ridge to the plateau.

18 Mitre Ridge 220m Hard Severe *   (1933)
One of the great classic ridges of the Cairngorms. Although there is
some vegetation and a little loose rock, it is a fine natural line with
rewarding situations. After the first pitch (avoidable by the winter start),
the climbing is not more than Very Difficult. The first pitch takes the big
groove set midway between the lowest rocks and the right corner of
the ridge. Start up slabs and follow the corner directly to a short bulging
wall. Climb the wall in the corner to a small stance (35m). Follow the
general line of a rising shelf to below a deep-cut chimney on the west
face. Climb the chimney and enter a shallow gully which leads to a
shoulder on the ridge. A short wall blocks progress. Make a delicate
traverse right, then go straight up to the steep wall below the First Tower
(30m). Above and to the left is a large grass platform which may be
gained directly by a short inset right-angled corner or, slightly easier,
by moving left across a slab and climbing a splintered chimney. Climb
the wall above the platform and ascend right to the col between the
two towers. There are now three variations to climb the Second Tower.
By far the best (Bell's Variation) is to follow a shelf to the right-hand
corner and climb a very exposed crack on the west face. Step back left
from the crack and finish straight up. The other alternatives are to climb
the tower by a steep crack from the col, or to turn the tower on the left.
From the top of the Second Tower, finish along a narrow horizontal
arete over the final tower.
Winter: V,6 ***   (1953)
One of the finest winter expeditions in the area. In good conditions, the
initial groove makes a superb start. Otherwise, it can be avoided by a
line of weakness at the right-hand corner of the ridge which joins the
route above the groove. The short wall after the shoulder is a definite
crux in powder conditions. Above, climb the splintered chimney to the
platform. The Second Tower can be turned on the left or Bell's Variation
can be climbed (V,7). The final arete provides an impressive finish.

   The west wall of Mitre Ridge is very steep and impressive, but it has
more holds than seems likely. Two obvious corner-gully systems run
up on either side of a 100m subsidiary cuneiform-shaped buttress
which stands out from the wall of the ridge above the First Tower.
Cumming-Crofton Route follows the left-hand corner to the arete
between the First and Second Towers; Commando Route takes the
right-hand corner to a point where it forks – the left fork joins the
top of Cumming-Crofton, and the right fork runs up to the final col
on the ridge.

BEINN A' BHUIRD
MITRE RIDGE

WEST WALL

ST

FT

26
26a

27

25

20a

23 24

25
26
27

22

21
20

FT First Tower
ST Second Tower
20 Cumming-Crofton
21 The Chancel

22 The Empty Quarter
23 Commando Route
24 Ghurka

25 Chindit
26 Slochd Wall
27 The Primate

19 The Sacrament 175m E2   (1992)
A traditional mountaineering route between Mitre Ridge Direct and Cumming-Crofton Route.
1. 30m Cumming-Crofton Route, pitch 1.
2. 25m 4c Climb the wall above the belay to enter the corner which leads to a ledge on the crest.
3. 15m 4a Go straight up the edge (as for Cumming-Crofton variation) to the foot of the First Tower.
4. 25m 5b Climb the right-hand of twin cracks to the top of the tower; a strenuous and serious pitch.
5. 20m Scramble along the ridge to the notch below the Second Tower.
6. 20m 4c Climb the crest of the ridge to the left of Bell's Variation. Delicate to start.
7. 40m Scramble to the plateau.

20 Cumming-Crofton Route 165m Severe **   (1933)
This steep and sustained climb is the most outstanding pre-war route in the Cairngorms. Start directly below the corner.
1. 30m Go straight up to a small platform, then climb the prominent chimney, which has a hanging flake forming a constriction at mid-height, to a stance in a cleft at the top.
2. 15m Traverse right for 10m *via* a short smooth groove. When stopped by a vertical wall, return left by an airy traverse across a wall and over a bulge into the main corner.
3. 25m The general line is now up the corner. Climb the wall just to the right of the corner for 5m, then step left into the corner crack and climb to a broad platform.
4. 30m Climb a crack in the left wall, then traverse right and follow a sloping ledge to a short wall. Pursuing the same line, follow a loose gully to the ridge between the First and Second Towers.
5. and 6. 65m A suitable finish is to climb the Second Tower by Bell's Variation on the right.

Variation: VS 4c
A link pitch to join Mitre Ridge, allowing a fine finish. Start from the top of pitch 2 of the normal route.
1. 20m Continue in the corner for 3m, then traverse left to a protruding block. Follow the obvious crack straight up to the crest of the ridge.
2. 10m From there it is possible to traverse briefly left to join Mitre Ridge, but it is recommended to go straight up the edge to the foot of the First Tower.

A suitable continuation is *via* Mitre Ridge Direct (HVS 5b), starting with the awkward mantelshelf.

Winter: VI,6 **   (1977)

A superb, sustained and technically hard winter route, the scene of several epic attempts before its first ascent. Follow the summer line.

21 The Chancel 120m HVS   (1978)

This good route climbs the left edge of the cuneiform-shaped buttress, starting 5 metres right of Cumming-Crofton Route at a large block.

1. 20m 4c Climb a prominent cracked groove to a niche; belay on the right.

2. 20m 5b From the niche move up left and climb a shallow corner to a bulge (crux). Pull onto the left wall, then go left and up to belay on the second pitch of Cumming-Crofton Route.

3. 25m 4b Continue up an obvious ramp leading right, away from Cumming-Crofton Route, to a grass terrace girdling the face of the buttress.

4. and 5. 55m 4c From the mid-point of the terrace, climb the wall above, go left to a ledge, then continue straight up to easy ground below the Second Tower.

22 The Empty Quarter 95m E3 *   (1983)

The wall right of The Chancel, using an obvious shallow vertical corner towards the right side of the wall, gives an excellent well protected pitch.

1. 40m 5c Scramble up to a ledge, then move right onto the wall and go up to the corner. Climb it and exit left at the top. Follow a good crack leftwards until it is possible to move up to a little foot ledge under an overlap. Step up, go left under the bulge, then pull over and climb the wall *via* diagonal cracks to easier rock. Traverse left and climb an obvious fault to reach the terrace.

2. and 3. 55m 4c Finish up The Chancel, pitches 4 and 5.

23 Commando Route 140m IV,5   (1969)

This excellent winter route follows the corner-gully forming the right side of the cuneiform-shaped buttress. The difficulty is to reach the corner, which begins 20m up, by a tension move from a minor gully on the right. Once gained, follow the corner gully by its right fork in three steep and sustained pitches. It is probably worth VS in summer, being dangerously loose.

On the right of Commando Route lies the very steep Slochd Wall, with a prominent roof system at 30m. This wall provides three fine technically interesting routes on steep rock with surprising holds.

24 Ghurka 125m VS   (1977)
This route takes the minor gully forming the left boundary of the steep wall, using the start of Commando Route.
1. 35m Climb vegetated rock to where a group of cracks strike up the left wall.
2. 25m Climb cracks to the rib, which leads to the higher bay immediately below an overhanging *cul de sac*.
3. 15m Exit by the central slot (1 peg for aid, loose rock), gain a foothold on the lip of an overhang, and climb to the edge of slabs overlooking Slochd Wall.
4. 50m Climb a crack past a knob of rock at a steepening and continue straight up the exposed right edge to a rock peninsula at the plateau.
Winter: VI,7   (1984)
Follow the summer line, except exit from the *cul de sac* by the left-hand slot without aid.

25 Chindit 100m VS   (1979)
This route follows the left edge of the wall, making a short detour into the fault of Ghurka on the left. Start at the foot of North-West Gully. Climb the gully to the first depression, then traverse left onto the wall *via* a grass shelf to an obvious stance (15m). Climb diagonally left to the edge, then follow a crack for about 10m to a steepening. Traverse left under the steepening into Ghurka and regain the edge 2m above *via* a sloping foothold on the arete. Move up, then make an exposed rising traverse rightwards (4c) until it is possible to move back left to the edge. Follow the edge, then traverse left across the top of the fault (20m). Climb an obvious crack past a knob of rock at a steepening and continue straight up the exposed right edge to the final tower. Here one can go left to the plateau, but a good finish is to traverse right onto the front wall and finish straight up, as for Slochd Wall.
Variation: **Chindit Direct** E1 5b *
The fine direct version stays on the wall. From the steepening where the original route moves left, step right and go up to the overlap. Make a difficult mantelshelf into an obvious small corner and traverse from the corner up left to join cracks on the original route.

26 Slochd Wall 95m HVS ** (1969/1982)

This superb route ascends a large vertical corner which leads up from the left end of the roof system. Higher up, the corner diverges into two corners providing the left-hand and right-hand (original) finishes. Although both finishes are good, the left-hand finish makes a more sustained route. Start at the foot of North-West Gully.

1. 30m 5a Climb the gully to the first depression and traverse onto the wall *via* a grass shelf to gain an obvious stance (common with Chindit). Follow a crack rightwards and climb a steep slab trending slightly left alongside a small corner (old bolt runner) to a big overhang. Swing right under the overhang into a shallow corner and climb this (crux) into the main corner.

2. 15m 4c For the left-hand finish, traverse left to enter and follow another corner until it is possible to step right to a large ledge (the last few metres are common with Helter Skelter).

3. 20m 5a Climb the rib at the left end of the ledge for a short way, then swing left to regain the corner. Go straight up, turn the overhang on the left, then move diagonally left to the arete of Chindit; belay a little higher.

4. 30m Continue up the edge and finish by the final crack of The Primate.

Variation: **Right-Hand Finish** 5a

From the top of the first pitch, continue in the right-trending main corner, starting on the right wall for 3m, and join The Primate at the grass terrace.

27 The Primate 95m E1 (1979/1984)

The is the wide crack splitting the roof system right of Slochd Wall; the roof gives a fascinating sequence of moves. Start from the first stance of Slochd Wall.

1. 25m 4c Climb the obvious crack going out right to reach cracks which lead to a ledge below and right of the roof crack. If the initial crack is wet, one can start at two jammed blocks in North-West Gully.

2. 25m 5b Traverse left and follow the crack through the roof. Continue up the crack to a grass terrace below the final wall.

3. 45m Continue by short walls to a left-slanting groove in the head-wall. Climb the groove almost to the left edge and finish by the crack above.

28 Blue Deacon 100m IV,4   (1991)
The short fault right of Primate. Climb North-West Gully to the first
obvious break on the left wall (about 40m from the foot of Slochd Wall).
Go up left to a fault blocked by chokestones. Pass behind them and
continue straight up to finish in a depression just right of the final pitch
of Slochd Wall.

A route has been climbed starting at the jammed blocks in North-
West Gully and taking steep cracks going initially rightwards (HVS 5b).
The route deteriorates towards the top.

29 Helter Skelter 270m VS   (1978)
This rising girdle of Mitre Ridge, with a spectacular finish on Slochd
Wall, crosses some improbable pieces of rock for its grade. Start by
two large blocks on a ledge near the foot of South-East Gully. Move
right into a crack, climb this for 10m, then traverse right and belay
above an isolated overlap on East Wall Direct (25m). Move down right
into a grassy crack, traverse right, then climb to an overlap and traverse
right beneath it (4c) to gain a central crack line. Move up and right to
a steepening, cross The Bishop and belay just left of the orange scar
beneath an overhang (35m). Climb the groove left of the overhang,
cross Mitre Ridge Direct and climb diagonally right up a ramp to a fine
balcony overlooking Mitre Ridge Route (35m). Climb a slot-chimney in
the left corner of the balcony, then spiral round the crest on superb
holds to emerge above the chimney on Mitre Ridge Route. Move right
into Cumming-Crofton Route, climb the ramp of The Chancel and
belay on the large ledge. Follow the ledge into Commando Route, then
go up and right to belay on a bay below an overhanging slot (35m).
Descend slightly and gain a sloping foothold on the arete (as for
Chindit). Move up, then make an exposed rising traverse (4c, crux) to
a corner on Slochd Wall (left finish). Climb the corner for 3m, then move
right to the large ledge (20m). Move right beneath a corner on Slochd
Wall (right finish) and climb the left edge of the wall above. Finish up
the headwall as for The Primate.

30 North-West Gully 150m III   (1956)
This corner gully, tucked hard against the west wall of Mitre Ridge,
gives a good winter route which varies greatly in difficulty. After a period
of freeze and thaw, a superb 30m ice pitch may form. Early in the
season, under powder, it is much harder. The approach from the corrie
floor is by a graceful arete of snow which swings up round the base of
the ridge.

There is another shallower gully in the slabby buttress right of North-West Gully. This is **North-West Couloir**, Grade III. The buttress to its left has been climbed (Moderate), as has the one on its right in winter, **North-West Groove**, Grade III.

STOB AN T-SLUICHD
1107m (Map Ref 113 028)

This isolated top of Beinn a' Bhuird sports an array of miniature aretes and buttresses which face across to Mitre Ridge. The best defined arete is at the left end (**Pinnacle Ridge**; Difficult, Grade III). The broader buttress on the extreme right, beyond a wide scree chute, is **M and B Buttress** (Moderate). Between these two, are four more of less defined aretes. These have all been climbed in summer; on the first one left of M and B Buttress is **Token Groove** (Grade III), a shallow, left-trending groove system left of the main crest.

Graded List of Summer Climbs

This list includes all the summer rock routes from VS upwards in both this and the companion volume to the northern part of the Cairngorms.

E7
Aphrodite
Realm of the Senses
L'Elisir d'Amore

E6
Fer de Lance
Web of Weird
Improbability Drive
Cannibal
The Shetlander
The Existentialist

E5
Flodden
Slartibartfast
Run of the Arrow
Groanmaker
Perilous Journey
Ascent of Man
Naked Ape
Thor
Stone Bastion

E4
Cupid's Bow
The Israelite
Sans Fer
Dragon Slayer
Voyage of the Beagle
The Quickening
The Skater
Iron in the Soul
Missing Link
The Bedouin
Range War
Bombadillo
The Spire
The Hurting
The Snake
Chariots of Fire

Two's Company
An Saobh-chreideach
Billy Nomates

E3
Crazy Sorrow
The Giant
Flakes of Fear
Jezebel
Scarlet Fever
The Wicker Man
Idol Threat
The Outlands
Eye of Allah
Heart of Gold
Infidel
Slithy Tove
DD's Recurring Dreams
The Gathering
Death's Head Route
Vampire Direct
Henchman
King Crimson
The Harp
Cougar
Pointlace
Black Spout Wall
Bete Noir
In the Pink
The Empty Quarter
The Deluge

E2
Haystack
Friends Essential
Arc of a Diver
Scythe
The Sharp End
Crimson Cringe
Zircon
Alice Springs

Masque
Culloden
Twisted Sister
The Crow
Chimera
The Demon
Rib Tickler
Gulliver
Nevermore
Drainpipe Crack
Sous les Toits
Steeple
Talking Drums
The Pin
Snipers
The Sword of Damocles
The Sacrament
Cayman
North-East Cruiser
Falseface
The Prowl
Vampire
Post Mortem
Edgewood
Evil Spirits
Solitaire
Babes in the Wood
Fraud Squad
Goliath Eliminate
Tough-Brown Integral
Drop Out
The Vault

E1
Stiletto
Perestroika
Rolling Thunder
Dirge
Optical Illusion
Dubh Loch Monster
Mort
Three Step
Vixen
Tickler
Gadd's Route
Scalpel Direct

Desolation Crack
Chindit Direct
Falkenhorst
Raptor
High Step
Lonesome Pine
Weevil's Way
Dragonfly
Waterkelpie Wall
The Grinder
Yin and Yang
The Vicar
Chocolate Girl
Fox Moth
Twister
Independence
King Rat
Medium Rare
Rockover
The Stretcher
Mantichore
The Needle
Poison Dwarf
The Primate
The Nihilist
Pantheist
Sapphire
Prince of Darkness
Damien
The Blue Max
The Exorcist

HVS
The Devils Alternative
Katsalana
Ivory Tower
The Chancel
Mirage variations
Time Traveller
Bellows
Slochd Wall
Dark Horse
Umslopogaas
Magic Crack
Talisman Direct Start
Sand-Pyper Direct

Epitome
The Sting
Cutlass
The Bishop
Beelzebub
Barndance
Never Mind
Daddy Longlegs
War and Peace
Amethyst Pillar
Quickstep
Limbo Dance
Consolation Groove
Joker's Buttress
Snakebite
The Catwalk
Clonedyke
Tickled Pink
Ventriloquist
The Omen
Second Sight
Hood Route
Pushover
Crypt
Contra-flow
Predator
The Scent
Sgian Dubh
Goliath
Damnation
The Chute
Digeridoo
Abdel Wahab
Dogleg
Fool's Rib
A Likely Story
Windchill
Next to Last
Streaker's Root
The Gowk
The Tower of Babel
Devil Dancer
Salamander
Sheath
Cyclops
The Inquisition

Dinosaur/Pink Elephant

VS
Pinnacle Grooves
The Strumpet
The Citadel
No Blue Skies
Bastille
Gibber
Devil Dancer
Good Intentions
The Link (direct)
Trunk Line
Come Dancing
Homebrew
Brodan's Dyke
Hot Toddy
Tough-Guy
Hot Lips
The Last Oasis
Helter Skelter
Postern Direct
Windchill
Longbow Direct
The Chebec
Monarch of the Glen
Koala
The Mousetrap
Ghost Crack
Mack's Dilemma
The Dagger
The Gnat
Scabbard
Bloodhound Buttress
Vertigo Wall
Black Mamba
Lion of Judah
Pythagoras
Fingers Ridge Direct
Shotgun
Delicatessen
Vulcan
Doctor Janis
Prore
Sermon
Big De'il

Whispers
Glasnost
The Hin'most
The Clean Sweep
Nomad's Crack
Tough-Brown Ridge Direct
Parallel Gully B
The Last Tango
Hell's Bells
Jewell-Kammer Route
Sundance
Indolence
Djibangi
Tearaway
Carmine Groove
Salvation
Apres Moi
Speakeasy
Sawfly

Angel's Edgeway
The Carpet
Mariella
The Underworld
Ali Baba
Hackingbush's Horror
Fall-out Corner
Sabre
Pinnacle Face
The Fly
Bugaboo Rib
Hellfire Corner
The Only Game in Town
Hourglass Buttress
Phoenix Edge
Firewater
Styx
Pink Dwarf
Lamina

List of First Ascents

LOCHNAGAR

W 1893	12 Mar	Black Spout, Left Hand Branch	J.H.Gibson, W.Douglas
S 1895	16 Aug	Tough-Brown Traverse	W.Tough, W.Brown
S 1898	12 Nov	Raeburn's Gully	H.Raeburn, J.Rennie, H.Lawson

Popular until the main cave pitch collapsed in 1940.

S 1902	19 Oct	West Gully	H.Raeburn, A.M.Mackay, F.S.Goggs
S 1908	17 Apr	Black Spout Buttress	T.E.Goodeve, W.N.Ling, H.Raeburn
W 1913	21 Dec	Crumbling Cranny	Miss Inglis Clark, Mrs Hunter, H.Alexander
S 1926	1 Aug	Black Spout, Left Hand Branch	G.R.Symmers, F.King

First appearance of Symmers, who with Ewen climbed many of Lochnagar's natural lines, often on appalling rock and vegetation.

S 1926	1 Aug	Crumbling Cranny	G.R.Symmers, F.King
S 1927	21 Aug	Pinnacle Gully 1	G.R.Symmers, J.Silver
S 1928	26 Aug	Central Buttress	G.R.Symmers, N.Bruce
S 1930	10 Aug	Giant's Head Chimne	G.R.Symmers, W.A.Ewen
S 1930	17 Aug	Parallel Gully A	G.R.Symmers, W.A.Ewen
S 1932	3 Jul	Pinnacle Gully 2	W.J.Middleton, R.Lees, W.A.Ewen
S 1932	Jul	Shallow Gully	N.Bruce, H.A.Macrae
S 1932	18 Sep	Shadow Buttress A, Original Route	G.R.Symmers, W.A.Ewen
W 1932	27 Dec	Raeburn's Gully	G.R.Symmers, A.W.Clark, W.A.Ewen
W 1932	28 Dec	Pinnacle Gully 2	A.W.Clark, W.A.Ewen
S 1933	6 Aug	Gargoyle Chimney	G.R.Symmers, W.A.Ewen
S 1933	12 Sep	Douglas-Gibson Gully	C.Ludwig

An extraordinary solo ascent after 30 years of attempts on the route. Right branch: A.Nisbet, D.Wright, Sep 1979.

S 1933	16 Sep	Polyphemus Gully	G.R.Symmers, W.A.Ewen
S 1934	30 Aug	Shadow Buttress B, Original Route	G.R.Symmers. W.A.Ewen
S 1936	7 Jun	Eagle Buttress	J.H.B.Bell, W.G.McClymont, D.Myles
S 1939	28 May	Parallel Buttress	J.H.B.Bell, W.H.Murray

2 pegs for aid. FFA: J.Bruce, W.Stewart, 1953. Direct start W.D.Brooker, D.A.Sutherland, J.W.Morgan, 1949. Variation start D.Pyper, D.Reid, May 1961

S 1939	28 May	Backdoor Route (in descent)	J.H.B.Bell, W.H.Murray
S 1940	Aug	Eagle Ridge (Dundee Route)	W.S.Scroggie, J.G.Ferguson

The main section of the ridge was avoided.

S 1941   Jul Eagle Ridge   J.H.B.Bell, N.Forsyth
*1 peg for aid. The most significant of Bell's routes, and the one to most inspire
the next gereration. Perhaps FFA was the second ascent by S.Thompson, Mrs
Thompson, Jul 1944. Third ascent was free by W.D.Brooker, D.Sutherland 1949.*
S 1941   Jul Shadow Buttress A,   J.H.B.Bell, N.Forsyth
                   Bell's Route
S 1941   Jul Shadow Buttress B,   J.H.B.Bell, N.Forsyth
                   Bell's Route
1 peg for aid. FFA unknown
S 1941   Jul Slab Gully   J.H.B.Bell, N.Forsyth
S 1941   Jul Tough-Brown Ridge   J.H.B.Bell, N.Forsyth
                   Direct
2 pegs for aid. FFA: G.Strange, A.McIvor, 8 Aug 1976
S 1945   Jun Gully Route   G.Scott, W.T.Hendry
S 1946   19 May Gargoyle Direct   D.H.Haworth, G.J.Ritchie
S 1947   5 Oct Lemming's Exit   I.F.Roberts, G.A.Roberts
W 1948   Jan Central Buttress   S.R.Tewnion, J.Tewnion
The start of 8 years intensive development when Lochnagar reigned supreme.
W 1948   28 Mar Parallel Gully A   G.W.Ross, R.Still
W 1949   9 Jan Black Spout Buttress   J.Tewnion, C.Hutcheon,
                                          D.A.Sutherland, K.Winram
W 1949   1 May West Rib   W.D.Brooker, D.A.Sutherland,
                                          K.Winram
S 1949   29 May Sunset Buttress   W.D.Brooker, D.A.Sutherland
Combined tactics. FFA unknown
S 1949   11 Jun Jacob's Slabs   K.Winram, R.Porter
S 1949   13 Aug Route 1   D.A.Sutherland, W.D.Brooker
1 peg for aid. FFA unknown
S 1949   27 Aug Giant's Head Chimney   W.D.Brooker, D.A.Sutherland
                   Direct
S 1949   27 Aug Multiple Chimneys   W.D.Brooker, D.A.Sutherland
W 1949   27 Dec Shadow Buttress A,   W.D.Brooker, J.W.Morgan
                   Original Route
W 1950   29 Jan Giant's Head Chimney   W.D.Brooker, J.W.Morgan
W 1950   11 Mar Forsaken Gully   E.Lawrence, R.L.Mitchell
W 1950   28 Dec Douglas-Gibson Gully   T.W.Patey, G.B.Leslie
*Perhaps the most significant ascent of all as Patey bursts on the scene with
the first Grade V.*
W 1951   27 Jan Pinnacle Gully 1   T.W.Patey, C.Morrison
S 1951   10 Jun Causeway Rib   J.C.Stewart, W.D.Brooker
S 1951   30 Aug Shadow Chimney   T.W.Patey, M.D.Coutts
S 1951   15 Dec Scarface   T.W.Patey, G.B.Leslie, J.M.Taylor
W 1952   20 Jan Gargoyle Chimney   J.M.Taylor, W.D.Brooker
W 1952   20 Jan Tough-Brown Traverse   T.W.Patey, D.A.Aitken

| S | 1952 | 8 Jun | Parallel Gully B | T.W.Patey, J.M.Taylor, W.D.Brooker, C.M.Dixon, D.A.Aitken M.C.S.Philip, C.Morrison, J.Henderson |

Top half previously by I.M.Brooker, A.D.Lyall, 26 May 1952. Direct start: 1 peg for aid. D.Stuart, B.S.Findlay, Jun 1970. FFA: G.Strange, W.McKerrow, Jul 1976.

S	1952	13 Aug	Central Buttress Direct	T.W.Patey, C.Morrison
S	1952	31 Aug	Shadow Rib	T.W.Patey, J.M.Taylor
S	1952	31 Aug	Twin Chimneys Route	T.W.Patey, J.M.Taylor
S	1952	7 Oct	The Stack	T.W.Patey, J.M.Taylor, W.D.Brooker

Combined tactics. FFA unknown

| W | 1952 | 22 Nov | Shadow Chimney | F.R.Malcolm, D.J.Ritchie |
| W | 1952 | 29 Nov | The Stack | J.M.Taylor, T.L.Fallowfield |

Combined tactics, 1 peg for aid. FFA unknown

| W | 1953 | 24 Jan | Polyphemus Gully | K.Grassick, H.S.M.Bates |
| W | 1953 | 25 Jan | Eagle Ridge | T.W.Patey, J.M.Taylor, W.D.Brooker |

Combined tactics on the tower and summer crux. Hardest route of this generation and still respected today. The time of 4½ hours showed how advanced winter buttress climbing had become. FFA unknown

W	1953	25 Jan	Gelder Gully	M.C.S.Philip, J.Henderson, A.Grattidge
S	1953	28 Feb	Route 2	T.W.Patey, J.M.Taylor
W	1953	Dec	Shadow Buttress A, Bell's Route	W.D.Brooker, J.W.Morgan, J.M.Taylor
W	1954	27 Feb	Western Slant	T.W.Patey, J.W.Morgan, J.M.Taylor, L.S.Lovat
W	1954	20 Mar	Backdoor Route	T.W.Patey, A.O'F.Will, G.McLeod, A.Thom

Variation: B.S.Findlay, J.Higham 5 Feb 1988

S	1954	25 Sep	The Gutter	W.D.Brooker, H.M.S.Bates, J.Y.L.Hay
S	1954	27 Sep	The Clam	T.W.Patey, J.M.Taylor, F.R.Malcolm, A.Thom, M.Smith, G.H.Leslie
W	1954	5 Dec	Gargoyle Direct	R.H.Sellers, G.Annand

1 peg for aid. FFA unknown

W	1955	23 Jan	The Gutter	T.W.Patey, A.O'F.Will
W	1955	23 Jan	Shadow Buttress B, Bell's Route	T.W.Patey, A.O'F.Will
S	1955	May	Girdle Traverse	T.W.Patey, A.G.Nicol, A.O'F.Will
S	1955	21 Aug	Direct Route, Sinister Buttress	T.W.Patey, W.D.Brooker
S	1955	4 Sep	Pinnacle Face	J.Smith, J.Dennis

Same day as The Dagger and a similar breakthrough.

| W | 1956 | 4 Mar | Parallel Buttress | T.W.Patey, J.Smith, W.D.Brooker |

4 pegs for aid. FFA: D.F.Lang, N.W.Quinn, Jan 1969

| W | 1956 | 11 Mar | Route 1 | J.Smith, W.D.Brooker |

1 peg for aid. FFA unknown

| W | 1956 | 31 Mar | Eagle Buttress | W.D.Brooker, J.M.Taylor |

S 1956   1 Apr   Transept Route   R.H.Sellers, J.White, D.J.Ritchie
S 1956   16 Jun   The Link   K.A.Grassick, W.D.Brooker
     Direct start and finish: G.P.Muhlemann, G.S.Strange, 29 Jun 1974
W 1957   10 Mar   Amphitheatre Route   T.W.Patey, G.H.Leslie, S.Long
S 1957   6 Apr   Shylock's Chimney   T.W.Patey, J.R.Marshall
S 1957   20 Apr   Grovel Wall   T.W.Patey, W.D.Brooker
W 1958   22 Feb   Parallel Gully B   J.R.Marshall, G.Tiso
     One of the last great winter problems snatched by raiding Edinburgh climbers.
W 1958   Mar   Parallel Gully A,   A.G.Nicol, T.Weir, N.Tennent
                   Right Fork
W 1959   8 Feb   Shallow Gully   D.L.Macrae, F.G.Henderson
W 1961   Apr   Twin Chimneys Route   T.W.Patey, W.D.Brooker, C.M.Dixon
W 1966   16 Jan   Pinnacle Face   K.A.Grassick, J.Light, A.G.Nicol
     *Combined tactics, 3 pegs for aid but by the summer route. First ascent to plateau
     and FFA: D.Dinwoodie, A.McIvor, 1974. Direct Finish: J.Anderson, B.Sprunt,
     Mar 1980*
W 1966   4 Apr   West Gully   A.Fyffe, M.D.Y.Mowat
     Upper gully only: P.McIntyre, A.Nash, 21 Mar 1948
W 1967   15 Jan   Slab Gully   M.Forbes, M.Rennie
S 1967   11 June Mort   M.Forbes, M.Rennie
     *10 pegs for aid. FFA: D.Dinwoodie, R.A.Smith, Aug 1976. A great leap forward
     for Lochnagar showing the modern rock potential.*
S 1967   16 Sep   Crypt   M.Forbes, M.Rennie
     3 pegs for aid. FFA: D.Dinwoodie, R.A.Smith, 1975
W 1969   23 Dec   Tough-Brown Ridge   M.Rennie, N.D.Keir
                   Direct
     4 pegs for aid. FFA: D.F.Lang, N.W.Quinn, 3 Feb 1974
W 1970   2 Jan   Shadow Rib   J.Bower, B.S.Findlay, G.S.Strange
     Direct Start (as described): B.S.Findlay, G.S.Strange, 31 Jan 1990
W 1970   Mar   Forsaken Rib   J.Bower, G.R.Simpson
S 1970   Aug   Post Mortem   M.Forbes, M.Rennie
     Originally A3. FFA: A.Nisbet, S.Kennedy, 2 Aug 1981.
W 1972   12 Feb   Scarface   D.Stuart, G.S.Strange
W 1972   12 Feb   Giant's Head Direct   D.Dinwoodie, N.D.Keir
W 1972   5 Mar   Shadow Buttress B ,   A.J.Bolton, C.Butterworth
                   Original route
W 1972   18 Mar   Penumbra   C.Butterworth, P.Arnold
S 1972 Summer   Pysche   M.Freeman, B.T.Lawrie
     1 tension peg. FFA: D.Dinwoodie, R.A.Smith,1974
W 1973   25 Feb   Douglas-Gibson Gully   D.Dinwoodie, C.Heap, M.Ross,
                   Right Fork   D.Innes
W 1974   2 Feb   The White Spout   M.Freeman, N.D.Keir
W 1974   3 Feb   Centrist   M.Freeman, N.D.Keir
     1 peg for aid. FFA: S.Kennedy, N.Morrison, A.Nisbet, 20 Feb 1980
W 1974   17 Feb   Winter Face   N.W.Quinn, D.F.Lang
W 1974   20 Feb   Tower Variation,   A.J.Bolton, C.Butterworth

Polyphemus Gully
1 peg for aid
S	1974 Summer	Nymph	D.Dinwoodie, R.A.Smith
S	1974 14 Sep	The Straight-jacket	D.Dinwoodie, N.D.Keir

4 pegs for aid (unrepeated?)
W	1975 18 Jan	Causeway Rib	R.J.Archbold, G.S.Strange
W	1975 18 Jan	West Rib	R.A.Smith, G.Stephen
W	1975 23 Mar	Central Buttress Direct	M.Geddes, N.D.Keir

3 pegs for aid. FFA: A.Nisbet, D.Wright, Dec 1979
W	1975 31 Mar	Terrorist	N.D.Keir, D.Mardon

Some aid used (unrepeated?)
S	1975 May	Dirge	D.Dinwoodie, A.McIvor

1 tension peg. FFA: D.Dinwoodie, A.McIvor, 1976.
S	1975 29 Jun	Pinnacle Grooves	R.J.Archbold, G.S.Strange
S	1976 13 Jun	Mantichore	G.P.Muhlemann, G.S.Strange

2 pegs for aid. FFA: B.T.Lawrie, P.Tipton, 1978
S	1976 8 Aug	Parallel Buttress, Left Edge	A.McIvor, G.S.Strange
S	1976 8/10 Aug	Black Spout Wall	D.Dinwoodie, R.A.Smith

2 pegs for aid. FFA: B.T.Lawrie, N.Morrison, Sept 1983. An impressive ascent of a magnificent route.
S	1976 10 Aug	Fool's Rib	D.Dinwoodie, R.A.Smith
S	1976 10 Aug	Hood Route	D.Dinwoodie, R.A.Smith
S	1976 Aug	The Nihilist	B.T.Lawrie, D.Innes

Variation start: G.P.Muhlemann, G.S.Strange, 28 Aug 1983
W	1977 5 Feb	Grovel Wall	M.Freeman. A.Nisbet

Lower half previously G.Cohen and party, 1975. Upper half previously J.Bower, A.Corbett, G.R.Simpson, G.S.Strange, 1968.
W	1977 5 Mar	West End	G.P.Muhlemann, G.S.Strange
W	1977 12 Mar	Lemming's Exit	A.Robertson, A.Nisbet
W	1977 13 Mar	The Clam	R.A.Smith, D.Wright
S	1977 10 Jul	Epitome	R.J.Archbold, M.Freeman, G.P.Muhlemann

Variation: R.J.Archbold, H.Towler, Aug 1981
W	1977 12 Dec	Cathedral Chimney	M.Freeman, G.S.Strange
S	1978 5 Apr	Sciolist	A.McIvor, G.S.Strange
S	1978 12 Jul	Sylph	D.Dinwoodie, R.Renshaw
S	1978 16 Jul	Pantheist	D.Dinwoodie, R.A.Smith
S	1978	White Mischief	D.Dinwoodie, G.S.Strange
W	1978 16 Dec	Parallel Gully A, 1930s Route	A.Nisbet, N.McCallum
W	1979 27 Jan	The Link	J.Anderson, A.Nisbet

A significant ascent, the hardest route in the Cairngorms at the time.
W	1979 4 Feb	Crypt	B.Sprunt, A.Nisbet

1 tension peg. FFA: R.Anderson, M.Hamilton, Mar 1980

W 1979	Feb	The Girdle	Day 1: N.D.Keir, H.Towler Day 2: N.D.Keir, G.Muhlemann, A.Nisbet
W 1979	Feb	The French Connection	B.Sprunt, J-M.Boivin
W 1980	Feb	Douglas-Gibson Gully, Far-Left Fork	A.Nisbet, N.Spinks, J.Unwin
W 1980	8 Mar	Epitome	J.Fijalkowski, B.Sprunt

Axe rests used on this desperate route. Second ascent the next day: 1 nut for aid, no rests (no further repeats).

W 1980	8 Mar	Multiple Chimneys	A.Nisbet, M.Hutchinson
W 1980	9 Mar	Parallel Buttress, Left Edge	R.Anderson, M.Hamilton

(including the variation start)

W 1980	17 Mar	Pinnacle Grooves	A.Nisbet, S.Kennedy, M.McLeod

1 nut for aid. FFA: S.Richardson, J.Ashbridge, 23 Jan 1993

W 1980	21 Mar	The Straight-jacket	A.Nisbet, N.Spinks
S 1980	17 May	Tough-guy	R.J.Archbold, G.P.Muhlemann
S 1981	29 Jul	Dod's Diversion	G.S.Strange, G.Thompson, R.A.Smith
S 1981	7 Sep	The Outlands	W.Todd, B.T.Lawrie, D.Dinwoodie
W 1981	Dec	PG Corner	A.Paul, G.Reilly
S 1982	23 Jul	Crazy Sorrow	D.Dinwoodie, C.MacLean
S 1982	31 Jul	Katsalana	B.S.Findlay, G.S.Strange
S 1982	4 Aug	The Vault	D.Dinwoodie, C.MacLean
S 1982	4 Aug	Drainpipe Crack	D.Dinwoodie, C.MacLean
S 1982	5 Aug	Rolling Thunder	A.Fyffe, R.D.Barton
W 1982	Dec	Sunset Gully	I.Dalley, G.S.Strange
W 1982	Dec	Gremlin	M.Hamilton, G.S.Strange
W 1983	Jan	Transept Groove	R.J.Archbold, G.S.Strange
S 1983	Aug	Tough-Brown Integral	R.J.Archbold, G.S.Strange
W 1984	6 Jan	Psyche	A.Paul, D.Dinwoodie
W 1984	3 Mar	Douglas-Gibson Gully, Central Fork	A.Paul, D.Dinwoodie, C.MacLean
W 1984	17 Mar	The Link Direct	C.Dale, E.Todd

1 peg for aid (unrepeated?)

W 1984	19 Mar	Nymph	C.MacLean, A.Nisbet, A.Clifford

3 rests on axes (unrepeated?)

W 1984	21 Mar	Direct Route, A Shadow Buttress	C.MacLean, A.Nisbet

Time-Out Finish: A.D.Robertson, J.Currie 28 Jan 1995

W 1984	4 Apr	Pantheist	D.Dinwoodie, A.Nisbet

2 rests on axes (unrepeated?)

W 1984	25 Nov	Twin Chimneys Route, Rib Start	G.Livingston, G.S.Strange
W 1984	4 Dec	Slime Lords	G.Livingston, E.Clark

W 1984	18 Dec	Tough-guy	A.Nisbet, C.MacLean
	(first 3 pitches and escape ramp)		
W 1984	22 Dec	Solstice	G.S.Strange, G.Livingston
W 1984	24 Dec	The Ice Ox	G.Livingston, A.Matthewson
W 1984	26 Dec	Tough-guy	A.Nisbet, B.Davison
	(alternative start and true finish)		
W 1984	26 Dec	Katsalana	D.Hawthorn, G.Livingston
W 1985	6 Feb	Slice of Ice	C.MacLean, A.Nisbet
W 1985	7 Feb	Catabatic Corner	C.MacLean, A.Nisbet
W 1985	Feb	Dod's Diversion	M.Hind, C.Rice
		(final pitch)	
W 1986	19 Jan	Raeburn's Groove	D.Dinwoodie, A.Nisbet
W 1986	7 Mar	Trail of Tears	D.Dinwoodie, A.Nisbet
W 1986	30 Mar	Diedre of the Sorrows	D.Dinwoodie, A.Nisbet
	1 peg for aid		
W 1986	14 Dec	Judas Priest	B.S.Findlay, G.S.Strange
W 1987	Jan	Torquing Corpse	G.Livingston, M.Charlton
W 1987	13 Dec	Sepulchre	B.S.Findlay, G.S.Strange
W 1988	13 Mar	Eclipse	B.S.Findlay, G.S.Strange
W 1989	12 Apr	Route on D-G wall of Eagle Ridge	D.Dinwoodie, F.Templeton, R.Watt
S 1989	12 Jun	Infidel	A.Ross, C.Stewart, M.Sutherland
S 1989	17 Jun	An Saobh-chreideach	A.Ross (unseconded)
W 1992	25 Oct	Bell's Pillar	G.S.Strange, W.Church
W 1992	21 Nov	Moonshadow	S.Richardson, J.Ashbridge.
W 1992	21 Nov	Sunset Buttress	S.Richardson, J.Ashbridge
W 1992	24 Dec	White Mischief	A.Nisbet, J.Preston
W 1993	17 Oct	Settler's Rib	R.Webb, S.Richardson
W 1993	30 Dec	No Worries Groove	S.Richardson, G.Richardson
W 1994	22 Jan	Transept Route	S.Richardson, R.Everett
W 1994	19 Feb	Isis	B.S.Findlay, G.S.Strange
W 1994	6 Mar	Quick Dash Buttress	S.Richardson, R.Allen
W 1994	20 Mar	Vortex	B.S.Findlay. G.S.Strange
W 1994	11 Dec	Quick Dash Crack	B.S.Findlay, S.M.Richardson
W 1994	18 Dec	Reiver's Buttress	S.M.Richardson, R.Webb
W 1994	18 Dec	Sour Grapes	S.M.Richardson, R.Webb
W 1994	27 Dec	Trinity	B.S.Findlay, G.S.Strange
W 1995	2 Feb	Iffy	I.Jones, I.Oates
W 1995	4 Feb	Chevalier	S.M.Richardson, R.Webb
W 1995	25 Feb	Quasimodo	S.M.Richardson, A.D.Robertson
W 1995	19 Mar	Gully Route	B.S.Findlay, G.S.Strange
W 1995	25 Mar	Hiawatha	S.M.Richardson, G.Scott
S 1995	8 Jul	The Existentialist	W.Moir, P.Allen

COIRE NA SAOBHAIDHE

W 1975	Mar	The Watercourse	D.King, G.S.Strange

CNAPAN NATHRAICHEAN

W 1969	Dec	Shortcake	N.Keir
S 1976	Jun	All rock routes on Sleac Ghorm	D.Dinwoodie, A.McIvor

Some climbing was done here in the 1950s.

W 1977	Feb	The Plaid	G.S.Strange
W 1979	28 Jan	Four winter routes on Sleac Ghorm	S.Evans, A.Robertson, R.A.Smith
S 1989	May	Venom	I.Davidson, P.Stewart

EAGLES ROCK

S 1967	14 Jun	Lethargy	J.McArtney, D.Duncan

The start of a rapid development at the same time as on Creag an Dubh-loch, although F.R.Malcolm and others are believed to have climbed here in the 1950s.

S 1967	14 Jun	Indolencce	J.McArtney, D.Duncan
S 1967	16 Jun	Nomad's Crack	J.McArtney, D.Duncan
S 1967	17 Jun	Abstention	A.Fyffe, J.Glennie
S 1968	22 Jun	Nameless	D.Pyper, S.Wilkinson
S 1968	25 Aug	A Likely Story	G.N.Hunter. D.F.Lang

2 peg for aid. FFA: A.Fyffe, J.Grieve, Oct 1970

S 1968	28 Aug	Green Slab	G.N.Hunter, D.F.Lang
S 1968	Aug	Bumble	M.Main, B.T.Lawrie
S 1969	9 Jun	Gibber	A.Fyffe, J.Grieve
S 1969	17 Aug	The Waterfall	G.R.Simpson, G.S.Strange
W 1970	3 Jan	Lethargy	J.Bower, G.R.Simpson

The winter potential here was slow to be recognised.

S 1970	13 Jun	Whisper	A.Fyffe, R.Zorab
S 1970	28 Aug	Nimrod	G.N.Hunter, D.F.Lang
S 1971	8 May	Spectrum	G.S.Strange, D.Stuart, D.Dinwoodie
W 1971	1 Dec	Spectrum	D.Dinwoodie, J.Mothersele
W 1974	2 Jan	Bumble	N.D.Keir, J.Taylor

2 separate lines, each solo.

W 1974	2 Jan	The Waterfall	N.D.Keir, J.Taylor
S 1974	2 Jun	Flanker's Route	R.J.Archbold, G.S.Strange
S 1974	22 Jun	Stratus	R.J.Archbold, G.S.Strange
S 1974	Summer	Left Edge, A Likely Story Slab	I.Duckworth, G.Smith
W 1974	15 Dec	Sliver	R.J.Archbold, G.S.Strange
S 1975	4 May	Flamingo	R.J.Archbold, G.S.Strange
S 1975	4 May	The Stretcher	D.Dinwoodie, A.McIvor
S 1975	14 Jun	Taboo	A.Lawson, G.S.Strange
W 1976	31 Jan	Shiver	R.J.Archbold, G.S.Strange
S 1976	19 Jul	Jade Pavement	D.Dinwoodie, A.McIvor, J.B.Porteus
W 1976	12 Dec	Indolence	A.Nisbet, A.Robertson

W 1976	26 Dec	Nomad's Crack	A.Nisbet, A.Robertson
W 1976	28 Dec	Abstention	A.Nisbet, A.Robertson
W 1977	2 Feb	Gibber	A.Nisbet, N.Spinks
W 1977	20 Feb	Whisper	A.Nisbet, A.Robertson
W 1980	Winter	The Drool	D.Dinwoodie, A.Williams

Had surprisingly survived earlier attempts.

W 1980	Winter	Flamingo	N.Spinks and partner
S 1981	30 Aug	Vanguard	R.J.Archbold, T.Syme
S 1984	16 Jun	Fraud Squad	A.Ross, G.Reilly, C.Harper
S 1985	Summer	Verbal Diarrhoea	G.Reilly, A.Ross, F.Templeton
S	Unknown	Prohibition	Unknown

CREAG AN DUBH-LOCH

S 1928	Sep	South-East Gully	G.R.Symmers, N.Bruce
S 1930	May	South-East Buttress	G.R.Symmers, Burnett
W 1933	Feb	Central Gully	McHardy, Stewart
S 1940	Jul	North-West Gully	J.Scott, K.McLaren
S 1941	27 Jul	Labyrinth Route	J.H.B.Bell, N.Forsyth

A formidable route for its time.

S 1944	Summer	Central Gully Buttress	S.Thompson, Mrs Thompson
S 1946	5 May	North-West Gully Arete	W.T.Hendry, G.Lumsden
W 1947	26 Jan	South-East Gully	W.A.Russell, M.Smith, W.Stephen
W 1948	Mar	South-East Buttress	F.Patterson, A.Alexander
S 1948	8 May	Hanging Garden Route	J.H.B.Bell, Mrs Bell, W.S.Thomson

Left fork by A.Robertson, Summer 1976

| S 1951 | 8 Sep | Labyrinth Edge | W.D.Brooker, G.B.Leslie |
| S 1952 | 10 May | False Gully | T.W.Patey, W.D.Brooker, J.M.Taylor |

Lassoed flake on left arete of chimney pitch. The move was freed on the first ascent of Cayman, 1977, but may have been done before.

| S 1952 | 12 Aug | Sabre Edge | T.W.Patey, C.Morrison |

Combined tactices from the top of the pinnacle. FFA: J.Dennis, J.Smith, 3 Sep 1955

W 1952	29 Dec	North-West Gully	T.W.Patey, J.M.Taylor, W.D.Brooker, J.W.Morgan
S 1954	17 Apr	Bower Buttress	L.S.Lovat, T.W.Patey: W.D.Brooker, C.D.Thompson
S 1954	10 Oct	Vertigo Wall	T.W.Patey, G.McLeod, A.O'F.Will

Climbed in the rain in tricounis. A very bold venture on a futuristic line, 4 pegs for aid: climbed with 1 peg for aid by J.Smith, J.Dennis, 3 Sep 1955. FFA: M.Fowler, 1989

S 1955	Mar	Central Gully Buttress	T.W.Patey
S 1956	21 Oct	The Aqueduct	J.Smith, T.W.Patey
S 1956	21 Oct	Minotaur	T.W.Patey, J.Smith

W 1957   13 Jan Sabre Cut   T.W.Patey, F.R.Malcolm, A.Thom
First summer ascent uncertain.
S 1958   2 Jul Caterpillar Crack   R.W.P.Barclay, W.D.Brooker
2 pegs for aid. FFA: G.S.Strange, D.Stuart, 1970
S 1958   10 Jul Theseus Grooves   R.W.P.Barclay, W.D.Brooker
S 1958   26 Aug Waterkelpie Wall   R.W.P.Barclay, W.D.Brooker
*Combined tactics and 1 peg for aid. FFA: D.Dinwoodie, D.Stuart, mid 1970s.
Lower section: J.McArtney, D.Mercer, 2 Aug 1964 with 1 peg for aid. FFA:
A.Nisbet, P.Langhorne, Aug 1983. The orginal route and the direct start were
both breakthrough routes on the Central Gully Wall.*
W 1959   10 Feb Labyrinth Edge   W.D.Brooker, D.Duncan
Excellent conditions showed the winter potential.
W 1959   Feb   Hanging Garden   R.H.Sellers, G.Annand, J.Smith
                 Route, Right Fork
*Hanging Garden Route is probably the line of the 1959 ascent. First definite
ascent by D.Dinwoodie, G.S.Strange, 9 Dec 1972.*
S 1959   Nov   The Mousetrap   J.R.Marshall, R.Marshall,
                                             R.Anderson
Considered the hardest route in the Cairngorms at the time.
S 1964   25 Jul Dinosaur   J.W.Stenhouse, B.T.Lawrie
*1 peg for aid. FFA: it has become normal to go left on to Labyrinth Edge below
the aid move although it has been freed by D.Dinwoodie, A.McIvor, 1974. The
first route to tackle these somewhat intimidating slabs. Direct finish:
D.Dinwoodie, A.Beyts, 1976*
W 1964   19 Dec False Gully   K.Grassick, W.James, J.M.Taylor
*1 peg for tension. Ice finish: R.McHardy, A.Nisbet Mar 1978. Direct Finish:
S.M.Richardson, J.Ashbridge 4 Mar 1995.*
S 1965 23/24 Oct The Giant   D.Bathgate, J.Ewing, J.Brumfitt
*Much aid used (A2). An epic ascent including an enforce bivouac by the
Edinburgh Squirrels on a line that Aberdonians considered to be their property.
FFA: N.Estcourt, P.Braithwaite, Summer 1974.*
S 1966   9 Jul Yakaboo   G.N.Hunter, G.Millar
*Approx. 10 points of aid. Route now obsolete: known ascent with 1 peg for aid
but a free ascent not certain.*
W 1967   Mar   North-West Gully Arete D.Pyper, S.Wilkinson
S 1967   Jul   Culloden   A.D.Barley, R.R.Barley
*First route on the Broad Terrace Wall - ahead of its time: 4 pegs for aid. FFA:
J.Lamb, P.Whillance, 1975*
S 1967   Jul   Four Corners Route   R.Sharpe, K.Spence
*1 peg for aid on the first corner, A1 on the fourth corner. Ascent with 1 peg for
aid by D.Dinwoodie, G.S.Strange, Jun 1977.*
S 1967 16/17 Sep The Blue Max   B.W.Robertson, A.Fyffe,
                                             W.T.Wilkinson
*1 rurp for tension and a spike lassoed on the crux pitch, A1 on Quartz Corner
in the rain. Quartz corner FFA: A.Fyffe, J.Grieve, 7 Jun 1969. FFA: J.Fraser and
party, May 1975.*

S 1968   9 Jun King Rat   A.F.Fyffe, J.Bower
5 pegs for aid, some of this aid due to loose rock on the big roof. FFA: P.Thomas, M.Fowler, Jun 1977 taking a different line on the roof.

S 1968 15/16 Jun Cougar   M.Rennie, P.Williams
About 16 points of aid. FFA: D.Cuthbertson, M.Hamilton, Jun 1977. Both were influential ascents for their time on an intimidating wall, the 1977 ascent demonstrating the free climbing possibilities on this wall.

W 1969   12 Jan Theseus Grooves   J.T.Campbell, B.S.Findlay,
                                         G.R.Simpson, G.S.Strange

S 1969   1 Jun False Impression   B.S.Findlay, G.S.Strange
Direct finish: A.Fyffe, J.Savory, 7 Jun 1970.

S 1969   7 Jun Black Mamba   A.Fyffe, J.Grieve
An important day with 3 fine new routes and the start of a good week of climbing by this team.

S 1969   7 Jun Falseface   G.N.Hunter, D.F.Lang
13 points of aid used. Free ascent of pitch 2 and a new free pitch 3 by D.Wright, G.S.Strange, 18 Jul 1976. FFA: R.A.Smith, D.Dinwoodie, Jul 1977. Variation start: R.J.Archbold, G.S.Strange, Jul 1977.

S 1969   7 Jun Goliath   B.S.Findlay, M.Rennie
4 points of aid. FFA: I.Nicolson and party, 1970. Direct Start: S.Docherty, N.Muir, 22 May 1971, with 2 pegs and 2 nuts for aid. FFA: B.Davison, A.Nisbet, Aug 1983. Shelf Variation: J.McArtney, B.T.Lawrie, 1967.

S 1969   9 Jun Late Night Final   A.Fyffe, J.Grieve
S 1969   10 Jun The Kraken   J.Grieve, A.Fyffe
S 1969   12 Jun Catwalk   A.Fyffe, J.Grieve
S 1969   14 Jun Pink Elephant   J.Grieve, A.Fyffe
W 1970   31 Jan Mammoth   J.Bower, J.Furnell, N.Blenkinsop,
                                         I.Rae
W 1970   14 Mar Centaur   A.Fyffe, D.Whitcombe
Direct finish: D.Wright, N.D.Keir, 1975.

W 1970   Mar Bower Buttress   J.Bower, G.R.Simpson
S 1970   17 May Predator   B.S.Findlay, G.S.Strange
5 aid points. FFA: D.Dinwoodie, D.F.Lang, 9 Jul 1972. Direct start: D.Dinwoodie, R.Renshaw, 1978.

S 1970   18 Jun Dubh Loch Monster   I.Nicolson, D.Knowles
1 peg for aid. FFA: J.Lamb, P.Whillance, 1975.

S 1970   20 Jun Gulliver   I.Nicolson, D.Knowles
A bold lead for its day.

S 1970   20 Jun The Sword of   G.N.Hunter, D.F.Lang
                    Damocles
A controversial ascent using 9 pegs and 3 bolts for aid. Variation, which also eliminated some aid by D.Wright, G.S.Strange, 17 Jul 1976. FFA: D.Dinwoodie, R.A.Smith, Jul 1977. Smith trundled the Damoclean flake.

S 1971   8 May The Om   D.F.Lang, J.Littleford
S 1971   22 Sep The Last Oasis   J.Bower, J.Ingram
2 pegs for aid. FFA: D.Dinwoodie, R.A.Smith, 1976

W 1972   Winter   Eastern Ramp   J.Bower and party
W 1972   11 Mar Labyrinth Direct   A.J.Bolton, P.Arnold
*A very bold and early front-pointing solution to a last great problem. The crux
was climbed without resting, from a psychological belay of ice-screws and axes.
Unrepeated until 1979.*
W 1972   12 Mar Mistral   G.S.Strange, J.Tweddle
S 1972 Summer The Bower-Lang   J.Bower, D.F.Lang
                    Route
S 1972   4 Oct Dragon Slayer   D.Dinwoodie, B.T.Lawrie
1 peg and 2 nuts for aid. FFA: B.Davison, A.Nisbet, Aug 1983.
S 1972   8 Oct Vampire   D.Dinwoodie, G.S.Strange
*4 pegs and 1 nut for aid. FFA: B.T.Lawrie, A.Nisbet, Jul 1977. Direct corner:
B.T.Lawrie, M.Freeman, Jul 1977. 2 pegs and 1 nut for aid. FFA: D.Dinwoodie,
G.Livingston, Aug 1983.*
S 1973   19 May Cyclops   G.S.Strange, M.Freeman
S 1973   19 Aug Falkenhorst   L.Brown, D.F.Lang, G.S.Strange
2 slings on spikes, 2 pegs and 3 nuts for aid. FFA: W.Todd, A.Last, Jun 1977
S 1973 Summer Girdle Traverse,   J.Mothersele, D.Riley
                    Central Slabs
2 pegs for aid (unrepeated).
S 1973 Summer Nemesis   J.Mothersele, W.Nicholls
S 1974   Jul The Strumpet   D.Dinwoodie, R.A.Smith
W 1975   Feb The Aqueduct   J.Moreland, R.A.Smith
W 1975   Feb Yeti   J.Moreland, R.A.Smith
W 1975   22 Mar Caterpillar Crack   G.Stephen, D.Dinwoodie
4 points of aid (unrepeated?)
S 1975   Jun The Sting   L.Brown, P.Nunn
S 1976   8 May Rock Island Line   M.Freeman, G.Stephen
S 1976   10 Jul Death's Head Route D.Dinwoodie, J.Mothersele
3 points of aid. FFA: D.Dinwoodie, D.Hawthorn, Jun 1986
S 1976   11 Jul Mirage   D.Wright, G.S.Strange
Variations: G.Cohen, J.Hutchison, 1981
S 1976   17 Jul The Crow   D.Dinwoodie, A.McIvor
Flake lassoed and 2 points of aid .FFA: D.Dinwoodie, G.Livingston, Aug 1983
S 1976   Aug Sous les Toits   D.Dinwoodie, B.T.Lawrie
One abseil used. FFA: W.Moir, C,Whittit, 1990
W 1977   6 Jan Hanging Garden   A.Nisbet, A.Robertson
                    Route, Left Fork
W 1977   Feb The Snow Desert   R.A.Smith, D.Wright
S 1977   Jun Vixen   R.J.Archbold, G.P.Muhlemann
1 peg for aid. FFA: A.Paul, D.Hawthorn, Jul 1984
S 1977   Jun Dogleg   T.Syme, N.D.Keir
S 1977   Jul Cayman   D.Dinwoodie, G.S.Strange
*Independent Finish: R.Anderson, A.Russell, 17 Jun 1984. Croc Finish:
S.Richardson, R.Reid, 23 Jul 1994.*

W 1977   3/4 Dec   Vertigo Wall   A.Nisbet, A.Robertson
A bivouac, 6 pegs and 2 ice-screws for aid. FFA: A.Cunningham, A.Nisbet, Nov 1985. An amazing direct start by J.Anderson, S.Kennedy, Jan 1980 (1 peg for aid) failed just below the normal route after the onset of darkness.
S 1978   17 Jun   The Prowl   D.Dinwoodie, R.Renshaw,
                                          R.J.Archbold, G.S.Strange
S 1978   Jun   Ariadne   D.Dinwoodie, R.Renshaw
W 1979   Mar   Labyrinth Left-Hand D.Dinwoodie, A.Williams
1 nut for aid. FFA with variation: A.Nisbet, G.Harper 24 Feb 1983
W 1979   1 Apr   Trunk Line   N.D.Keir, H.M.Towler
S 1979   Jun   Sans Fer   M.Hamilton, K.Spence
First new route here for Hamilton and at E4 6b the start of the modern era.
W 1980   12 Jan   The White Elephant   R.Anderson, R.Milne
Lower section previously by N.Keir, D.Wright, Feb 1975. Late season alternative: J.Anderson, A.Nisbet, 31 Mar 1979. A week with the best conditions since 1972: three long hard routes were climbed.
W 1980   16 Jan   Goliath   A.Nisbet, N.Morrison
1 point of aid, repeated the next day then never since - remarkable conditions!
W 1980   19 Jan   The Mousetrap   M.Hamilton, K.Spence, A.Taylor
1 point of aid. FFA: D.Dinwoodie, J.Hall, 25 Jan 1986.
W 1980   30 Mar   The Last Oasis   A.Nisbet, N.Spinks
1 peg and 1 nut for aid. Direct and free finish: D.Hawthorn, F.R.Malcolm, Jan 1993
S 1980   11 May   Dragonfly   R.J.Archbold, G.S.Strange
S 1980   25 May   Coon's Yard   R.J.Archbold, G.S.Strange
1 peg for aid after rain started (unrepeated?)
S 1981   23 Jun   Raptor   D.Dinwoodie, J.Wyness
W 1982   Feb   Eastern Groove   C.Jamieson, A.Paul
S 1982   30 May   Slartibartfast   M.Hamilton, P.Whillance (alts),
                                          R.Anderson
The start of a two year blitz of improbable lines by Whillance and Hamilton.
S 1982   31 May   Bombadillo   P.Whillance, M.Hamilton,
                                          R.Anderson (alts)
S 1982   5 Jun   The Israelite   P.Whillance, J.Moore
S 1982   24 Jul   The Ascent of Man   M.Hamilton, R.Anderson
S 1982   1 Aug   The Naked Ape   P.Whillance, P.Botterill, M.Hamilton,
                                          R.Anderson
S 1982   4 Sep   The Wicker Man   P.Whillance, R.Anderson
W 1983   24 Feb   Labyrinth Buttress   A.Nisbet, G.Harper
S 1983   22/23 Jul Flodden   M.Hamilton, K.Spence, R.Anderson
S 1983   24 Jul   Friends Essential   M.Hamilton, K.Spence, R.Anderson
S 1983   28 Jul   Masque   M.Hamilton, P.Whillance
S 1983   29 Jul   Alice Springs   M.Hamilton, P.Whillance
S 1983   29 Jul   Range War   K.Spence, D.McCallum
S 1983   12 Aug   Voyage of the Beagle M.Hamilton, R.Anderson
Originally known as the Boysen Line after an earlier attempt.

S 1983 18 Aug Perilous Journey D.Dinwoodie, G.Livingston
S 1983   Aug The Sass Corner B.Davison, C.Ord
W 1984   9 Feb Black Mamba S.Allan, A.Nisbet
   1 peg for aid (unrepeated).
S 1984   9 Jun Cannibal M.Hamilton, R.Anderson
   An aptly named route for a couple of reasons.
S 1984   5 Aug The Snake D.Dinwoodie, G.S.Strange
S 1984 11 Aug Jezebel G.Livingston, A.Ross
S 1984 15 Aug The Improbability Drive G.Livingston, D.Dinwoodie
S 1984 22 Aug Iron in the Soul D.Dinwoodie, B.T.Lawrie
W 1985   6 Feb Blizzard Nightmare C.Jamieson, G.Livingston,
                                     G.S.Strange, E.Todd, C.Ord
W 1985 10 Nov Treeline Groove A.Nisbet, M.Stringer
W 1986 25 Jan The Rattrap S.Allan, A.Nisbet
   3 points of aid. This route was done in a single push of 19 hours aided by
   moonlight and a good knowledge of this part of the cliff.
S 1986   1 Jul Slithy Tove D.Dinwoodie, D.Hawthorn
S 1986 18 Jul The Groanmaker D.Dinwoodie, C.Fraser
S 1986 15 Jul Heart of Gold A.Ross, M.Sutherland
S 1986 20 Jul Hotblack Desiato A.Ross, F.Templeton
W 1987   Jan Sabre Edge S.Stewart, G.Ettle
   Combined tactics (unrepeated?)
W 1987   Feb Nemesis S.Stewart, G.Ettle
W 1987   Feb Late Night Final S.Stewart, G.Ettle
W 1987 21 Feb Four Corners Route A.Cunningham, A.Nisbet
S 1987   5 Jul Idol Threat R.Anderson, G.Nicoll
S 1987   5 Jul The Web of Weird D.Dinwoodie, G.Thomson
   Hybrid Vigour Start: R.Campbell, P.Thorburn, Jul 1994. Pitch 3: R.Campbell,
   summer 1995 (unseconded). Pitch 4: P.Thorburn, N.Craig, R.Campbell,
   summer 1995.
S 1987 10 Aug Fer de Lance D.Dinwoodie, J.Hall
S 1989 27 Jul The Bedouin W.Moir, C.Stewart
W 1991 17 Jan The Titan G.Ettle, S.Blagbrough
S 1991   7 Sept The Eye of Allah W.Moir, C.Forrest
W 1991 16 Nov The Golden Thread S.Richardson, J.Ashbridge
W 1992   3 Feb Dogleg G.Ettle, A.Nisbet
W 1993   Jan The Sting D.Dinwoodie, D.Hawthorn
W 1993   Jan The Sass Corner D.Hawthorn, C.Ord
S 1994 30 Jul The Fox Moth S.Richardson, G.Muhlemann
W 1995 26 Feb North-West Buttress W.Church, G.S.Strange
S 1995 16 Jul Chimera S.Richardson, C.Cartwright
S 1995   9 Aug The Shetlander W.Moir, N.Morrison, N.Ritchie
S 1995   9 Aug Billy Nomates W.Moir, N.Morrison, N.Ritchie
S 1995 10 Aug DD's Recurring Dreams N.Morrison, W.Moir
S 1995 10 Aug The Gathering N.Morrison, W.Moir

BROAD CAIRN BLUFFS

S	1948	21 Nov	Rakes Rib	K.Winram, E.L.Smith, M.Smith
S	1952	3 May	Coffin Chimney	J.M.Taylor, T.W.Patey
W	1970	Mar	Coffin Chimney	A.Fyffe, R.Zorab
W	1974	3 Mar	Funeral Fall	M.Freeman, N.D.Keir
W	1975	Jan	Yoo-Hoo Buttress	T.MacLellan, A.Nisbet, V.Frost
W	1975	Jan	Rakes Rib	D.Boyne, L.Brown, A.Espie, B.Robertson
S	1983	30 Jul	Solitaire	G.S.Strange, B.S.Findlay
S	1992	2 Sep	Two's Company	S.Richardson, J.Ashbridge
S	1994	1 Aug	The Only Game in Town	A.Fyffe, A.Liddell

BEINN A' BHUIRD: COIRE NA CICHE

W	1948	28 Feb	Twisting Gully	K.Milne, J.Davison, J.Reid
S	1949	20 Aug	Slugain Buttress	W.D.Brooker, D.A.Sutherland
S	1949	21 Aug	Sickle	W.D.Brooker, D.A.Sutherland
S	1953	10 May	Hourglass Buttress	A.Thom, F.R.Malcolm

1 peg for aid. FFA unknown. Direct start: A.O'F.Will, T.W.Patey, Apr 1955. An early VS, and a classic.

| S | 1953 | 28 Jun | Trident | A.Thom, E.Gordon, F.R.Malcolm, S.Anderson |

Combined tactics used. Freed on second ascent in 1953/4.

S	1953	30 Jun	Quartzvein Route	Q.T.Crichton, F.L.Swinton
S	1953	18 Oct	Jason's Chimney	A.Thom, F.R.Malcolm, A.O'F.Will
S	1953	18 Oct	Grey Tower, Chimney Route	A.Thom, F.R.Malcolm, A.O'F.Will
W	1954	17 Jan	Little Tower Gully	F.R.Malcolm, A.Thom
S	1955	Aug	The Carpet	F.R.Malcolm, G.Malcolm, R.W.P.Barclay, G.Adams

Combined tactics and several pegs for aid. Pegs soon eliminated and the route became a companion classic to Hourglass Buttress. FFA unknown.

S	1955	28 Aug	Sandy Crack	F.R.Malcolm, A.O'F.Will, G.McLeod
W	1957	10 Feb	Slugain Buttress	G.Adams, D.McRae
W	1959	Jan	Quartzvein Route	W.A.Christie, J.W.Vigrow
W	1959	Mar	Sickle	A.Thom, R.Wiseman
S	1964	25 May	Three Step	R.H.Ford, R.A.North

A controversial ascent as aid was used to solve an outstanding problem. FFA: C.MacLean, A.Paul, 1 Aug 1982.

| S | 1965 | 28 Aug | Lamina | M.Rennie, R.Stirton, J.Bower |
| W | 1967 | 15 Jan | Trident | J.Bower, M.C.MacLennan |

2 pegs for aid. FFA: G.S.Strange, B.S.Findlay, 3 Nov 1985. 7 days after the first ascent of In the Pink, an E3.

| S | 1968 | 2 Jun | The Watchtower | J.Bower, A.Fyffe |
| W | 1970 | 19 Mar | The Carpet | J.Bower, G.Boyd |

Combined tactices and 3 pegs for aid but still very hard for its time:unrepeated for 13 years. FFA: D.Hawthorn, A.Nisbet, 1983

W 1970   29 Mar Hourglass Buttress   J.Bower, G.Boyd
2 pegs for aid. FFA: A.Cunningham, A.Nisbet, Nov 1985
S 1970   6 Sep Vatican Steps   G.N.Hunter, D.F.Lang
W 1973   1 Mar Sandy Crack   C.Anderson, R.J.Archbold, N.D.Keir
1 nut for aid (unrepeated?)
S 1973   8 Sep Homebrew   R.J.Archbold, N.D.Keir, A.Lawson
S 1974   31 Mar Jason's Chimney   M.Freeman, N.D.Keir
S 1976   18 Jul Hell's Bells   S.Falconer, G.Reilly, I.Reilly,
                                         G.Stephen
S 1976   Sept High Step   J.Moreland, D.Wright
S 1977   2 Jul Hot Toddy   R.J.Archbold, N.D.Keir
W 1982   Feb Neptune's Groove   A.Nisbet, G.S.Strange
S 1982   24 Jul The Grinder   G.S.Strange, H.Towler
S 1982   1 Aug Joker's Crack   D.Dinwoodie, K.Murphy
S 1982   Aug Quickstep   R.F.Allen, A.Nisbet
*An unsuccessful attempt to find the line of Silk Cut, unrecorded in the
mid-1970s.*
S 1983   Aug Limbo Dance   G.Reilly, F.Templeton
W 1984   Dec Thief's Corner   R.Clothier, D.Hawthorn
S 1985   7 Jul Pigs on the Wing   D.Hawthorn, K.Murphy
W 1985   Nov Grey Tower, Chimney   W.Moir, N.Ritchie
                  Route
S 1986   17 Aug Dans Macabre   E.Todd, D.Thomson
W 1986   13 Dec The Watchtower   C.Forrest, W.Moir, N.Ritchie
W 1987   29 Nov Grey Tower,   R.Everett, S.Richardson
                  Left-hand Route

BEINN A' BHUIRD: COIRE AN DUBH LOCHAIN

W 1911   Apr Main Rake   H.Alexander, A.A.Longden, A.M.Watt
S 1949   1 May May Day Route   J.Tewnion, E.L.Smith, W.A.Russell,
                                         M.Smith
S 1949   21 Aug Crow-step Route   C.Petrie, M.Smith
S 1949   21 Aug Polypody Groove   J.Tewnion, E.L.Smith
Rib variation: A.Nisbet, 1984, probably climbed before
S 1950   Jul Central Rib   K.Winram, C.Petrie
W 1950   26 Nov Winter Rib   J.Tewnion, G.Dey, M.Smith
S 1952   7 Jun Birthday Route   K.A.Grassick, J.G.Lillie, R.Preshaw
S 1953   15 Mar Tantalus Gully   G.C.Greig, M.Smith, K.Winram
W 1957   10 Feb Tantalus Gully   R.Ellis, M.Scott
S 1964   Jul Bloodhound Buttress   M.Higgins, J.C.Innes
*1 peg for aid. Climbed with a top rope on the crux pitch,
T.W.Patey,W.W.Hutchison, Sep 1953.FFA: D.Dinwoodie, B.T.Lawrie,
A.McIvor, mid 1970s.*
S 1965   9 Oct Tearaway   A.Fyffe, M.D.Y.Mowat
W 1967   15 Feb May Day Route   N.D.Keir, B.S.Findlay
W 1969   Jan Polypody Groove   D.W.Duncan, G.R.Simpson

| W 1972 | 30 Jan | Faux Pas | J.Bower, B.Clarke, A.Morgan |
| W 1975 | 15 Feb | Bloodhound Buttress | R.A.Smith, G.Stephen |

7 pegs for aid. FFA: A.Cunningham, A.Nisbet, 6 Dec 1986

W 1977	Apr	Crow Step Route	R.J.Archbold, G.Cohen
S 1977	9 Jul	Come Dancing	S.Falconer, G.Stephen
S 1978	24 Jun	Sniffer Buttress	A.Nisbet, N.Spinks
S 1978	25 Jun	The Scent	A.Nisbet, N.Spinks
S 1981	10 Aug	The Streak	A.Nisbet
S 1981	10 Aug	Hooker's Route	A.Nisbet, N.Spinks

Hook and an 8 foot pole for aid.

W 1982	Feb	Tail-end Slabs	A.Nisbet, G.S.Strange
S 1982	Aug	The Last Tango	R.F.Allen, A.Nisbet
S 1989	23 Jul	Desolation Crack	S.N.Smith, G.S.Strange
W 1987	12 Dec	The Vital Spark	I.Barron, S.Kennedy
W 1987	12 Dec	Birthday Route	I.Barron, S.Kennedy

BEINN A' BHUIRD: DIVIDING BUTTRESS

S 1948	4 Apr	Slab and Arete	J.Tewnion, M.Smith
S 1949	28 May	Sentinel Route	K.Winram, M.Smith
W 1967	15 Jan	The Ramp	D.Cameron, G.S.Strange
W 1970	14 Nov	Sentinel Gully	G.S.Strange, D.Stuart
W 1970	14 Nov	Sentinel Route	M.Rennie, D.Riley
S 1974	Summer	Jewell-Kammer Route	J.Jewell, P.Kammer
S 1982	30 Jul	Streaker's Root	R.J.Archbold, H.Towler, D.Wallace
S 1983	Jul	The Fringe	A.Nisbet, M.Ross, D.Strickland
S 1983	Jul	Parkie's Route	A.Nisbet, M.Ross
S 1990	17 Jun	Sawfly	R.J.Archbold, S.N.Smith, G.S.Strange
S 1990	17 Jun	The Gnat	R.J.Archbold, S.N.Smith, G.S.Strange
S 1991	4 Aug	Weevil's Way	R.Ross, G.S.Strange

BEINN A' BHUIRD: COIRE NAN CLACH

S 1984	8 Jul	Twister	G.S.Strange, R.Ross
S 1988	15 Aug	Chocolate Girls	N.Ritchie, W.Moir
S 1988	15 Aug	Twisted Sister	W.Moir, N.Ritchie, C.Stewart
S 1990	Jun	Bete Noir	N.Ritchie, C.G.Munro
S 1990	Jun	Abdel Wahad	N.Ritchie, C.G.Munro

BEINN A' BHUIRD: GARBH CHOIRE

| S 1933 | 4 Jul | Mitre Ridge | E.A.M.Wedderburn, P.D.Baird, E.J.A.Leslie |
| S 1933 | 4 Jul | Cumming-Crofton Route | M.S.Cumming, J.W.Crofton |

Variation: R.J.Archbold, H.Towler, 5 Sep 1981. Two very significant routes, the hardest pre-war climbs in the Cairngorms and also of classic quality. Many of the earlier routes were on bad rock and vegetation.

S 1943   Jun   Commando Route   Sgt. Major Langlands, A.D.M.Cox
S 1943   Jun   North-West Gully   Sgt. Major Langlands, A.D.M.Cox
                  (in descent)
First ascent: M.Smith, J,Tewnion, 19 Sep 1948
S 1943   Jun   South-East Gully   J.Hunt, A.Y.Greenhaugh
S 1950   30 Jun   Consolation Gully   J.Tewnion, K.Winram
S 1952   24 Aug   Back Bay Gully   G.C.Greig, M.Smith, K.Winram
S 1953   8 Mar   Laminated Crag   K.Winram, M.Smith
W 1953   2 Apr   Mitre Ridge   W.D.Brooker, T.W.Patey
A "matter of fact"ascent of a classic hard route, combined tactics used. Direct
and free: J.Anderson, A.Nisbet, Apr 1984
S 1953   Jul   Squareface   T.W.Patey, J.M.Taylor
W 1954   31 Mar   Approach Gully   T.W.Patey, G.B.Leslie, A.G.Nicol,
                                  J.M.Taylor
W 1954   31 Mar   Back Bay Gully   T.W.Patey, G.B.Leslie, A.G.Nicol,
                                  J.M.Taylor
W 1954   31 Mar   The Flume   J.M.Taylor, G.B.Leslie
S 1954   29 Aug   Mandarin Buttress   T.W.Patey, A.Watson, K.Winram,
                                  M.Smith
S 1954   29 Aug   East Wall Direct   T.W.Patey
W 1956   15 Apr   Consolation Gully   T.W.Patey, R.H.Sellers, R.Harper
W 1956   16 Dec   North-West Gully   R.H.Sellers, G.Adams
W 1959   Feb   South-East Gully   R.H.Sellers, G.Annand
W 1959   March   Mandarin Buttress   W.A.Christie, W.B.Gault
S 1959   Aug   Angel's Edgeway   W.B.Gault, A.Kane (pitch 2)
As described: B.S.Findlay, G.S.Stange, 17 Jun 1989
W 1966   13 Mar   Nomad's Gully   M.D.Y.Mowatt, A.McR.Corbett
W 1967   Feb   North-West Couloir   M.Rennie, D.W.Duncan
W 1969   9 Mar   Commando Route   P.F.McDonald, I.G.Rowe
1 peg for tension on both known ascents
S 1969   31 Aug   Slochd Wall   M.Rennie, G.S.Strange
Mostly aid (A3). FFA: B.T.Lawrie, A.Nisbet, 3 Jul 1979. Left finish: R.J.Archbold,
H.Towler, D.J.Wallace, 31 Jul 1982
W 1970   25 Mar   Back Bay Gully,   N.D.Keir
                  Left Branch
W 1971   27 Mar   Comala's Ridge   G.R.Simpson, G.Boyd
W 1972   Jan   Squareface   C.Butterworth, R.C.Maguire
W 1973   1 Apr   Salamander   D.F.Lang
W 1974   23 Feb   East Wall Direct   N.D.Keir, J.Mothersele, R.A.Smith
Original route (W): T.W.Patey, A.G.Nicol, 31 Mar 1954
W 1974   15 Dec   The Flume Direct   D.F.Lang, N.W.Quinn
S 1975   28 Jun   Mitre Ridge Direct   G.Stephen, A.McIvor
S 1975   28 Jun   Crucible Route   R.J.Archbold, G.S.Strange
W 1977   26 Feb   Cumming-Crofton   R.Renshaw, G.S.Strange
                  Route
W 1977   Apr   North-West Groove   R.J.Archbold, G.Cohen

S 1977   3 Jul Ghurka   R.J.Archbold, N.D.Keir
1 peg for aid. Demonstated that the west face had better holds than previously
thought and opened the way for several fine routes (unrepeated).
W 1978   Apr Crucible Route   R.J.Archbold, D.Dinwoodie
1 peg for tension (unrepeated?)
S 1978   27 May The Chancel   D.M.Nichols, G.S.Strange
S 1978   28 May The Bishop   D.M.Nichols, G.S.Strange
S 1978   3 Jun Helter Skelter   R.J.Archbold, W.McKerrow
S 1978   4 Jun Surgeon's Slab   R.J.Archbold, W.McKerrow
S 1978   4 Jun Witch Doctor   R.J.Archbold, W.McKerrow
S 1979   9 Jul The Primate   J.Anderson, A.Nisbet
Pitch 1 by G.S.Strange, R.Ross, 8 Jul 1984
S 1979   15 Jul Chindit   R.J.Archbold, N.D.Keir
Direct: D.Dinwoodie, C.Jamieson, 31 Jul 1982
W 1980   2 Mar Alchemist's Route   R.J.Archbold, D.M.Nichols
S 1981   5 Sep Rhombus   R.J.Archbold, H.Towler
W 1982   11 Feb Gold Coast   A.Nisbet, C.MacLeod
1 peg for aid (unrepeated?)
S 1982   31 Jul Slochd Wall, Right   A.Paul, G.Reilly
                   Edge
S 1983   6 Aug The Empty Quarter   D.Dinwoodie, G.S.Strange
W 1984   15 Feb The Grail   A.Nisbet, A.Clifford
W 1984   16 Feb The Actress   A.Nisbet, A.Clifford
1 peg for aid (unrepeated?)
W 1984   22 Dec Ghurka   C.MacLeod, A.Nisbet
W 1987   31 Jan Flume Left-Hand   W.Moir
W 1988   3 Apr Black Danube   I.Barron, S.Kennedy
W 1991   24 Mar Blue Deacon   R.J.Archbold, B.S.Findlay,
                                             G.S.Strange
S 1992   13 Sep The Sacrament   S.Helmore, S.Richardson
W 1995   18 Feb The Cardinal   S.M.Richardson, R.Webb

STOB AN T-SLUICHD

S 1948   4 Jul Pinnacle Ridge   G.W.Ross, A.E.Anton
S 1949   28 May M and B Buttress   G.Mathieson, I.M.Brooker
W 1977   11 Apr Pinnacle Ridge   M.Freeman, G.S.Strange
W 1983   30 Jan Token Groove   B.S.Findlay, G.S.Strange

GLEN CLOVA

W 1910   1 Jan Craig Rennet   H.G.Drummond, J.A.Parker
W 1910   2 Jan Backdoor Gully   H.G.Drummond, J.A.Parker
S 1911   3 Jan Pinnacle Ridge,   H.G.Drummond, H.Alexander,
                   Craig Maud   J.B.Miller
W 1915   May B Gully   H.Raeburn, W.Galbraith, W.A.Reid
S 1915   May B Gully Buttress   H.Raeburn, W.Galbraith, W.A.Reid
S 1931   27 Jul Scorrie Buttress   A.L.Cram, R.M.McIntyre

S 1931	15 Nov	The Deep Crack	Grampian Club members
S 1934	Feb	Diagonal Crack, Juanjorge	R.Scott, J.Beedie
S 1935	Nov	Glen Doll Gully	J.D.B.Wilson, D.A.Rait
S 1939	28 May	The Comb	J.G.Ferguson, W.S.Scroggie
S 1939	4 June	Slanting Gully	G.S.Ritchie, J.Brown, A.Powley, E.Urquhart

First winter ascent by F.Old and party in the 1950s.

S 1939	15 Oct	Maud Buttress, Cairn Damph	J.H.B.Bell, D.Myles
S 1946	Aug	Romulus and Remus	G.S.Ritchie, E.Maxwell, P.D.Ritchie, L.Ferguson
S 1948	3 Oct	Gimcrack Gully, Juanjorge	K.Winram, J.Tewnion, W.A.Russell
S 1948	14 Nov	Hooker's Joy	E.L.Smith, A.Alexander, M.Smith
S 1948	Nov	B Gully Chimney	R.F.Entwhistle, A.M.Kinnear, E.R.Robertson, J.B.Hyde
S 1950	5 Mar	The Pyramid	J.Tewnion, K.Winram
W 1953	15 Feb	Look C Gully	C.L.Donaldson, J.R.Marshall

The best winter route in the Clova area. There are rumours of an earlier ascent.

W 1954	27 Feb	Glen Doll Gully	G.Smith, E.W.Thomson, N.W.Thomson
W 1954	Feb	Curving Gully, Craig Maud	G.Smith, E.W.Thomson, J.Sime
W 1954	Feb	North Gully, Craig Rennet (in descent)	G. Smith, E.W.Thomson, J.Sime
W 1950's		Gimcrack Gully	F.Old, D.F.Lang
W 1950's		Chokestone Gully, Corrie of Bonhard	F.Anderson and party
W 1962	29 Dec	B Gully Chimney	D.Crabb, D.F.Lang
W 1965	Mar	Slanting Gully, Craig of Gowal	G.N.Hunter, S.A.M.Viveash
S 1968	10 Aug	The Gowk	G.N.Hunter, D.F.Lang

1 tension traverse. FFA: G.Reilly, I.Reilly, B.Simpson, M.Webster, 1974.

W 1970	Winter	Girdle Traverse, Corrie Fee	M.Forbes, G.Miller
W 1972	30 Jan	Wet Knees	N.D.Keir, A.Lawson
W 1972	5 Feb	A Gully Buttress	A.MacDonald, J.McKenzie,

3 pegs for aid on alternative line.

W 1975	20 Jan	The Comb	I.Robb, J.Thomson
W 1975	Feb	The Skivver	G.Reilly, W.Taylor
W 1975	1 Mar	Central Route	I.Reilly, A.Paul
W 1975	Nov	The Pyramid	A.Paul, G.Reilly, I.Reilly, W.Taylor
W 1979	Feb	The Gowk	E.Cameron, G.N.Hunter
W 1979	31 Dec	Hogmanay Gully	A.J.Thomson, I.D.Shepherd, S.F.Cameron

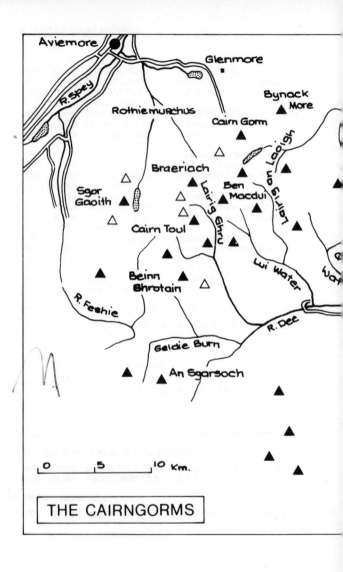

THE CAIRNGORMS